HISTORICAL MANUAL
OF
ENGLISH PROSODY

HISTORICAL MANUAL
OF
ENGLISH PROSODY

GEORGE SAINTSBURY

Introduction by Harvey Gross

SCHOCKEN BOOKS · NEW YORK

First published in 1910

First SCHOCKEN PAPERBACK *edition 1966*

Copyright © 1966 by Schocken Books Inc.

Library of Congress Catalog Card No. 66–16648

Manufactured in the United States of America

CONTENTS

BOOK I

INTRODUCTORY AND DOGMATIC

CHAPTER I

CHAPTER II

SYSTEMS OF ENGLISH PROSODY—THE ACCENTUAL OR STRESS

CHAPTER III

SYSTEMS OF ENGLISH PROSODY—THE SYLLABIC

CHAPTER IV

SYSTEMS OF ENGLISH PROSODY—THE FOOT

v

CHAPTER V

RULES OF THE FOOT SYSTEM

CHAPTER VI

CONTINUOUS ILLUSTRATIONS OF ENGLISH SCANSION ACCORDING TO THE FOOT SYSTEM

BOOK II

HISTORICAL SKETCH OF ENGLISH PROSODY

CHAPTER I

FROM THE ORIGINS TO CHAUCER—THE CONSTITUTION OF ENGLISH VERSE

CHAPTER II

FROM CHAUCER TO SPENSER—DISORGANISATION AND RECONSTRUCTION

CHAPTER III

FROM SHAKESPEARE TO MILTON—THE CLOSE OF THE FORMATIVE PERIOD

BOOK III

HISTORICAL SURVEY OF VIEWS ON PROSODY

CHAPTER I

BEFORE 1700

CHAPTER II

FROM BYSSHE TO GUEST

CHAPTER III

LATER NINETEENTH-CENTURY PROSODISTS

BOOK IV

AUXILIARY APPARATUS

CHAPTER I

GLOSSARY

CHAPTER II

REASONED LIST OF POETS WITH SPECIAL REGARD TO THEIR PROSODIC QUALITY AND INFLUENCE

Arnold, Matthew (1822-1888)—Barham, Richard H. (" Thomas Ingoldsby ") (1788-1845)—Beaumont, Sir John (1583-1623)— Blake, William (1757-1827)—Bowles, William Lisle (1762-1850)—Browne, William (1591-1643)—Browning, Elizabeth Barrett (1806-1861)—Browning, Robert (1812-1889)—Burns, Robert (1759-1796) — Byron, George Gordon, Lord (1788-1824)—Campbell, Thomas (1777-1844)—Campion, Thomas (?-1619) — Canning, George (1770-1827) — Chamberlayne, William (1619-1689)—Chatterton, Thomas (1752-1770)— Chaucer, Geoffrey (1340?-1400)—Cleveland, John (1613-1658) —Coleridge, Samuel Taylor (1772-1834)—Collins, William (1721-1759) — Congreve, William (1670-1729) — Cowley, Abraham (1618-1667)—Cowper, William (1731-1800)— Donne, John (1573-1631)—Drayton, Michael (1563-1631)— Dryden, John (1630-1700)—Dixon, Richard Watson (1833-1900) — Dunbar, William (1450?-1513? or -1530?) — Dyer, John (1700?-1758?)—Fairfax, Edward (d. 1635)—Fitzgerald, Edward (1809-1883)—Fletcher, Giles (1588-1623), and Phineas (1582-1650)—Fletcher, John (1579-1625)—Frere, John Hookham (1769-1846)—Gascoigne, George (1525?-1577)—Glover, Richard (1712-1785)—Godric, Saint (?-1170)—Gower, John (1325?-1408) — Hampole, Richard Rolle of (1290?-1347) — Hawes, Stephen (d. 1523?) — Herrick, Robert (1591-1674) — Hunt, J. H. Leigh (1784-1859) — Jonson, Benjamin (1573?-1637)—Keats, John (1795-1821)—Kingsley, Charles (1819-1875)—Landor, Walter Savage (1775-1864)—Langland, William (fourteenth century)—Layamon (late twelfth and early thirteenth century)—Lewis, Matthew Gregory (1775-1818)— Locker (latterly Locker-Lampson) Frederick (1821-1895)— Longfellow, Henry Wadsworth (1807-1882)—Lydgate, John (1370-1450?)—Macaulay, Thomas Babington (1800-1859)— Maginn, William (1793-1842)—Marlowe, Christopher (1664-1693)—Milton, John (1608-1674)—Moore, Thomas (1779-1852)—Morris, William (1834-1896)—Orm—O'Shaughnessy, Arthur W. E. (1844-1881)—Peele, George (1558?-1597?)— Percy, Thomas (1729-1811)—Poe, Edgar (1809-1849)—Pope, Alexander (1688-1744)—Praed, Winthrop Mackworth (1802-1839)—Prior, Matthew (1664-1721) — Robert of Gloucester (*fl. c.* 1280)—Rossetti, Christina Georgina (1830-1894) and Dante Gabriel (1828-1882)—Sackville, Thomas (1536-1608)— Sandys, George (1578-1644)—Sayers, Frank (1763-1817)— Scott, Sir Walter (1771-1832)—Shakespeare, William (1564-1616) — Shelley, Percy Bysshe (1792-1822) — Shenstone,

CHAPTER III

ORIGINS OF LINES AND STANZAS

CHAPTER IV

BIBLIOGRAPHY

INTRODUCTION

I

FLUCTUATIONS on the critical market indicate it is a good time to buy shares in prosody. After a period of relative quiescence, critical interest turns again to this vexing and much vexed study. I underline *critical* because the best of recent studies approaches prosody not as a sub-category of proscriptive grammar, or a species of clinical acoustics, but as deeply involved with literary theory and humanistic literary criticism. Prosody was never a popular part of literary study; it was shamefully neglected during the flourishing decades of the New Criticism. Too many prosodists came to their subject burdened by party-line notions, crank theories, and polemical biases; too many prosodists were conspicuously uninterested in poetic values while showing passionate dedication to metrical paradigms, unprovable classical influences, and statistical boondoggling. More recently, the evangelists of scientism have been spreading the good news of 'computational metrics,' coded messages, and the mystiques of information theory and computer analysis.

There is little to be gained in railing against the prevailing spirit of the age. But until the quantifiers of behavioral science can devise an instrument sensitive enough to respond to the rhythmic organization of even the simplest poem, prosody must remain inextricably bound up with matters of taste and value. After we have accumulated and analyzed the statistics, we still face pragmatic questions of criticism: what is good and bad prosody; what distinguishes mere skill in metrics from transcendent handling of rhythmic forms?

An adequate theory of rhythm would not make prosody an exact science; however, until we have such a theory, we will never quite understand how, in the words of R. P. Blackmur, rhythm "move(s) perception into meaning and . . . move(s) meaning into words."[1] I have suggested in my *Sound and Form in Modern Poetry* that prosody *is* meaning, that the sounds a poem makes are symbolic of human percept and affect. Rhythm is both imitative of human behavior and expressive of human feeling. Rhythm is a 'symbol' of feeling, as Susanne Langer suggests; perhaps it is not isomorphic with our inner life, but in some way, as yet unexplained, correspondent to the movements of human process. Meter, with its flow of syllables, stresses, and feet, may set up a self-referring system, a *Gestalt*, to which our sensibilities respond *as if* to actual feelings.

This is not the place, for obvious reasons, to develop a complex theory of rhythm; but much stimulating work in semiotics, aesthetics, and literary systematics points clear directions. Rhythm is a 'cognition': the abstract form of change; the 'meaning' of rhythm resides in the nature of time itself. Meter, the specialized form of rhythm, is an abstraction from a realm of linguistic possibilities; consequently no mere linguistic 'facts' (given us by phoneticians or oscillo-

---

[1] "Lord Tennyson's Scissors" in *Form and Value in Modern Poetry* (New York, 1957), p. 374.

graphic analysis) can explain what is intimately a part
of symbolic process.

Until a theory of rhythm has been developed, we
must proceed empirically, trusting our own responses.
I know of no objective method that unlocks the
rhythmic secrets of a good poem; what I can offer is
a combination of scansion and critical analysis that
may explain why certain arrangements of syllables
and stresses urge language into song. Let me illustrate
with two metrically different versions of Thomas
Wyatt's *They Flee from Me:*

> They flee from me that sometime did me seek,
> With naked foot stalking within my chamber.
> Once have I seen them gentle, tame, and meek,
> That now are wild, and do not once remember
> That sometime they have put themselves in danger
> To take bread at my hand; and now they range,
> Busily seeking in continual change.

* * *

> They flee from me, that sometime did me seek,
> With naked foot stalking in my chamber.
> I have seen them gentle, tame, and meek,
> That now are wild, and do not remember
> That sometime they have put themselves in danger
> To take bread at my hand; and now they range,
> Busily seeking with a continual change.

The first version comes from Tottel's *Songs and
Sonnets*, published in 1557; the second from an early
manuscript, *Egerton 2711*, in the collection of the
British Museum. We scan and compare some crucial
lines:

MS   With ná|ked foót | stálk|ing in | my chám|ber

Tottel   With ná|ked foót | stálk ing | with in | my chám|ber

MS   I | have seén | them gén|tle, táme, | and meék

Tottel   Ónce have | I seén | them gén|tle, táme, | and meék

MS   That nów | are wíld, | and | do nót | re mém|ber

Tottel   That nów | are wíld | and dó | not ónce | re mém|ber

The editor of the *Songs and Sonnets* added syllables
and words; his not very clear intention was to steady
Wyatt's rhythm and bring the meter closer to canons
of regular syllable count and alternate stressing.
Wyatt was working the native rhythm of four basic
stresses but subtly, and with exact effect, occasionally
shifting the lines into pentameters. I scan the lines as
pentameters, indicating the lighter, purely *metrical*
stresses by (✓). That Wyatt had some notion of what
he was about, and was not merely stumbling toward
better things (the metric of Spenser and Sidney), is
revealed in the skillfully counterpointed (or to use
Saintsbury's term—*equivalenced*) fifth line:

To táke | breád at | my hánd; | and nów | they ránge . . .

Even the editor of Tottel knew when to leave well
enough alone. The reversal of the extremely sensitive
second foot touches the deepest springs of feeling:
whether this particular rhythmic form symbolizes
vital process or whether the break in the prevailing
pattern generates another kind of significant "shape
in time" (Ezra Pound's phrase) makes a theoretical
but no practical difference. This rhythmic form directly tells our nervous systems something about
human feeling; the described action moves first into

metaphor (the beloved as tame fawn, taking bread), then, transformed by the rhythm, moves into the realm of the unparaphrasable.

Other lines show similar prosodic effects. Although Tottel's editing of the second line fills out the requisite five feet, the MS version, despite the monosyllabic foot in the third position, offers an inevitable rhythm. Here sound and sense merge. *Stalking within* suggests a comic situation: as if the young lady, lost in darkness, could not find her way to her lover's bed. *Stalking in*, with its strong stress on *stalk-* and its lighter emphasis on *in*, allows the proper semantic reenforcement. It is the *stalking* which is crucial. And the strong monosyllabic foot, presiding at the line's metrical center, counterpoints the rhythm; we hear the older strong stress meter and the new syllable stress meter combining in disproportioned but hauntingly beautiful music.

2

A friend reports that the late R. P. Blackmur, "when he wanted to know something about prosody," consulted Saintsbury. Blackmur possessed the subtlest, most adventurous critical imagination of his generation. That he valued Saintsbury, who was rarely subtle and more often perverse than adventurous, may seem incongruous. But Saintsbury remains the most authoritative historian of the subject. He had a vast knowledge of English poetry, from the very beginnings to his own contemporaries, "Mr Swinburne and Mr. Meredith." He had a gift for metrical analysis: I frequently take exception to Saintsbury's evasive, self-

contradicting 'dogmatics'; I rarely find myself dis-
agreeing with his admirable scansions. The reader
might look at his scansion of Blake's *Mad Song* on
pp. 93–94; if the term 'good ear' is more than an emo-
tional noise of approval, I would say that Saintsbury
has a very good ear indeed.

The *Historical Manual of English Prosody* is based
on Saintsbury's three-volume *A History of English
Prosody*. While the monumental *History* is designed
as a comprehensive survey, the shorter *Manual* is intended for students in schools and colleges. It is meant
as an introduction and a book of useful reference; the
student would do well to read Saintsbury's short
Preface and to follow his recommendations on the use
of the *Manual*. It is a singularly complete book: it
not only treats prosody as practical metrics but also
gives a succinct and valuable historical account of
prosodical theory. Its full complement of apparatus,
including analytic table of contents, glossary of terms,
lists and bibliography, makes this an invaluable *vade
mecum;* a careful reading is an education in the history of English poetry as well as in the history of
versification.

Saintsbury's limitations are partly those of the
Victorian age and partly those of his own energetic,
idiosyncratic temperament. Saintsbury wholeheart-
edly assented to the Idea of Progress and to the notion
that the nineteenth century was the final goal of the
historical process. Saintsbury believed English prosody was struggling, from the twelfth century onwards,
toward the perfection of the two-valued "foot system." As a result, Saintsbury's judgments are tinged
by a naïve teleology; we discover historical assess-
ments of this kind:

In still earlier or 'Old' English verse (the foot system) is not discernible at all; in the earliest period of 'Middle English' it is discernible, struggling to get itself into shape. Later, with advances and relapses, it perfects itself absolutely. (p. 22)

Because Saintsbury holds it as gospel truth that the foot system does not "get itself into shape" until later in the Elizabethan Age, he tends to undervalue the poets of the earlier Tudor periods. Skelton's very beautiful

> Mirry Margaret
> As midsommer flower,
> Gentyll as faucon
> Or hauke of the tower . . .

deserves more than the epithet 'doggerel'; its metrical structure is clearly based on native strong-stress principles.

Saintsbury acknowledged (as any good post-Hegelian would) the dialectical swing of English prosody. He saw "advances and relapses," periods of imputed 'health' and periods of dissolution and decay. Such moralism, a besetting fault of his times, has no place in describing what are, after all, matters of technique. Saintsbury (like Yvor Winters after him) gets very close to saying that there is good and evil prosody, that dissolute poets and decadent periods generate a corrupt metrical style.

The most serious objections voiced to Saintsbury's approach to prosody are his thoroughgoing empiricism and his theoretical laxity. Saintsbury is a practical critic; he brings to his subject a minimum of formal preconception. He operates mainly on his own catholic (perhaps too catholic) tastes and his bumptious en-

thusiasm. T. S. Eliot calls Saintsbury a "Critic with
Gusto . . . an erudite and genial man with an insatiable
appetite for the second-rate, and a flair for discovering
the excellence which is often to be found in the second-
rate."[2] In Saintsbury's defense, we should note that
along with poets now sunk into oblivion, he calls to
our attention (but not for expected disapproval) the
prosodical innovations of Walt Whitman and Gerard
Manley Hopkins.[3]

Saintsbury's most irritating posture is his stubborn
pretense that stress does not play the crucial role in
determining the metrical foot. He insists that syllables are either "long or short"; he cunningly evades
saying what precisely are the features that make syllables long or short (see pages 31 and 32). Saintsbury
obviously does not hold to the Latin and Greek rules
of quantity; indeed, he has only contempt for those
"who commit whoredom with the enchantress of classical metric." When we examine Saintsbury's actual
scansions, we see that stress does define a syllable as
"long":

$$
\begin{array}{llll}
\breve{} \ \bar{} & \breve{} \ \bar{} & \breve{} \ \bar{} & \breve{} \ \bar{} \\
\end{array}
$$

The plain | was grass | y, wild | and bare,
Wide, wild, | and o | pen to | the air,
Which | had built | up ev | e ry where
An un | der-roof | of dole | ful gray.   (p. 110)

No "long" syllable in these lines is unstressed. We
note Saintsbury's recognition of "equivalence" or substitution: a spondee for an iamb in the first foot of the
second line; a monosyllable for an iamb in the first

---

[2] *To Criticize the Critic* (New York, 1965), p. 12.
[3] See *A History of English Prosody*, III, p. 391.

foot of the third line; an anapest for an iamb in the
final foot of the third line. Saintsbury reads the word
ev-e-ry-where and not, as most people pronounce it,
ev'ry-where. Saintsbury scans 'em the way he sees 'em;
he admits few elisions in his system. His prosody is
graphic with a vengeance; he scans the printed word
as it stands on the page. Such literal-mindedness
sometimes leads to mistakes; he reads Marlowe's line
from *Tamburlaine* (see p. 64)

The gol|den ball | of Heav|en's e ter|nal fire

forgetting that *Heaven* is conventionally monosyllabic
in Elizabethan verse.

Indirectly, Saintsbury's ambiguity about length
and stress makes better theoretical sense than most
recent, highly sophisticated linguistic and acoustic investigations of meter. Saintsbury's persistent vague-
ness and "strange empiricism" confirm the brilliant
deductions of Wimsatt and Beardsley.[4] Scansion, the
graphic notation of meter, *abstracts* from a wide variety of phonetic behavior. Once a metrical pattern has
been established, it makes little difference whether a
line reveals (under close phonetic scrutiny) two levels
of stress or twenty. Two basic principles apply: 1) a
metrical *Gestalt* will tend to override small variations
in rhetorical (speech) stress; 2) actual scansion can
take into account only *relative stress.* We may illustrate
(1) in this line:

He found | her by | the o|cean's moan|ing verge . . .

Because *we have been prepared* to hear this line as

4 W. K. Wimsatt, Jr., and Monroe C. Beardsley, "The Concept of Meter:
An Exercise in Abstraction," in *Hateful Contraries* (Lexington, Ky., 1965).

iambic, the normally weak syllable *by* becomes strong, falling, as it does, under the metrical ictus. If we turn the line into fashionable prose and destroy the pattern,

He found her by the best methods of modern research . . .

the normal stress falls on *her*, not *by*.

The principle of relative stress explains how, within an established metrical context, certain normally weak syllables become strong, and conversely, certain normally strong syllables become weak:

In héar|ing óf | the ó|cean, ánd | in sight
Of thóse | ríbbed wínd | streaks rún|ning ín|to white . . .

In the fourth foot of the first line, *and* accumulates metrical strength, falling between the two weak syllables *-cean* and *in*. Similarly, in the third foot of the second line, *streaks* loses strength and must be accounted metrically weak in the scansion. I would, however, regard the second foot as holding two strong-stressed syllables: an authentic spondee.

3

Saintsbury lived from 1845 to 1933; his life spanned both the Victorian and Modern periods of literature. His work in prosody appeared at exactly the same time that Eliot and Pound were first writing their characteristically 'modern' poems. Of course, Saintsbury knew nothing of Eliot at Harvard or

Pound among the Imagists; his investigations stopped with such figures of the *fin de siècle* as Henley and Dowson. But the newest poets (now venerable figures of academic respectability) were sophisticated prosodists; Eliot's first book was called *Ezra Pound: His Metric and Poetry*. Pound himself experimented with dozens of metrical forms and told us about Provençal technique, *vers libre*, and that rhythm "was a shape cut in time." Eliot and Pound regarded prosody as part of literary criticism; what they noted about meter was embodied in a context of literary analysis and evaluation.

A few of the New Critics, notably John Crowe Ransom and Yvor Winters, maintained interest in the study of metrics. During the later forties and early fifties, poets turned away from free verse and began experimenting with traditional forms. Prosody turned from freedom back to restriction; prosodists turned back to the time-honored methods of foot-scansion. Which perhaps makes George Saintsbury the latest thing!

HARVEY GROSS

University of California, Irvine
January, 1966

PREFACE

THE not unfavourable reception of the first two volumes of a larger work on English Prosody suggested, to the author and to the publishers, that there might be room for a more compressed dealing with the subject, possessing more introductory character, and attempting the functions of a manual as well as those of a history. It did not, however, seem that the matter could be satisfactorily treated in extremely brief form, as a primer or elementary school-book. The subject is one not very well suited for elementary instruction ; and in endeavouring to shape it for that use there is a particular danger of too positive and peremptory statement in reference to matters of the most contentious kind. Catechetical instruction has to be categorical ; if you set hypotheses, or alternative systems, before young scholars, they are apt either to distrust the whole thing or to become hopelessly muddled. And the opposite danger—of unhesitating adoption of positive state-ments on doubtful points—must have been found to be only too real by any one who has had to do with education. Schoolboys cannot be too early, or too plentifully, or too variously supplied with good *examples* of verse ; but they should be thoroughly familiar with the practice before they come to the principles.

To the Senior Forms of the higher Secondary Schools, on the other hand, and to students in those Universities which admit English literature as a subject, this function of it is quite suitable and well adapted, and it is for their use that this volume is planned (as well as for that of the general reader who may hardly feel inclined to tackle three large octavos). An effort will be made to include everything that is vital to a clear understanding of the subject; while opportunity will, it is hoped, be found for insertion of some information, both of a historical and of a practical kind, which did not seem so germane to the larger *History*. It has been a main object with me in preparing this book, while reducing prosodic theory to the necessary minimum, but keeping that, to "load every rift" with prosodic fact; and I could almost recommend the student to devote himself to the Contents and the Index, illustrated by the Glossary, all of which have been made exceptionally full, before attacking the text.

The work, like the larger one of which it is not so much an abstract as a parallel with a different purpose, cannot hope to content those who think that prosody should be, like mathematics or music, a science, immutable, peremptory, abstract in the other sense. It will not content those who think—in pursuance or independently of such an opinion—that it should discard appreciation of the actual poetry, on which, from my point of view, it is solely based. It will, from another point, leave dissatisfied those who decline the attempt to reduce this poetry to some general but elastic laws, and who concentrate themselves on the immediate musical or rhetorical values (as they seem to them) of individual poems, or passages, or even (as is not uncommon) lines. Nor will it provide, what some seem to desire, a tabular analysis of every verse-form in the language, for reasons explained in the proper place (*v. inf.* p. 336 *note*). But, from past experience, it seems that it may find some public ready for it; and it is perhaps not wholly fatuous to hope that it may help to create a larger.

GEORGE SAINTSBURY

EDINBURGH,
ALL SOULS' DAY,
1910

BOOK I

INTRODUCTORY AND DOGMATIC

CHAPTER I

INTRODUCTORY

PROSODY, or the study of the constitution of verse, was, not so long ago, made familiar, in so far as it concerned Latin, to all persons educated above the very lowest degree, by the presence of a tractate on the subject as a conclusion to the Latin Grammar. The same persons were further obliged to a more than theoretical knowledge of it, in so far as it concerned that language, by the once universal, now (as some think) most unwisely disused habit of composing Latin verses. The great majority of English poets, from at least the sixteenth century, if not earlier, until far into the nineteenth, had actually composed such verses ; and even more had learnt the rules of them, long before attempting in English the work which has given them their fame. It is sometimes held that this fact—which as a fact is undeniable—has had an undue influence on the way in which English prosody has been regarded ; that it must have exercised an enormous influence on the way in which English poetry has been produced may be denied, but hardly by any one who really considers the fact itself, and who is capable of drawing an inference.

It was, however, a very considerable time before any attempt was regularly made to construct a similar scientific or artistic analysis for English verse itself. Although efforts were made early to adjust that verse to the complete forms of Latin—and of Greek, which is in some respects prosodically nearer than Latin to English,—

although such attempts have been constantly repeated and
are being continued now,—it has always been impossible
for any intelligent person to make them without finding
curious, sometimes rather indefinite, but extremely palp-
able differences and difficulties in the way. The differences
especially have sometimes been exaggerated and more
often mistaken, and it is partly owing to this fact that, up
to the present moment, no authoritative body of doctrine
on the subject of English prosody can be said to exist.
It is believed by the present writer that such a body of
doctrine ought to be and can be framed — with the
constant proviso and warning that it will be doctrine
subject, not to the practically invariable uniformity of
Science, but to the wide variations of Art,—not to the
absolute compulsion of the universal, but to the comparative freedom of the individual and particular. The in-
quiries and considerations upon which this doctrine is
based will be found, at full, in the larger work referred to
in the Preface. In the first Book, here, will be set forth
the leading systems or principles which have actually
underlain, and do underlie, the conflicting views and the
discordant terminology of the subject, and this will be
followed by perhaps the most valuable part, if any be
valuable, of the whole—a series of selected passages, scanned
and commented, from the very beginning to the very end
of English poetry. In the second, a survey will be given
of that actual history of the actual poetry which ought
to be, but has very seldom been, the basis of every discussion on prosody. In the third a brief conspectus will
be supplied of the actual opinions which have been held
on this subject by those who have handled it in English.
The fourth will give, in the first place, a Glossary of Terms,
which appears to be very much needed ; in the second,
a list of poets who have specially influenced the course of
prosody, with reasoned remarks on their connection with
it ; in the third, a selected list of important metres with
their origins and affiliations ; any further matter which may
seem necessary following, with a short Bibliography to

conclude. The object of the whole is not merely to in-
culcate what seems to the author to be the best if not
the only adequate general system of English prosody, but
to provide the student with ample materials for forming
his own judgment on this difficult, long debated, often mistaken, but always, if duly handled, profitable and delectable
matter.

CHAPTER II

SYSTEMS OF ENGLISH PROSODY—THE ACCENTUAL
OR STRESS

Classical
prosody
uniform in
theory.

THE great difficulty attending the study of English prosody, and the cause of the fact that no book hitherto published can be said to possess actual authority on the subject, arises from the other fact that no general agreement exists, or ever has existed, on the root-principles of the matter.[1] Classical writers on metre, of whom we possess a tolerable stock, differed with each other on many minor points of opinion, and from each other in the ways in which they attacked the subject. But they were practically agreed that "quantity" (*i.e.* the difference of technical "time" in pronunciation of syllables) and "feet"—that is to say, certain regular mathematical combinations of "long" and "short" quantity—constituted metre. They had indeed accent— the later Greeks certainly and the Latins probably—which was independent of, and perhaps sometimes opposed to, quantity; but except in what we call the ante-classical times of Latin and the post-classical times of both Latin and Greek, it had nothing to do with metrical arrangement. They had different values of "long" and "short"; but these did not affect metre, nor did the fact that in both languages, but especially in Greek, a certain number of

[1] Or, it may be added, on its terminology; whence it results that there is no subject on which it is so difficult to write without being constantly misunderstood. It is perhaps not surprising that some people almost deny the existence of English prosody itself, and decline at any rate to take it seriously; while others talk about it in ways which half justify the sceptics.

syllables were allowed to be "common"—that is to say, capable of taking the place of "long" or "short" alike. The central system of prosodic arrangement (till the flooding of the later Empire with "barbarians" of various nationality and as various intonation and modes of speech broke it down altogether) remained the same. "Longs" and "shorts" in the various combinations and permutations possible, up to three syllables most commonly, up to four in fewer cases, and possibly up to five in still fewer, made up *lines* which experiment discovered to be harmonious, and practice adopted as such. These lines were sometimes used continuously (with or without certain internal variations of feet, considered equivalent to each other), as in modern blank verse ; sometimes arranged in batches corresponding more or less to each other, as in modern couplet or stanza poetry.

On the other hand, though English prosodists may sometimes agree on details, translated into their different terminologies, the systems which lie at the root of these terminologies are almost irreconcilably different. Even the reduction of these systems to three types may excite protest, though it is believed that it can be made out without begging the question in favour of any one.

English not so.

The discord begins as early as possible ; for there are some who would maintain that "accentual" systems and "stress" systems ought not to be identified, or even associated. It is quite true that the words are technically used [1] with less or more extensive and intensive meaning ; but definitions of each are almost always driven to adopt the other, and in prosodic systems they are practically inseparable. The soundest distinction perhaps is that

"Accent" and "stress."

---

[1] It is inevitable, in dealing with this subject, that technicalities, historical and literary references, etc., should be plentifully employed. To explain them always in the text would mean endless and disgusting delay and repetition ; to give notes of cross-reference in every case would bristle the lower part of the page unnecessarily and hideously. Not merely the Contents and Index, but the various Glossaries and Lists in the Fourth Book have been expressly arranged to supply explanation and assistance in the least troublesome and most compendious manner. But special references will be given when they seem absolutely necessary.

"accent" refers to the habitual stress laid on a syllable in ordinary pronunciation; "stress" to a syllable specially accented for this or that reason, logical, rhetorical, or prosodic purely.

English prosody as adjusted to them.

According to this system (or systems) English poetry consists of syllables—accented or unaccented, stressed or unstressed—arranged on principles which, whatever they may be in themselves, have no analogy to those of classical feet. According to the more heedless and rough-going accentualists—the view is expressed, with all but its utmost crudity, in Coleridge's celebrated Preface to *Christabel*[1]— all you have got to do is to look to the accents. Cruder advocates still have said that "accents take the place of feet" (which is something like saying that points take the place of swords), or that unaccented syllables are "left to take care of themselves." It has also been contended that the number and the position of accents or stresses give a complete and sufficient scheme of the metre. And in some late forms of stress-prosody the regularity, actual or comparative, which used to be contended for by accentualists themselves is entirely given up; lines in continuous and apparently identical arrangement may have two, three, four, five, or even more stresses. While yet others have gone farther still and deliberately proposed reading of verse as a prose paragraph, the natural stresses of which will give the rhythm at which the author aimed.[2] Some again would deny the existence of any normal form of staple lines like the heroic, distributing them in "bars" of "beats" which may vary almost indefinitely.

On the other hand, there are some accentualists who hardly differ, in more than terminology, from the upholders of a foot-and-quantity system. They think that there is no or little time-quantity in English; that an English "long" syllable is really an accented one only, and an English short syllable an unaccented. They would not neglect the

[1] See on this in Book III.
[2] See the article in Glossary on "Musical and Rhetorical Arrangements of Verse," and Rule 41, *infra*, p. 35.

unaccented syllables ; but would keep them in batches similar to, if not actually homonymous with, feet. In fact the difference with them becomes, if not one of mere terminology, one chiefly on the previous question of the final constitution and causation of "long" and "short" syllables. Of these, and of a larger number who consciously or unconsciously approach nearer to, though they do not actually enter, the "go-as-you-please" prosody of the extreme stressmen, the majority of English prosodists has nearly always consisted. Gascoigne, our first writer on the subject, belonged to them, calling accent itself "emphasis," and applying the term "accent" only to the written or typographical symbols of it ; while he laid great stress on its observance in verse. With those who adopt this system, and its terminology, the substitution of a trochee for an iamb in the heroic line is "inversion of accent," the raising or lowering of the usual pronounced value of a syllable, "wrenching of accent," and so on. And the principal argument which they advance in favour of their system against the foot-and-quantity scheme is the very large prevalence of "common" syllables in English— an undoubted fact ; though the inference does not seem to follow.

The mere use of the word "unaccented" for "short" Its diffi-culties and "accented" for "long" does no particular harm, though it seems to some clumsy, irrational, and not always strictly correct even from its own point of view, while it produces unnecessary difficulty in the case of feet, or "sections," with *no* accent in them—things which most certainly exist in English poetry. But the moment that advance is made upon this mere question of words and names, far more serious mischief arises. There can be no doubt that the insistence on strict accent, alternately placed, led directly to the monotonous and snip-snap verse of the eighteenth century. In some cases it leads, logically and necessarily, to denial of such feet as those just mentioned —a denial which flies straight in the face of fact. Although it does not necessarily involve, it most frequently leads also to, the forbidding, ignoring, or shuffling off of trisyllabic feet, which are the chief glory and the chief charm of English poetry, as substituted for dissyllabic. And, further still, it leads to the most extraordinary confusion of rhythms—accentualists very commonly, if not always, maintaining that, inasmuch as there are the same number of accented syllables, it does not matter whether you scan

‒ ◡ ‒ ◡ ‒ ◡◡ ‒

When | the Bri|tish war rior queen |

iambically or

‒ ‒ ◡ ‒ ◡ ‒ ◡◡ ‒

When the | British | warrior | queen

trochaically,

‒ ◡ ◡ ‒ ◡◡ ‒ ◡ ◡ ‒ ‒   ‒ ◡◡ ‒ ‒

In the hex|ameter | rises the | fountain's | silvery | column

dactylically or

‒ ◡ ◡ ‒ ◡◡ ‒ ◡ ◡ ‒   ‒ ◡◡ ‒ ‒

In | the hexam|eter ri|ses the foun|tain's sil|very col|umn

anapæstically.

Further still, and almost worst of all, it leads to the enormities of fancy stress above referred to, committed by people who decline to regard as "long" syllables not accented in ordinary pronunciation.

and insuf-
ficiencies. But its greatest crime is its hopeless inadequacy, poverty, and "beggarly elementariness." At best the accentual prosodist, unless he is a quantitative one in disguise, confines himself to the mere skeleton of the lines, and neglects their delicately formed and softly coloured flesh and members. To leave unaccented syllables "as it were to take care of themselves" is to make prosody mere singsong or patter.

Finally, it may be observed that, in all accentual or stress prosodies which are not utterly loose and desultory, there is a tendency to multiply exceptions, provisos, minor classifications to suit particular cases, and the like, so that English prosody assumes the aspect, not of a combination of general order and individual freedom, but of a tangle of by-laws and partial regulations. Unnecessary when it is not mischievous, mischievous when it is strictly and logically carried out, the accentual system derives its only support from the fact above mentioned (the large number of common syllables to be found in English), from the actual existence of it in *Old* English before the language and the poetry had been modified by Romance admixture, and from an unscientific application of the true proposition that the classical and the English prosodies are *in some respects* radically different.

It will, however, of course be proper to give examples of the manner in which accentual (or stress) scansion is worked by its own partisans and exponents. Their common formula for the English heroic line in its normal aspect is $5xa$: [1]

Examples of its application.

What oft | was thought, | but ne'er | so well | exprest.

If they meet with a trisyllabic foot, as in

And ma|ny an am|orous, ma|ny a hu|morous lay,

they either admit *two* unaccented syllables between the accents, or suggest "slur" or *synalœpha* or "elision" ("man-yan"), this last especially taking place with the definite article "the" ("th'"). But this last process need not be insisted on by accentualists, though it must by the next class we shall come to.

It is common, if not universal, for accentual prosodists to hold that two accents must not come together, so that they are troubled by that double line of Milton's where the ending and beginning run—

Both stood

Both turned.

---

[1] This formula seems due to Latham, the compiler of a well-known work on Language. The foot-division mark | has been sometimes adopted (by Guest) and defended (by Professor Skeat, who, however, does not personally employ it) as a substitute for the accent mark. For arguments against this which seem to the present writer strong, see *H.E.P.* i. 8, and iii. 276, 544-545.

They admit occasional "inversion of accent" (trochaic substitution)—especially at the opening of a verse,—as in the line which Milton begins with

Máker ;

but, when they hold fast to their principles, dislike it much in other cases, as, for instance, in

fálls to | the gróund.

And they complain when the accent which they think necessary falls, as they call it, on one of two weak syllables, as in

And when. |

This older and simpler school, however, represented by Johnson, has been largely supplemented by another, whose members use the term "stress" or *ictus* in preference to "accent," and to a greater or less extent give up the attempt to establish normality of line at all.

Its various sects and supporters. Some of them [1] admit lines of four, three, or even two stresses, as, for instance—

His mín|isters of vén|geance and pursúit. |

Others [2] break it up into "bars" or "sections" which need not contain the same or any fixed number of "beats" or "stresses," while some again [3] seem to regard the stresses of a whole passage as supplying, like those of a prose paragraph, a sufficient rhythmical skeleton the flesh of which —the unaccented or unstressed part—is allowed to huddle itself on and shuffle itself along as it pleases.

This school has received large recent accessions ; but even now the greater number of accentualists do little more than eschew the terms of quantity, and substitute for them those of accent, more or less consistently.   Many of

[1] Of whom the most important by far is Mr. Bridges, though he has never, I think, reduced the number to two, or increased it above five. Others, however, have admitted *eight* !

[2] *E.g.* Mr. Thomson, Dr. M'Cormick, M. Verrier.

[3] *E.g.* Mr. J. A. Symonds, Mr. Hewlett.

them even use the classical names and divisions of feet;
and with these there need not, according to strict necessity,
be any quarrel, since their error, if it be one, only affects
the constitution of prosodic material before it is verse at
all, and not the actual prosodic arrangement of verse as
such.

CHAPTER III

SYSTEMS OF ENGLISH PROSODY—THE SYLLABIC

History of the syllabic theory. A STRICTLY syllabic system of prosody has hardly at any time been a sufficient key, even in appearance, to English verse. But it has preserved a curious insistence of pretension, and the study of it is of great and informing prosodic interest. It is, of course, French in origin—French prosody, except in eccentric instances, has been from the first, and is to the present day, strictly syllabic. It is innocuous in so far as in the words "octosyllable," "decasyllable," "fourteener," and the like, the irreducible syllabic minimum (save by licence of certain metres) is conveniently indicated. In so early an example as Orm (*v. inf.*) we find it carried out exactly and literally. But the inherited spirit of Old English, surviving and resisting all changes and reinforcements of vocabulary, accent, and everything else, will have none of it. In the *fif*teener [1] itself; in its sequel and preserver, ballad measure; in octosyllabic couplet—not merely in the loose form of *Genesis and Exodus*, but to some extent even in the strict one of *The Owl and the Nightingale*; in almost all mixed modes, when once they have broken free from direct copying of French or Provençal, it is cast to the winds. It can only be introduced into Chaucer, as far as his heroic couplet is concerned, by perpetual violations of probability, document, and rhythm. Even in Gower, the principal repre-

[1] For the almost necessary precedence, owing to the inflexional *e*, of the *four*teener by this, and for expansion and explanation of other historic facts mentioned in this chapter, see Scanned Conspectus and Books II. and III.

14

sentative of it, and one who probably did aim at it, there
are some certain, and many probable, lapses from strict
observance. But in the linguistic and phonetic changes
of the fifteenth century, with the consequent decadence
of original literary poetry, the principle of syllabic liberty
degenerates into intolerable licence, and the doggerel
which resulted, after triumphing or at least existing for
some generations, provoked considerable reaction in
practice and a still more considerable mistake in principle.

Wyatt, Surrey, and their successors in the middle of
the century and the first half of Elizabeth's reign, are
pretty strict syllabically; and it was from their practice,
doubtless, that Gascoigne—one of the last of the group, but
our first English preceptist in prosody—conceived the idea
that English has but one foot, of two syllables. Spenser's
practice in the *Shepherd's Kalendar* is not wholly in accordance with this; but even he came near to observing it
later, and the early blank-verse writers were painfully
scrupulous in this respect.

But it was inevitable that blank verse, and especially
dramatic blank verse, should break through these restraints;
and in the hands of Shakespeare it soon showed that the
greatest English verse simply paid no attention at all
to syllabic limitations; while lyric, though rather slower,
was not so very slow to indulge itself to some extent, as
it was tempted by "triple-timed" music. The excesses,
however, of the decayed blank verse of the First Caroline
period joined with those of the enjambed couplet, though
these were not strictly syllabic, to throw liberty into
discredit; and the growth and popularity of the strict
closed couplet encouraged a fresh delusion—that English
prosody *ought* to be syllabic. Dryden himself to some
extent countenanced this, though he indemnified himself by
the free use of the Alexandrine, or even of the fourteener,
in decasyllabics. The example of Milton was for some
time not imitated, and has even to this day been misunderstood. About the time of Dryden's own death, in the

temporary decadence of the poetic spirit, syllabic prosody made a bold bid for absolute rule.

In the year 1702 Edward Bysshe, publishing [1] the first detailed and positive manual of English prosody, laid it down, without qualification or apology, that "the structure of our verses, whether blank or rhyming, consists in a certain number of syllables ; not in feet composed of long or short syllables, as the verses of the Greeks and Romans." And although all Bysshe's details, which, as will be seen below, were rigidly arranged on these principles— so that he made no distinction between verse of triple time (though he grudgingly and almost tacitly admitted it) and verse of double, as such,—were not adopted by others, his doctrine was always (save in a very few instances to be duly noticed later) implicitly, and often explicitly, the doctrine of the eighteenth century. Nor has this ever lost a certain measure of support ; while it is very curious that the few foreign students of English prosody who have arisen in late years are usually inclined to it.

One difficulty in it, however, could never escape its most peremptory devotees ; and a shift for meeting it must have been devised at the same time as the doctrine. It was all very well to lay down that English verse *must* consist of a certain number of syllables; but it could escape no one who had ever read a volume or even a few pages of English poetry, that it *did* consist of a very uncertain number of them. The problem was, therefore, how to get rid of the surplus where it existed. It was met by recourse to that very classical prosody which was in other respects being denied, and by the adoption of ruthless "elision" or "crushing out" of the supposed superfluities. This involved not merely elision proper—the vanishing or metrical ignoring of a vowel at the end of a word before

a vowel (or an *h*) at the beginning of another, "th$\left(\overset{,}{e}\right)$ Almighty," "t$\left(\overset{,}{o}\right)$ admire." Application of a similar pro-

---

[1] See Bibliography and Book III.

cess to the interior of words like " vi$\binom{'}{o}$let," " di$\binom{'}{a}$mond,"
was inculcated, and in fact insisted on ; and even where
consonants preceded and followed a vowel of the easily
slurrable kind, as in " wat*e*ry," the suppression of the *e*

and sometimes even of other vowels—" del$\binom{'}{i}$cate "—was
prescribed.

There may possibly be two opinions (though it seems Its results.
strange that there should be) on the æsthetic results of
this proceeding.   To the present writer they seem utterly
hideous ; while the admission of the full syllables seems
melodious and satisfying.   It may also be pointed out
that there is a very tell-tale character about the fact that
not a few prosodists who defend " elision " in principle
defend it only as a metrical fiction, and even lay down
positively that the elided syllables are *always* to be pronounced.[1]   But it is far less matter of opinion—if it is
even matter of opinion at all—first, that this process of
mangling and monotonising English poetry is unnecessary;
and, secondly, that it is inconsistent with the historic
development of the language and the literature.   That it
is unnecessary will, it is hoped, be demonstrated in the
next of these Introductory Chapters ; and that it is unhis-
torical the whole body of the historical survey to follow
will show.   And another objection of great importance can
be made good at once and here.   The rigid observance of
the syllabic system produces, and cannot but produce, an
intolerable monotony—a monotony which has made the
favourite verse of the eighteenth century positively (if
perhaps excessively and unreasonably) loathsome to succeeding generations.   It would be condemned by this, if
it had no other fault ; while it has, as a matter of fact,
hardly a virtue.   It was tried once for all by Orm, and failed
once for all, in the beginning of modern English, and it
has never been tried in practice or maintained in theory

---

[1] This, it may be pointed out, is in flat contradiction to the older
doctrine of, for instance, Dryden, that no vowel can be cut out before
another in scansion which is not so in pronunciation.

since without validating inferior poetry and discouraging good.[1]

[1] Examples here can hardly be needed. At any rate, one (Shenstone's, *v. inf.*, own) may suffice :

> The loose wall *tottering* o'er the trembling shade.

Cautions.

Here syllabic prosody would pronounce, and in strictness spell, "tott'ring." —This is perhaps as good a place as any to make some remarks on the connection of syllables with English prosody. In that prosody there are no *extrametrical* syllables, except at the end of lines, and (much more doubtfully) at the cæsura, which is a sort of end. Every syllable that occurs elsewhere must be part of, or constitute, a foot ; and it is for this reason that the "Rules" following begin with feet, not syllables. It is practically impossible, in many, if not in most cases, to tell the prosodic value of an English syllable, or an English word, till you see it in actual verse. —Again, although there are, of course, innumerable instances where a foot coincides with a word, the composition of the foot out of syllables belonging to different words, as in

> The thun|*der of* | the trum|*pets of* | the night,

or

> To set|*tle the* | success|*ion of* | the state,

is usually more effective. —And, lastly, although there have, at different times, been strange prejudices against the use of monosyllables and of polysyllables, these prejudices are, in both cases, wholly unreasonable.

CHAPTER IV

SYSTEMS OF ENGLISH PROSODY—THE FOOT

ALTHOUGH the accentual and the syllabic systems—sometimes separate, but oftener combined—have, on the whole,
dominated English preceptist prosody almost from the
time when it first began to be formally studied, there has,
until very recently, been a constant tendency to blend
with these, if not the full acceptance, at any rate a certain
borrowing, of the terminology of a *third* system—the foot-
and-quantity one, so well known in the classical prosodies.
Not before Bysshe (*c.* 1700) do you find any positive
denial of "feet." Gascoigne (*c.* 1570) talks of them ; Milton
speaks of "committing short and long" ; Dr. Johnson,
though using a strict accent-and-syllable scheme, admits
(whether with absolute accuracy or not does not matter)
that "our heroic verse is derived from the iambic." And
in more modern times, from Mitford downwards, arguments
against the applicability of the terms in English have not
unfrequently been found consistent with an occasional, if
not a regular, employment of them.

In fact, nothing but a curious suspicion, as of something
cabalistical in them, can prevent their use, or the use of
some much more clumsy and inconvenient equivalents—
bars, beats, sections, what not ;[1] for that use is based on the
most unalterable of all things, except the laws of thought,
the laws of mathematics. Everybody, whatsoever his
prosodic sect, admits that verse consists of alternations
of two values—some would say of more than two, but that

---

[1] The most recent, perhaps, and the most unfortunate competitor is
"stress-unit "—for there are most certainly feet (*i.e.* constitutive divisions
of lines) which include no stress at all.

only complicates the application of an unchanged argument. Now the possible combinations of two different things, in successive numerical units of two, three, four, etc., are not arbitrary, but naturally fixed ; and the names of feet— iambic, trochaic, dactylic, etc.—are merely tickets for these combinations.

Particular objections to its systematic use.

The reasons of the objection have been various, and are perhaps not always fully stated, or even fully appreciated, by those who advance them. It is most common perhaps now (though it was not so formerly) to find the objection itself lodged thus—that the so-called English iambs, anapæsts, etc., are different things from the feet so called in Greek or Latin. This is sufficiently met by the reply that they are naturally so, the languages being different, and that all that is necessary is that the English foot should stand to English prosody as the Latin or Greek foot does to Latin or Greek, that is to say, as the necessary and constituent middle stage between the syllable and the line. But a less vague and, in appearance at least, more solid objection is that the Latin and the Greek foot were con- stituted out of definite " quantities " attaching to definite syllables, and that there is "no syllabic quantity in English," though there may be vowel quantity. And this objection is generally, if not always, based on or backed by a further one, that " quantity " depends directly on *time* of pronuncia- tion ; while this again is supported, still further back, by elaborate discussions of accent and quantity,[1] by denials that accent can constitute quantity, and by learned expatiations in quest of proof that Greeks and Romans scanned their verses as they did *not* pronounce them— that there was a sort of amicable pitched battle, always going on, between quantity and accent.

Now it can be easily shown that, even if these con-

---

[1] A full account of these would occupy a book bigger than the larger *History*. Among the latest and most curious attempts on the subject is one to mark off certain metrical rhythms as " accentual," certain others as " quantitative." This (which partly results from the superfluous anxiety to discover and isolate the sources of length and shortness) makes some- thing very like a chimera or a hotch-potch of English verse.

tentions as to classical verse be accepted (and some of
them are very doubtful), they supply no sort of bar to the
application of the foot system, with such quantity as it
requires, to English. It is quite true that the proportion
of syllables of absolutely fixed quantity — that is fixed
capacity of filling up what corresponds to the long or short
places of a classical verse—is, in English, very small. There
are some which the ear discovers by the awkwardness of
the sound when they are forced into a "short" place. So
also there are some which—by the coincidence of vowel
quality, position, and absence of accent—it is practically
impossible to put into a "long" place, such as the second
syllable of "Deity." Nor are what are called "long vowel
sounds"—the sounds of "rite," "fate," "beat," "Europe,"
"omen," "awkward," etc.—always sufficient to make a
syllable inflexibly long ; though they may be sometimes.
Again, the extremest "shortness" of vowel sound, as in
"and" or "if," will not prevent such syllables from being
indubitably long in certain values and collocations. In
other words, that peculiarity of being "common"—that is
to say, of being capable of holding either position—which
was far from unknown in the classical languages, is very
much more prevalent in English. It would be quite false
to say that every syllable in English is common ; but it is
scarcely at all false to say that almost every English *mono*-
syllable is, and an extremely large proportion of others.

The methods and movements by which this commonness is turned into length or shortness for the purposes of
the poet are obvious enough, and in practice undeniable ;
though the processes of professional phonetics sometimes
tend to obscure or even to deny them. Every well-educated
and well-bred Englishman, who has been accustomed to
read poetry and utter speech carefully, knows that when he
emphasises a syllable like "and," "if," "the," etc., it
becomes what the Germans would call *versfähig*—capable
of performing its metrical duty—in the long position ; that
when he does not, it is not so capable. Every one knows
in practice, though it may be denied in theory, that similar

lengthening [1] follows the doubling of a consonant after a short vowel, or the placing of a group of consonants of different kinds after it—the vowel-sound running, as it were, under the penthouse of consonants till it emerges. Extreme loudness and sharpness would have the same effect in conversation, but, unless very obviously suggested by sense, would escape notice in silent reading. Not very seldom, the mere art of the poet will get weight enough on a short syllable to fit it for its place as " long," or conjure away from a long one length enough to enable it to act as " short."

At any rate, it is with these two values, and with syllables endowed with them by custom, incidental effect, place, sense, the poet's sleight of hand, or otherwise, that the English poet deals ; and has dealt ever since a period impossible to nail down with exactness to year or decade, but beginning, perhaps, early in the twelfth century and perfecting itself in the thirteenth and later. And impartial examination of the whole facts from that period shows that he deals with them on a system, in early times no doubt almost or quite unconsciously adopted, but perfectly recognisable. In still earlier or " Old " English verse this system is not discernible at all ; in the earliest period of " Middle " English it is discernible, struggling to get itself into shape. Later, with advances and relapses, it perfects itself absolutely. Its principles are as follows :—

Intermediate rules of arrangement. **Every English verse consists of a certain number of feet, made up of long and short syllables, each of which is of equal consequence in the general composition of the line.**

The correspondence of the foot arrangements between different lines constitutes the link between them, and determines their general character.

Some interim rules of feet (expanded in note). **But this correspondence need not be limited to repetition of feet composed of a fixed and identical number of syllables in the same order; on the contrary, the best verse admits of large substitution of feet of different syllabic length, provided—(1) that these are equal or nearly equal in prosodic value to those for which they are substituted;**

---

[1] In metrical quantity, not in vowel sound.

(2) that the substituted feet go rhythmically well with those next to which they are placed.[1]

[1] A fuller list of observed rules for English verse generally will be found in the next chapter, but between the two a set of remarks, specially on the foot, may be extracted from the larger *History*, vol. i. pp. 82-84.

Every English verse which has disengaged itself from the versicle[1] **is composed, and all verses that are disengaging themselves therefrom show a *nisus* towards being composed, of feet of one, two, or three syllables.**
The foot of one syllable is always long, strong, stressed, accented, what-not.[2]
The foot of two syllables usually consists of one long and one short syllable, and though it is not essential that either should come first, the short precedes rather more commonly.
The foot of three syllables never has more than one long syllable in it, and that syllable, save in the most exceptional rhythms, is always the first or the third. In modern poetry, by no means usually, but not seldom, it has no long syllable at all.

The foot of one syllable is practically not found except
a, **In the first place of a line.**
b, **In the last place of it.**
c, **At a strong cæsura or break, it being almost invariably necessary that the voice should rest on it long enough to supply the missing companion to make up the equivalent of a " time and a half " at least.**
d, **In very exceptional cases where the same trick of the voice is used apart from strict cæsura.**
The foot of two syllables and that of three may, subject to the rules below, be found anywhere.
 But :
These feet of two and three syllables may be very freely substituted for each other.
There is a certain metrical and rhythmical norm of the line which must not be confused by too frequent substitutions.
In no case, or in hardly any case,[3] **must such combinations be put together so that a juxtaposition of more than three short syllables results.**

---

[1] Of Anglo-Saxon and very early Middle English poetry. See Scanned Conspectus and Book II.

[2] Except, to speak paradoxically, when it is nothing at all. The pause-foot or half-foot, the "equivalent of silence," is by no means an impossible or unknown thing in English poetry, as, for instance, in Lady Macbeth's line, I. v. 41—

Under | my bat|tlements. | ∧ Come, | you spirits,

where | spirits, | though not actually impossible, would spoil the line in one way, and "come," as a monosyllabic foot, in another.

[3] The exceptions, and probably the only ones, are to be found, if any-

But, for the purpose of this present book, illustration and example are of much more value than abstract exposition ; and to them we shall now turn.

Here, for instance, is a line from Tennyson's "Brook":

> Twinkled the innumerable ear and tail.

The different systems applied to a single verse of Tennyson's,

Now the system which regards syllabic precision first of all, with a minor glance at accent, but rejects "feet," surveys this line and pronounces it passable with the elision

> Twinkled *th'* innumerable ear and tail,

but rather shakes its head at the absence of accent, or the slight and weak accent, in "innumer*a*ble," and the "inversion" of accent in "twìnkled."

The system which looks at accent first of all pronounces that there are only *four* proper accents [stresses] here :

> Twìnkled the innùmerable èar and tàil.

Both these systems, moreover—the syllabic, as far as it recognises accent ; the accentual, of necessity,—regard "twinkled" as the admittance (pardonable, censurable, or quite condemnable, according to individual theory) of "wrenched accent," "inverted stress," or something of the kind—as a thing abnormal and licentious.

The foot system simply scans it—

> $$- \;\smile\; \smile\; \smile - \; \smile - \; \smile\; - \; \smile\; -$$
> Twinkled | the innu |mera|ble ear | and tail ;

regarding "twinkled" as a trochee substituted in full right for an iamb, and "the innu-" as an anapæst in like case ; "merā" as raised, by a liberty not out of accordance with the actual derivation, to a sufficiently long quantity for its position, and the other two feet as pure iambs.

and their application examined.

Now let us examine these three views.

In the first place, the bare syllabic view (which, it is fair

where, in some modern blank verse, where two tribrachs, or a tribrach and an iamb or anapæst, succeed each other.

to say, is almost obsolete, save among foreigners, though in consistency it ought to find defenders at home) takes no account of any special quality in the line at all. It is turned out to sample ; the knife is applied at "th' " to fit specification ; and there you are. It differs only from Southey's favourite heroic ejaculation

Aballiboozabanganorribo!

in being less "pure."

The syllabic-*plus*-accentual view passes it ; but with certain reservations. "Twinkled" is an "aberration," a "licence" perhaps (in some views certainly), a more or even less venial sin, while "-āble" with *a* in a stressed or accented place is a case for more head-shaking still. The line is saved ; yet so as by fire.

So is it under the looser stress-accentual system, but by a fire more devouring still. According to this latter, all rhythmical similarity with its companion five-stress lines is lost on the one hand, and on the other a jumble, with difficulty readable and absolutely heterogeneous, is created in the line itself. Your first rhythmical mouthful is "twink-," then you gabble over "led the innū-" till you rest on this last ; then you repeat the process (as soon as you have breath enough) with "-merable ear," and finally you reach "and tail." But you never find your fifth stress, and instead of continuous blank verse you make the context a sort of clumsy Pindaric.[1]

Even if this last description be regarded as exaggerated, it will remain a sober fact that, in all these handlings, either the beauty of the line is obscured altogether, or it is smuggled off as a "licence," or it is converted into something individual, separated from its neighbours, and possessing no kinship to them.

Yet the line, though not "a wonder and a wild desire," is a good one ; and (therein differing from their eighteenth-century ancestors) the syllabists and accentualists would

---

[1] It is difficult to see how this effect can be avoided by those who think that accents or stresses, governing prosody, vary in Milton from *eight* to *three*.

mostly nowadays allow this, though their principles have
to submit it to *privilegia* and allowances to make it out.

The foot arrangement makes no difficulty, needs no
privilegium, and necessarily applies none. The line is at
once recognised by the ear as a good line and correspondent to its neighbours, which, as a body, and also at
once when a few have been read, informed that ear
that they were five-foot lines of iambic basis. Therefore
it will lend itself to foot-arrangement on that norm. The
five feet may be iambs, trochees, anapæsts, spondees,
tribrachs, and *perhaps* (this is a question of ear) dactyls
and pyrrhics. These may be substituted for each other
as the ear shall dictate, provided that the general iambic
base is not overthrown or unduly obscured.

Further, these feet are composed of long and short
syllables, the length and shortness of which is determined
to some extent by ordinary pronunciation, but subject to
various modifying influences of position and juxtaposition.
Under those laws to which all its companions are equally
and inevitably subject, *mutatis mutandis,* it makes itself
out as above :

$$- \cup \quad \cup \cup - \cup - \cup -$$

Twinkled | the innu|mera|ble ear | and tail—

trochee, anapæst, iamb, iamb, iamb. The justification of *ā*
in " āble " has already been partly given ; it may be added
that in the actual pronunciation of the word by good
speakers there is a " secondary accent " (as they call it) on
the syllable.

Here there is no straining, no "private bill" legislation,
no separating of the line from its fellows, only a reasonable
Reign of Law with reasonable easements.

Application
further to
his " Holly-
hock " song. Let us now take a more complicated instance, also
from Tennyson. In that poet's first volume there was
a "Song" which, unlike most of its fellows, remained
practically unaltered amid the great changes which he
introduced later. It has, I believe, always been a special
favourite with those who have been most in sympathy with
his poetry. But, nearly twenty years after its first appear-

ance, it was described by no ill-qualified judge (an admirer of Tennyson on the whole) in the words given in the note:[1] and I believe it had been similarly objected to earlier. Now what were the lines that excited this cry of agonised indignation ? They are as follows:—

> A spirit haunts the year's last hours
> Dwelling amid these yellowing bowers:
>   To himself he talks ;
> For at eventide, listening earnestly,
> At his work you may hear him sob and sigh
>   In the walks ;
>   Earthward he boweth the heavy stalks
> Of the mouldering flowers :
>   Heavily hangs the broad sunflower
>   Over its grave in the earth so chilly ;
>   Heavily hangs the hollyhock,
>   Heavily hangs the tiger-lily.

Now it is not very difficult to perceive the defects of this extremely beautiful thing in the eyes of a syllabic-accentualist, as this critic (whether knowing it or not) probably was.

The syllabists have always, by a perhaps natural though perhaps also irrational extension of their arithmetical pre-possession, disliked lines of irregular length on the page. Bysshe would have barred stanzas ; a very few years before Tennyson's book, Crowe, then Public Orator at Oxford, had protested against the exquisite line-adjustments of the seventeenth century. To the pure accentualists the thing might seem an unholy jumble, accented irregularly, irregularly arranged in number, seemingly observing different rhythms in different parts.

Now see how it looks under the foot system :

> A spi|rit haunts | the year's | last hours
> Dwelling | amid | these yel|lowing bowers :
>   To himself | he talks ;

---

[1] Having already called it "an odious piece of pedantry," the critic (*Blackwood's Magazine*, April 1849) adds : " What metre, Greek or Roman, Russian or Chinese, it was intended to imitate we have no care to inquire : the man was writing English and had no justifiable pretence for torturing our ears with verse like this."

For at e|ventide, lis|tening ear|nestly,
At his work | you may hear | him sob | and sigh
  In the walks ;
  Earth|ward he bow|eth the hea|vy stalks
Of the moul|dering flowers :
  Hea|vily hangs | the broad | sunflower
  O|ver its grave | in the earth | so chilly ;
  Hea|vily hangs | the hol|lyhock,
  Hea|vily hangs | the ti|ger-lily—

the feet being sometimes, at the beginning of the lines, monosyllabic, and of course of one long syllable only

(Earth-, Hea-|, O-|) ; sometimes dissyllabic, iambic mainly, but occasionally at least *semi*-spondaic—

$$\smile - \smile \quad - \qquad \smile \quad - \qquad \triangledown \quad -$$

A spir|it haunts | the year's | last hours ;

often trisyllabic, and then always anapæstic—

$$\smile\ \smile - \quad \smile\ \smile \quad - \quad \smile\smile \quad - \quad \smile\triangledown$$

For at e|ventide list|ening earn|estly.

Even so early in the present book this should need little comment ; but it may be the better for some. It is an instance of substitution carried out boldly, but unerringly ; so that, iamb and anapæst being the coin of interchange and equivalence, the rhythm is now iambic, now anapæstic chiefly, the two being not muddled, but *fluctuant*—a prosodic part-song. And the foot system brings this out straightforwardly and on its general principles, with no beggings or assumptions whatever for the particular instance. Moreover, the structure of the piece may be paralleled freely from the songs in Shakespeare's plays.[1]

Such application possible always and everywhere. It is indeed sometimes said that such methods of scansion as these may apply very well to nineteenth-century poets, but that they are out of place in regard to older ones. This is demonstrably false. The method applies alike, and in like measure obviates all difficulties, in examples of the thirteenth, fourteenth, fifteenth, sixteenth, seventeenth, and eighteenth centuries. It is as applicable

[1] Such as " Under the Greenwood Tree."

to the early and mostly anonymous romancers and song-writers as to Tennyson, it accommodates Shakespeare as well as Browning. To Milton as to Shelley, to Dryden and Pope as to the most celebrated of our modern experimenters, say to Miss Christina Rossetti or Mr. Swinburne, it " fits like a glove." The rules in the next chapter, and the subjoined examples fully scanned in Chapter VI., will show its application as a beginning ; the whole contents of this volume must give the fuller illustration and confirmation.[1]

[1] For cautions and additions, as well as explanations, see Glossary, especially under " Foot," " Stress-unit," " Quantity," etc.

CHAPTER V

RULES OF THE FOOT SYSTEM

§ A. FEET

(These Rules are not imperative or compulsory precepts, but observed inductions from the practice of English poets. He that can break them with success, let him.)

Feet composed of long and short syllables.

1. English poetry, from the first constitution of literary Middle English to the present day, can best be scanned by a system of *feet*, or groups of syllables in two different values, which may be called for convenience *long* (–) and *short* (⌣).

Not all combinations actual.

2. The nature of these groups of syllables is determined by the usual mathematical laws of permutation; but some of them appear more frequently than others in English poetry, and some hardly occur at all.

Differences from "classical" feet.

3. Although, in the symbols of their constitution, these feet resemble those of the classical prosodies, it does not follow that they are identical with them, except mathematically,[1] the nature of the languages being different; and, in particular, their powers of combining in metre are far from being identical, so that combinations of feet which are successful in Greek and Latin need by no means be successful in English. Success is indeed almost limited to instances where the metrical constituents are restricted to iambs (⌣ –), anapæsts (⌣ ⌣ –), and trochees (– ⌣), with the spondee (– –) as an occasional ingredient.

[1] See above, Rule 2. It should be hardly necessary to remark that the explanations and exemplifications of these rules are to be furnished by the whole book, and that the Glossary in particular should be in constant use.

4. The iamb ($\cup$ –), the trochee (– $\cup$), and the anapæst ($\cup\cup$–) are by far the commonest English feet; in fact, the great bulk of English poetry is composed of them. The three usual kinds —iamb, trochee, anapæst.

5. The spondee (– –) is not so unusual as has sometimes been thought; but owing to the commonness of most syllables, especially in *thesis*, it may often be passed as an iamb, and sometimes as a trochee. The spondee.

6. The dactyl (– $\cup\cup$), on the other hand, though observable enough in separate English words, does not seem to compound happily in English, its use being almost limited to that of a substitute for the trochee. Used in continuity, either singly or with other feet, it has a tendency, especially in lines of some length, to rearrange itself into anapæsts with anacrusis. In very short lines, however, this "tilt" has not always time to develop itself. The dactyl.

7. The pyrrhic ($\cup\cup$) may occur in English, but is rarely wanted (see note above on spondee). The pyrrhic.

8. The tribrach ($\cup$ $\cup$ $\cup$), however, has become not unusual. The tribrach.

9. Other combinations (for names see Glossary) than these are certainly rare, and are perhaps never wanted in English verse, though they are plentiful in prose. (See Rule 41 and Glossary.) Others.

§ B. Constitution of Feet

10. The quality, or contrast of quality, called "quantity," which fits English syllables for their places as long or short in a foot, is not uniform or constant. Quality or "quantity" in feet.

11. It does not necessarily depend on the amount of time taken to pronounce the syllable; though there is probably a tendency to lengthen or shorten this time according to the prosodic length or shortness required. Not necessarily "time,"

12. It does not wholly depend on the usual quantity [1] of nor vowel "quantity."

[1] *E.g.* "fāte" or "fāst" as opposed to "făt"; "meet" to "dĕter"; "rīte" to "fĭt"; "ōmen" to "ŏtter"; "dūpe" to "bŭt."

the vowel sound in the syllable; for long - sounding vowels are not very seldom shortened, and short=sounding ones are constantly made long.

Accumulated consonants,

13. An accumulation of consonants after the vowel will lengthen it prosodically, but need not necessarily do so.

or rhetorical stress,

14. Strong rhetorical stress will almost always lengthen if required.

or place in verse will quantify.

15. The place in verse, if cunningly managed by the poet, will lengthen or shorten.

Commonness of monosyllables.

16. All monosyllables are common, the articles being, however, least susceptible of lengthening, and the indefinite perhaps hardly at all.

§ C. EQUIVALENCE AND SUBSTITUTION

Substitution of equivalent feet.

17. The most important law of English prosody is that which permits and directs the interchange of certain of these feet with others, or, in technical language, the substitution of equivalent feet.

Its two laws.

18. This process of substitution is governed by two laws : one in a manner *a priori*, the other the result of experience only.

Confusion of base must be avoided.

19. Substitution must not take place in a batch of lines, or even (with rare exceptions) in a single line, to such an extent that the base of the metre can be mistaken.

(Of which the ear must judge.)

20. Even short of this result of confusion the ear must decide whether the substitution is allowable.

Certain substitutions are not eligible.

21. As a result of experience we find that the feet most suitable — if not alone suitable — as substitutes for the iamb—the commonest foot=staple—are the trochee, the anapæst, and the tribrach; that the dactyl substitutes well, if not too freely used, for the trochee.[1] These equivalences are reciprocal.

[1] The combination of dactyl and trochee in English, however, will not produce the same effect as the combination of dactyl and spondee in Latin or Greek.

§ D. Pause

22. Next to equivalence, the most important and valuable engine in the constitution of English verses is the variation of the middle or internal pause.

Variation of pause.

23. Except in very long lines — which always tend to pause themselves either at the middle or at *two* places more or less equidistant—there is no reason why the pause of an English line should not be at any syllable from the first to the penultimate, and none why it should or should not occur at the end of a line, couplet, or even stanza — though in the last-named case rather special reasons are required for its omission. Not every line need necessarily have any pause at all.

Practically at discretion.

24. The effect of blank verse depends more upon pause-variation than upon anything else; and by this variation, accompanied by stop or overrun ("enjambment") at the end of the line, *verse-paragraphs* are constituted, which can contain verse-*clauses* or *sentences*, in like manner brought into existence by pauses.

Blank verse specially dependent on pause.

§ E. Line-Combination

25. Lines, composed as above of feet, can be used in English either continuously on the same or equivalent patterns, or in batches of two or more.

Simple or complex.

26. The batches of two almost necessarily require rhyme to indicate and isolate them, especially if the individual lines are of the same length. Other batches [stanzas] might, as far as any *a priori* objection goes, consist of unrhymed lines, symmetrically correspondent, or irregular [Pindaric].

Rhymes necessary to couplet.

27. It is, however, found in practice, despite the examples of Campion, Collins, and one or two others, that rhymeless batching or stanza-making is very seldom successful.[1]

Few instances of successful unrhymed stanza.

[1] Rules 26 and 27 do not apply to *un*metrical verse, such as the old alliterative couplet-line, or the rhythmed prose-verse of *Ossian*, Blake, and Whitman.

Unevenness of line in length.

28. There is neither *a priori* objection nor *a posteriori* inconvenience to be urged against the construction of stanzas or batches in lines of very uneven length.

Stanzas to be judged by the ear.

29. Every stanza-scheme must undergo, and is finally to be judged by, the test of the ear, and that only.

Origin of commonest line-combinations.

30. The commonest and oldest line=combinations—octosyllabic couplet, "common" or "ballad" measure, "long" and "short" measure, etc.—in some cases demonstrably, in all probably, result from the breaking up of the old long line ("fifteener" or "fourteener"), which itself came from the metricalising of the O.E. double stave.

§ F. RHYME

Rhyme natural in English.

31. It is natural to English poetry—*i.e.* Middle and Modern English, or English poetry proper—to rhyme; and, except in the case of blank verse, no unrhymed measure for the last seven centuries has ever produced large quantities of uniformly satisfactory quality.

It must be "full,"

32. Rhyme in English must be "full," *i.e.* consonantal (on the vowel *and* following consonant or consonants), not merely assonantal (on the vowel only). Assonance by itself is insufficient.

and not identical.

33. It should not, according to modern usage, be *identical*—that is to say, the rhyming syllables should not consist of exactly the same vowels and consonants. But exceptions to this may be found in good poets, especially when the *words* are not the same.

General rule as to it.

34. Good rhyme has necessarily varied, at different times, with pronunciation; but a certain rough rule may be seen prevailing not uncommonly, that vowels in rhyme may take the value which they have in words other than those actually employed.[1]

Alliteration.

35. What is sometimes called "*head*-rhyme" (*i.e.* "alliteration") has now no place in English as rhyme at all, nor does it constitute either metre or stanza; but it

---

[1] Thus Dryden rhymes "travell*er*" to "st*ar*," giving the *er* the value it has in "cl*er*k."

is a permissible, and often a very considerable, ornament to verse.

36. Rhyme is either single (on the last syllable only), double (on the two last), or triple (on the three last). Beyond three the effect would be burlesque, and this is hard to keep out of triple rhyme, and even sometimes seems to menace the double. *Single, etc., rhyme.*

37. In serious poetry the fuller in sound the single rhyme is the better. *Fullness of sound.*

38. Rhyme is usually at the end of the line ; but it may be "internal"; that is to say, syllables at one or even more than one place within the line may rhyme to the syllable at the end or to each other, and syllables within one line may rhyme to those at corresponding places within another. *Internal rhyme permissible,*

39. But this has a dangerous tendency to break the lines up. *but sometimes dangerous.*

§ G. Miscellaneous

40. The effect of English poetry at all times, but especially for the last hundred years, has been largely dependent on *Vowel=music*. This is by no means limited to the practice of what used to be called "making the sound suit the sense," though the two sometimes coincide. Vowel-music, not without occasional assistance from consonants, establishes a sort of *accompaniment* to the intelligible poetry—a prosodic *setting*. *Vowel-music.*

41. In the management of this, as of rhyme, pause, enjambment, and even the selection and juxtaposition of feet themselves, the poet often, if not as a rule in the best examples, uses particular sleights of fingering and execution parallel to those of the musical composer and performer. The results of this may appear to constitute verse=sections different from the feet. But these, however, never supersede feet, and are always resolvable into them ; nor do they ever supply criteria for anything except the individual line or passage. They stand to prosody proper very much as delivery or elocution does to rhetoric. The conveniences of this "fingering," or *"Fingering."*

poetic elocution, as well as sense and other things, may sometimes bring about *alternative* scansions, but all these connect themselves with and are obedient to the general foot system.[1]

Confusion
of rhythms
intolerable.

42. Despite this possibility of alternative scansion, and the other and commoner possibility of substitution of individual feet, iambic and trochaic, dactylic and ana-pæstic, metre or rhythm remain entirely distinct. Any system which regards these as merely different names for the same thing is self=condemned as disregarding the evidence, or rather verdict, of the ear.

[1] For elucidation and example see below, in Glossary, as above note, p. 8. The " sections " referred to are not those of Guest.

CHAPTER VI

CONTINUOUS ILLUSTRATIONS OF ENGLISH SCANSION ACCORDING TO THE FOOT SYSTEM

I. OLD ENGLISH PERIOD

Scansion only dimly visible.

No better examples can be taken for this than two already used by Dr. Sievers—the close of the *Phœnix* with its illuminative Latin admixture, and a bit of *Beowulf* (205 *ff.*) (dotted foot division added in first case):

> Háfað : us alýfed : *lucis* | *auctor*
> Þœt we mó:tun hér : *meru*|*eri*
> ʒóddædum be:ʒiétan : *gaudia in* | *coelo*
> Pǽr we : mótun : *maxima* | *regna*.

> Hǽfde se ʒoda || Géata téoda
> cémpan ʒecórene || þara þe ne cenóste
> findan míhte || fíftener súm
> súndwudu sóhte || sécʒ wísade
> láʒucræftig món || lándʒemýrcu.

In these the general trochaic run and the corresponding tendency to dactylic substitution, which are so evident in the Latin, as it were *muffle* themselves in the English; and the contrast, so strikingly brought out in the mixed passage, is not really less evident in the pure Anglo-Saxon one. The muffling is the result, partly of the imperfect substitution, or rather the actual presence of syllables not digested into the metre; partly of the overbearing middle pause, which, suggesting another in each section, chops the whole up into disconnected grunts or spasmodic phrases.

37

II. Late Old English with *Nisus* towards Metre

(*"Grave" Poem. Guest's text, spelling, and accentuation; the usual marks for the latter being substituted for his dividing bars, and foot division added in dots.*

> Thé wes : bóld ge:býld ‖ er : thú i:bóren : wére,
> Thé wes : mólde i:mynt ‖ er : thú of : móder : cóme,
> Ác hit : nés no i:díht :‖ né theo : deópnes i:méten,
> Nés gyt i:lóced ‖ hu : lóng hit the : wére.

Here an immense advance is made. The rhythm is still trochaic, though it is by no means certain that it does not show symptoms of *iambicisation*. It is far more well marked; and one of the means of the marking is that the "ditch in the middle"—the formal pause,—though no doubt technically and even rhetorically existing, is overrun by the suggested feet as long as the trochee is kept. But if this pause holds its place it suggests *iambic* scansion—

> The | wes bold | gebyld ;

and something like the whole future of English poetry lies in the suggestion. Do not omit to notice the metrical assistance given by the epanaphora, or repetition of the same word and phrases in the same place, and by the imperfect and irregular assonances emphasising the divisions.

III. Transition Period

Metre struggling to assert itself in a New Way.

Part of the verses of St. Godric.

> Sainte : Mari:e Vir:gine
> Moder Je:su Cris:tes Na:zarene
> Onfang : schild : help thin : Godric,
> Onfang : bring he : gelich : mit the : in God:es ric.

A distinct effort at iambic stanza, such as that of the great Ambrosian hymn, *Veni Redemptor gentium.*

It is not surprising if the experimenter stumbles, if the old trochaic rhythm is sometimes in his head, and if, in the last verse, he either overruns or divides and makes a quintet. The struggle towards feet—and new feet—is there, and rhyme, if imperfect, is there also.

IV. EARLY MIDDLE ENGLISH PERIOD

Attempt at merely Syllabic Uniformity with Unbroken Iambic Run and no Rhyme.

Orm.

And nu | icc wi|le shæ|wenn yuw
    summ-del | withth God|ess hellp|e
Off thatt | Judiss|kenn follk|ess lac
    thatt Drih|htin wass | full cwem|e.

The moral of this (whether it be written as above in eights and sevens or continuously as " fifteeners ") is unmistakable, as stated before: the writer, for all his scrupulous indication of short *vowels*, seems to care no more than if he were a modern Frenchman for *syllabic* quantity, or even for accent. He will have his fifteen syllables, his pause at the eighth, and his sing-song run of seven dissyllabic batches and a feminine ending. But, will he nill he, he impresses—with whatever sing-song effect and whatever merciless iteration—the iambic beat throughout his whole enormous work.

V. EARLY MIDDLE ENGLISH PERIOD

Conflict or Indecision between Accentual Rhythm and Metrical Scheme.

Layamon.

1 { Þa an|swære|de Vor|tiger—
  { of ælc | an vu|ele he | wes wær.

2 { Nulle : ich heom : belauen‖
  { bi mine : quike live.

3 { For Hen|gest is | hider | icumen,
  { He is | mi fa|der and ich | his sune.

4 { And ich : habbe : to leof-monne‖
  { his dohter : Rowenne.

These four couplets (continuous in the original) exhibit
perfectly the process which was going on. (2) is a rather
shapeless example of the old scarcely metrical Anglo-Saxon
line with a roughly trochaic rhythm ; and (4) is not very
different. But (3) is a not quite successful, though recognisable, attempt at a rhymed (it is actually assonanced)
iambic dimeter or octosyllabic couplet. And (1) is this
couplet complete at all points in rhythm, metre, and rhyme
—capable, in fact, of being exactly quantified and rendered
exactly into modern English, all but the dropped final *e* :

$$\breve{}\ \ -\ \ \breve{}\ -\ \ \breve{}\ \ -\ \breve{}$$

Then an|swered|[e] Vor|tiger

$$\breve{}\ -\ \ \breve{}-\ \breve{}\ -\ \ \ \breve{}\ \ -$$

of ilk |an e|vil he | was ware.

VI. EARLY MIDDLE ENGLISH PERIOD

The Appearance and Development of the " Fourteener."

The exact origin [1] of the "fourteener," "septenar " (as
the Germans call it), "long Alexandrine " (as it was very
improperly termed in England for a time), "seven-foot "
or "seven-accent " line—to give its various designations—
is a matter of conjecture. The "fifteener " of Orm with
the redundant syllable lopped off ; a variation with iambic
or "rising stress " rhythm substituted for trochaic or falling,
and a syllable added in the popular Latin metre of

Meum est propositum in taberna mori ;

with other things ; most probably of all, a shortened
metrification of the old long line, to represent the frequent
inequality of its halves better than the octosyllabic couplet
—have been suggested. It holds, however, such an important place in English prosody from the early thirteenth
to the late sixteenth century, and its resolution into the
ballad couplet or "common measure " is of so much greater
importance still, that it can hardly have too much
attention.

---

[1] More will be found on this and the origin of other metres in Bk. IV.

The extraordinarily prosaic and "stumping" cadence of the *Ormulum* perhaps obscures the connection, especially as this rigid syllabisation makes trisyllabic feet impossible. But the true rhythm appears, though still with a redundant syllable, in the famous *Moral Ode*, the older versions of which are dated before Orm. The oldest, as it is supposed to be, of these shows the form in full existence—

Ich em | nu al|der thene | ich wes | a win|tre and | a la|re.

But the youngest—

Ich | am el|der than | ich wes | a win|ter and eke | on lo|re—

gives a priceless improvement; for even if "nu" has dropped out, the resulting monosyllabic foot is quite rhythmical, the trisyllabic "-ter and eke" is unmistakable, and the life and spirit that it gives to the verse equally so. In the course of the thirteenth century the form develops immensely. As a continuous one, it furnishes the staple of the *Chronicle* and *Saints' Lives*, attributed—the former certainly and the latter probably in at least some cases— to Robert of Gloucester. As thus in Lear's complaint :

Mid yox|ing and | mid gret | wop ‖ þas | began | ys mone
Alas ! | alas ! | þe luþor wate | that fyl|est me | þos one :
Þat | þus | clene | me bryngst | adoun ‖ wyder | schal I | be broȝht?
For more | sorwe | yt doþ | me when ‖ it co|meth in | my thoȝht.

. . . . . .

Le|ve doȝ|ter Cor|deille, ‖ to sþo|e þou seid|est me
Þat as muche | as ych | hadde y | was worþ | pei y | ne lev|ed the.

But before long it shows, though it may be still written on, an evident tendency to break up into ballad measure, as in the (also thirteenth-century) *Judas* poem :

Hit wes upon a scere-Thursday
That ure Laverd aros,
Ful milde were the wordes
He spec to Judas :
"Judas, thou most to Jursalem
Oure mete for to bugge,
Thritti platen of selver
Thou bere upo thi rugge.

VII. EARLY MIDDLE ENGLISH PERIOD

The Plain and Equivalenced Octosyllable.

We have seen how, in Layamon, the regular rhymed octosyllabic couplet or iambic dimeter ("four-stress line," etc.) shows itself, either as a deliberate alternative to the old long line, or as a half-unconscious result of the endeavour to adjust it to the new metrical tendencies of the language. And we saw, also, that its examples in Layamon himself vary from absolute normality to different stages of licence or incompleteness. Before long, however, we find *two* varieties establishing themselves, with more or less distinct and definite contrast. The first, which seems to keep French or Latin examples more or less strictly before it, is exemplified in *The Owl and the Nightingale*, and scans as follows :

> Wi nul|tu singe | an oth|er theode,
> War hit | is much|ele mo|re neode ?
> Thu nea|ver ne | singst in | Irlonde,
> Ne thu | ne cumest | nogt in | Scotlonde :
> Hwi nul|tu fa|re to Nor|eweie ?[1]
> And sing|en men | of Gal|eweie ?
> Thar | beoth men | that lut|el kunne
> Of songe | that is | bineothe | the sunne.

Here, it will be observed, there is practically no licence except a few doubtful *e*'s, and that of omitting one syllable and making the line "acephalous" iambic or catalectic trochaic. This form was followed largely, and, from Chaucer and Gower onwards, by most poets, except Spenser, till the time of Chatterton, Blake, and Coleridge in *Christabel*.

Side by side with it, however, a form embodying the special characteristic of the new English prosody—

---

[1] Or possibly

> Hwi nul|tu fa|re to | Nor[e]weie,

which is more likely as to "farè" ("farè[n]"), and looks forward to the fashion in which we now say "Norway," but "Galloway." The remark will extend to not a few other scansions.

equivalent substitution—exhibits itself in full force in the mid-thirteenth-century *Genesis and Exodus*, as well as in other miscellaneous poems and in the romances.   Here are specimens from *Genesis and Exodus*, 2367-2376 :

> Josep | gaf ilc | here twin|ne srud,
> Benia|min most | he ma|de prud ;
> Fif we|den best | bar Ben|iamin
> Thre hun|dred plates | of sil|ver fin,
> Al|so fele | o|there | thor-til,
> He bad | ben in | is fa|deres wil,
> And x | asses | with se|mes fest ;
> Of all | Egyp|tes welth|e best
> Gaf he | is brethe|re, with her|te blithe,
> And bad | hem ra pen hem hom|ward swithe.

And from *Richard Cœur de Lion*, 3261-3268 :

> Nay quod | Kyng Rich|ard, be God | my lord,
> Ne schal | I nevyr | with him | acord !
> Ne hadde ne|vyr ben | lost A|cres toun
> Ne had|de ben | through hys | tresoun.
> Yiff he yil|de again | my fad|erys tresour
> And Jeru|salem | with gret | honour,
> Thenne | my wrath|e I hym | forgive
> And ne|vyr ellys | whyl that | I live.

Here, it will be observed, the foot of *three* syllables— generally, if not always, an anapæst—and even, it would seem, that of one sometimes, are freely substituted for that of *two*, adding immensely to the variety, spirit, and freedom of the line.   The first " ne hadde " is perhaps run together.

VIII. EARLY MIDDLE ENGLISH PERIOD

The Romance-Six or " Rime Couée."

At an uncertain period in the thirteenth century this makes its appearance—no doubt directly imitated from the French, but probably also in part a derivative of the application of metrical tendency to the aboriginal line-couplet.   Its French name [1] is not, to our eyes, appropriate

---

[1] For origin and explanation see Glossary.

—one would rather call it "waisted" or "waisted-and-tailed rhyme"; and as it is very largely (in fact, with the plain couplet predominantly) used in the English romances, "romance-six" as opposed to "ballad-four" seems a good name for it. It sometimes, however, extends to three, four, or even six sets of two eights and a six, and is found both plain and equivalenced, as thus:

> The brid|des sing|e, it is | no nay,
> The spar|hauk and | the pap|ejay,
> that joy|e it was | to here.
> The thrus|telcok | made eek | his lay,
> The wo|de dowv|e upon | the spray
> She sang | ful loud|e and clere.
> (Chaucer, *Sir Thopas.*)

> As soon|e as the em|peroure yil|dyd the gast,
> A prowd|e gar|son came | in haste,
> Sir Syn|agote | hight he—
> And broght | an hun|dred hel|mes bright
> Of har|dy men | that cowd|e wel fight
> Of felde | wolde ne|ver oon flee.
> (*Le Bone Florence of Rome*, 778-783.)

The plain form, as Chaucer, of malice prepense, showed in the above, is particularly liable to sing-song effect.

IX. Early Middle English Period

Miscellaneous Stanzas.

(*a*) A very considerable number of these were introduced, sometimes no doubt by direct imitation of French or (as in the case of the "Burns-metre," [1]) Provençal originals, sometimes by the ingenuity of the individual poet, working on the plastic material of the blended language, according to the new metrical foot-system. They all scan easily by this, as may be seen in a stanza of *Tristrem*, one of the Harleian Lyrics, and a "Burns stanza" from the York Plays; while anapæstic substitution, amounting to something like "triple time" as a whole, appears in the Hampolian extract.

---

[1] See again Bk. IV. for fuller information on this.

> The king | had a douh|ter dere,
> That mai|den Y|sonde hight,
> That gle | was lef | to here
> And romaun|ce to rede | aright.
> Sir Tram|tris hir | gan lere,
> Tho, | with al | his might,
> What al|le poin|tès were
> To se | the sothe | in sight,
>   To say,
> In Yr|lond nas | no knight,
> With Y|sonde | durst play.
>   (*Sir Tristrem*, 1255-63.)

(*Three*-foot iambic with single-foot "bob." All final *e*'s sounded or elided. One monosyllabic, and two or three trisyllabic, substitutions.)

> Bytuen|e Mershe | ant A|veril
>   when spray | bigin|neth to springe,
> The lut|el foul | hath hi|re wyl
>   on hy|re lud | to synge ;
> Ich lib|be in ∧|∧ love-|longinge
> For sem | lokest | of al|le thynge,
> He may | me ∧|∧ blis|se bringe,
>   icham | in hire | baundoun.
> An hen|dy hap | ichab|be y-hent,
> Ichot | from hevene | it is | me sent,
> From alle | wymmen | mi love | is lent
>   ant lyht | on A|lysoun.
>   (*Alison*, Harleian MS. p. 27, ed. Wright.)

(From the other stanzas it appears that the middle quatrain should consist of three eights and a six, and that something has dropped—supplied now by carets. Otherwise the scheme is clear.)

> Fro thaym | is lost[e] | both[e] game and glee.
> He bad|de that they | schuld mais|ters be
> Over all[e] kenn[e] thing, outy-taen a tree
>   He taught | them to be
> And ther-|to went[e] | both she | and he
>   Agagne | his wille.
>   ("York " Plays, vi. § 2.)

(The final *e*'s are beginning to be neglected, and the whole is probably in strict iambics *here*, though vacillation between four- and five-foot lines is not absolutely impossible. But there is trisyllabic substitution elsewhere, though not very much. It may be remembered that there is little of it in Burns's own examples of this metre. Closer still to his is the following):

> *Eve.* Sethyn [1] it | was so | me knyth | it sore,
> Bot syth|en that wo|man witte|lles ware,
> Mans mais|t[i]rie | should have | been more
> Agayns | the gilte.
> *Adam.* Nay at | my speech|e would thou ne|ver spare
> That has | us spilte.

> (*Ibid.* § 24.)

(*b*) My tru|est trea|sure so trai|torly ta|ken,
> So bit|terly bound|en with by|tand band|es,
> How soon | of thy ser|vants wast thou | forsa|ken
> And loathe|ly for *my* | life hurled | with hand|es
> (Horstmann's *Hampole*, i. 72.)

(Probably, when first written, the ultimate *e*'s of the even lines were sounded; but even this is not certain, and the superiority of the shortening would soon have struck the ear.)

(*c*) More elaborate stanza from the Drama:

> Myght|ful God | veray, ‖ Ma|ker of all | that is
> Thre per|sons without|en nay, ‖ oone God | in end|les blis,
> Thou maid|è both night | and day, ‖ beest, | fowle | and fish,
> All crea|tures that | lif may ‖ wrought | thou at | thy wish,
> As thou | wel myght:
> The sun, | the móyn|è, ve|rament
> Thou maid|è: [and] | the fir|mament,
> The star|rès al|so full | fervent
> To shyn|e thou maid|e ful bright.
> ("Townley" Plays, iii. p. 23, E. E. T. S.)

X. Early Middle English Period

Appearance of the Decasyllable.

The idea that the new metres in English were in-variably direct copies of those already existing in French

[1] The MS. has the contraction "Sĕn."

(or Latin) seems to be decisively negatived by the fact
that the decasyllabic line—the staple, not indeed in couplet
but in long batches or *tirades*, of the earlier French *chansons de geste*—makes a rare appearance in English verse
before the late fourteenth century. But it does appear,
thereby, on the other hand, negativing the notion that
Chaucer " introduced " it, and suggesting that it was,
in part at least, a genuine *experiment*—not in imitation, but
in really independent development, of the possibilities of
English metre. Here are scanned examples of different
periods.

(*a*) Uncertain in *intention*, but assuming distinct couplet
cadence :

> Cristes | milde | moder | seynte | marie,
> Mines | liues | leome | mi leou|e lefdi,
> To the | ich buwe | and mi|ne kneon | ich beie,
> And al | min heor|te blod | to the | ich offrie.
> > (*Orison of Our Lady* (*c.* 1200).)

(*b*) Expansion of octosyllable in single line :

> And nu|tes amig|deles | thoron|ne numen.
> > (*Genesis and Exodus*, 3840 (*c.* 1250).)

(*c*) In couplet :

> And swore | by Je|su that | made moon | and star
> Agenst | the Sara|cens he | should learn | to war.
> > (*Richard Cœur de Lion*, 2435-36 (before 1325 ?).)

(*d*) Overflow of octosyllable into decasyllable ; probably, in the first place, from the equivalenced lines lending
themselves to another run :

> The bugh|es er | the ar|mes with | the handes,
> And the | legges, | with the | fete | that standes.
> > (In Hampole's *Prick of Conscience*, 680, 681
> > (before 1350), with scores of others.)

XI. LATER MIDDLE ENGLISH PERIOD

The Alliterative Revival—Pure.

The examples of this revival (see Book II.) cannot, of
course, in their nature, be strictly *scanned*. But it is

important to bring out the change of *rhythm* as compared with the older examples (*v. sup.* p. 37).

(To prevent confusion with positive *metrical* scansion, I have made the scanning bars dotted, and have doubled the foot-division line for the middle pause in the first extract.)

> Hit bi-:fel in that fo : rest ‖ there fast : by-side,
> Ther woned : a wel old cherl |:| that was : a couherde.
>
>   (*William of Palerne.*)

(Notice that the *nisus* towards anapæstic cadence over-runs the break both in the metre and, as at "-glent," "stor," "-port" below, in the half line.)

> Wende, wor:thelych wyght : vus won:ez to seche,
> Dryf ouer : this dymme wa:ter if thou : druye findez,
> Bryng bod:worde to bot : blysse : to vus alle.
>
>   (*Cleanness.*)

> Thenne ho gef: hym god-day : and wyth a : glent laghed,
> And as ho stod : ho stonyed hym : with ful : stor wordes,
> " Now he that spedes : uche spech : this dis:port yelde,
> Bot that ye : be Gaw:ayn hit gotz : in mynde."
>
>   (*Gawain and the Green Knight.*)

XII. Later Middle English Period

The Alliterative Revival—Mixed.

The metrical *additions*, on the other hand (see Book II.), and those poems which, while employing alliteration, sub-ject it to metrical schemes, scan perfectly, as :

> Quen thay | hade play|ed in halle,
> As long|e as her wyll|e hom last,
> To cham|bre he con | hym calle
> And to | the chem|ne thay past.
>
>   .   .   .   .
>
> " A' mon | how may | thou slepe,
> This mor|ning es | so clere ?"
> He watz | in droup|ing depe
> Bot thenne | he con | hir here.
>
>   ("Wheels" of *Gawain and the Green Knight.*)

Fro spot | my spyryt | ther sprang | in space,
My bo|dy on balk|e ther bod | in sweven,
My gost|e is gon | in God|es grace,
In a|ventur|e ther mer|vayles meven.

(*The Pearl*, ii.)

Mone | makeles | of mighte,
Here co|mes ane er|rant knighte,
Do him | reson|e and righte
For thi | manhead.

("Wheel" of *The Awntyrs of Arthur*, xxvii.)

XIII. LATER MIDDLE ENGLISH PERIOD

Potentially Metrical Lines in Langland (see Book II.).

Decasyllables :

For Ja|mes the gen|tel bond | it in | his book.

(A. i. 159.)

Thus I | live lov|eless lik|e a lu|ther dogge.

(A. v. 97.)

Alexandrines :

And ser|ved Treu|the soth|lyche | somdel | to paye.

(C. viii. 189.)

Adam | and A|braham | and Y|say the | prophete.

(B. xvi. 81.)

Fourteeners :

But if | he wor|che well | there-with | as Do|wel him | techeth.

(B. viii. 56.)

Of a|ny sci|ence un|der son|ne the se|ven arts | and alle.

(B. xi. 166.)

A large number might be added where the pronunciation which was shortly to come in necessarily makes such lines, though they may not have been intended as such ; for instance—

Take we | her words | at worth, | for her | witness | be true ;

(B. xii. 125.)

and even octosyllables will appear—

Ne no say robe in rich[e] pelure ;

(A. iii. 277.)

partly explaining to us the chaos of lines in fifteenth-century poetry.

XIV. LATER MIDDLE ENGLISH PERIOD

Scansions from Chaucer.

Octosyllable :

> Hit was | of Ve|nus re|dely,
> This tem|ple ; for | in por|treyture,
> I saw | anoon | right hir | figure
> Na|ked fle|tyn*ge* in | a see.
> And al|so on | hir heed, | parde,
> Hir ro|se gar|lond white | and reed,
> And | hir comb | to kemb|*e* hir heed,
> Hir dow|ves, and | daun Cu|pido,
> Hir blin|de son|*e*, and Vul|cano,
> That in | his fa|ce was | ful broun.
>
> (*House of Fame*, i. 130-139.)

(*Two* "acephalous" lines, initial monosyllabic feet, or trochaic admixtures ; some unimportant elisions before vowels and *h* ; middle pause not kept in lines 1, 4, 6, and 10.)

Rhyme-royal :

> And down | from then|nès fast*e* | he gan | avise
> This li|tel spot | of erthe | that with | the see
> Embra|cèd is, | and ful|ly gan | despise
> This wrec|ched world, | and held | al vanite,
> To re|spect of | the pleyne | feli|cite
> That is | in heven|*e* above.   And at | the laste
> Ther he | was slayn | his lo|king down | he caste.
>
> (*Troilus and Criseyde*, v. 1814-20.)

(Metre quite regular, but pause much varied—practically *none* in line 5. Elisions as above, but *e*'s not valued, or elided, in *erthe, pleyne*. Final couplet hendecasyllabic, as indeed most are.)

(*a*) Riding rhyme or heroic couplet :

> Whan that | April|le with | his shou|res soote
> The droght|e of March | hath per|ced to | the roote,
> And bath|ed ev|ery veyn|e in swich | licour
> Of which | vertu | engen|dred is | the fleur ;

Whan Ze|phirus | eek with | his swe|te breeth
Inspi|red hath | in ev|ery holt | and heeth
The ten|dre crop|pes, and | the yon|ge sonne
Hath in | the Ram | his half|e cours | y-ronne,
And smal|e fowel|es ma|ken me|lodye,
That sle|pen al | the nyght | with o|pen eye,—
So pri|keth hem | Nature | in hir | corages,—
Thanne long|en folk | to goon | on pil|grimages,
And pal|meres for | to se|ken straun|ge strondes,
To fer|ne hal|wes, kowth|e in son|dry londes ;
And spec|ially, | from ev|ery shi|res ende
Of En|gelond, | to Caun|turbury | they wende,
The hoo|ly blis|ful mar|tir for | to seke
That hem | hath hol|pen whan | that they | were seeke.

(Opening paragraph of Canterbury Tales.)

(Very regular ; but possible trisyllabic feet wherever "every" occurs, and a certain one in "Caunt|erbury|." Pause almost indifferently at 4th and 5th syllables. French-Latin accent in " Natùre." Many hendecasyllables or redundances ; but all made by the *e* in one form or another.)

(*b*) " Acephalous " or nine-syllable lines :

Twen|ty bo|kes clad | in blak | or reed. (*Prol.* 274.)

(*c*) Alexandrines :

Westward, | right swich | ano!ther in | the op|posite.
(*K. T.* 1036.)

So sor|weful|ly eek | that I | wende ver|raily.
(*Sq. T.* 585.)

XV. Later Middle English Period

Variations from Strict Iambic Norm in Gower.

(*a*) Trochaic substitution :

Under | the gren|e thei | begrave.
(*Conf. Am.* i. 2348.)

(*b*) Anapæstic substitution :

Sometime | in cham|bre sometime | in halle.
(iv. 1331.)

Of Je|lousi|e, but what | it is
(v. 447.)

(*if the dissyllabic " ie " is insisted on*).

And thus | ful oft|e about|e the hals.

(v. 2514.)

It was | fantosm|e but yet | he heard.

(v. 5011.)

(It will be observed that in these four instances, all acknowledged by Professor Macaulay, the final *e* is required to make the trisyllabic foot, though the first instance differs slightly from the others. I should myself add a large number where Mr. Macaulay sees only "slur," but in which occur words like "ever" (i. 3), "many a" (i. 316, 317), or syllables like "eth," which *must* be valued in one case at least here—

To break*eth* and renn*eth* al aboute,   (*Prol.* 505.)

where Mr. Macaulay reads "tobrekth," and where the copyists very likely made it so.)

(*c*) Acephalous lines :

Very rare if the *e* be always allowed.   Perhaps non-existent.

XVI. Transition Period

Examples of Break-down in Literary Verse.

(*a*) Lydgate's decasyllabic couplet :

Ther he | lay to | the lar|kè song [∪ —]
With no|tès herd|è high | up in | the ayr.
The glad|è mor|owe ro|dy and | right fayr,
Phe|bus al|so cast|ing up | his bemes
The high|e hyl|les ∧ | gilt with | his stremes.

(*Story of Thebes,* 1250 *sqq.*)

(3, tolerable ; 2, ditto, with hiatus at cæsura ; 1, last foot missing ; 4, "acephalous" ; 5, syllable missing at cæsura.)

(*b*) His rhyme-royal :

This is | to sein | —douteth | never | a dele—
That ye | shall have | ∧ ful | posses|sion
Of him | that ye | ∧ cher|rish now | so wel,
In hon|est man|er, without|e offen|cioun,
Because | I know|e your | enten|cion
Is tru|li set | in par|ti and | in al
To loue | him best | and most | in spe|cial.

(*Temple of Glass,* st. 16.)

(*Two* examples (2 and 3) of the so-called "Lydgatian" missing syllable at cæsura.)

(*c*) A typical minor, John Metham, in *Amoryus and Cleopes*, stanza 1 :

The charms | of love | and eke | the peyn | of Amo|ryus | the knyght
For Cleo|pes sake | and eke | how bothe | in fere
Lovyd | and af|tyr deyed, | my pur|pos ys | to indight.
And now, | O god|dess, I thee | beseche | off kun|ning that | have | syche
   might,
Help me | to adorne | ther charms | in syche | maner
So that | qwere this | matere | doth yt | require
Bothe ther | lovys I | may compleyne | to loverys | desire.

(A fourteener, a decasyllable, an Alexandrine, a *six*teener, and three decasyllables, the last very shaky either as that or as an Alexandrine! In fact, sheer doggerel of the unintended kind.)

XVII. Transition Period

Examples of True Prosody in Ballad, Carols, etc.

(*a*) *Chevy Chase* :

The Per|cy out | of Northum|berland,
And a vow | to God | made he,
That he | would hunt | in the moun|tains
Of Chev|iot within | days three,
In the mau|gre of dough|ty Doug|las
And all | that ever with | him be.

(It must be observed that this modern spelling *exactly* represents the old prosodically. The reader will then see that there are no liberties, on the equivalent system, except the *crasis* of "-viot" and "ever." The former, insignificant in any case, is still more so here, for the actual Northumbrian pronunciation is or was "Chevot"; while if "ever" changes places with "that," there is not even any crasis needed. For a piece so rough in phrase, and copied by a person so evidently illiterate, the exactness is astonishing.)

(*b*) "E.I.O.":

To doom | we draw | the sooth | to schaw
   In life | that us | was lent,
Ne la|tin, ne law, | may help ane haw,[1]
   But rath|ely us | repent.
The cross, | the crown, | the spear | bees bown,
   That Je|su rug|ged and rent,
The nail|ès rude, | shall thee | conclude
   With their | own ar|gument.
   With E | and O take keep | thereto,
     As Christ | himself | us kenned
   We com|e and go | to weal | or woe,
     That dread|ful doom | shall end.

(Spelling modernised as before, but not a word altered.)

XVIII. TRANSITION PERIOD

Examples of Skeltonic and other Doggerel

(*a*) Skelton :

I.

Mirry | Marga|ret
As mid|somer flower,
Gen|tyll as fau|coun
Or hauke | of the tower—
With sol|ace and glad|ness,
Much mirth | and no mad|ness,
All good | and no bad|ness :—
So joy|ously,
So maid|enly,
So wom|anly.
Her de|menyng
In ev|ery thyng
Far far | passyng
That I | can indite
Or suffyce | to write.
     (*Crown of Laurel.*)

II.

But to make | up my tale,
She bru|eth nop|py ale,
And ma|kethe there|of sale,
To travel|lers, ‖ to tink|ers,
To sweat|ers, ‖ to swink|ers,
And all | good ‖ ale-drink|ers
That will noth|ing spare
But dryncke | till they stare
And bring | themselves bare,
With "now | away | the mare,
And let | us slay Care,
As wise | as an hare."
     (*Elinor Rumming.*)

(*b*) Examples from Heywood and other interludes.

(1) Continuous long doggerel :

I can|not tell | you: one knave | disdains | another,
Wherefore | take ye | the tone | and I | shall take | the other.

---

[1] As in "hips and haws."

We shall | bestow | them there | as is most | conven|ient
For such | a coup|le. I trow | they shall | repent
That ev|er they met | in this | church here.

(2) Singles :

(Shortened six.)
This | wyse him | deprave,

(Octosyllable.)
And give | the ab|solu|tion.

(Irregular decasyllable.)
The aboun|dant grace | of the | powèr | divyne

(Alexandrine.)
Preserve | this aud|ience | and leave | them to | inclyne.

(Irregular fourteener.)
Then hold | down thine | head like | a pret|ty man |
and take | my blessing.

(In all these examples the doggerel is probably *intended* ; that is to say, the writers are not aiming at a regularity which they cannot reach, but cheerfully or despairingly renouncing it.)

XIX. Transition Period

Examples from the Scottish Poets.

(*a*) Barbour (regular octosyllables) :

The kyng | toward | the vod | is gane,
Wery, | for-swat | and vill | of vayn ;
Intill | the wod | soyn en|terit he,
And held | doun to|ward a | valè,
Quhar throu | the vod | a vat|tir ran.
Thiddir | in gret | hy went | he than,
And | begouth | to rest | hym thair,
And said | he mycht | no for|thirmair.

(*One* "acephalous" line.)

(*b*) Wyntoun (octosyllables somewhat freer) :

Thir sev|yn kyng|is reg|nand were
A hun|der ful|ly *and for*|ty year,
And fra | thir kyng|is thus | can cess
In Ro|me thai che|*sit twa con*|sulès.

(IV. ii. 157-160.)

(*c*) Blind Harry (regular decasyllables on French model):

Than Wal|lace socht | quhar his | wncle | suld be ;
In a | dyrk cawe | he was | set|dul|fullè,
Quhar wat|ter stud, | and he | in yrn|yss strang.
Wallace | full sone | the brass|is wp | he dang ;
Off that | myrk holl | brocht him | with strenth | and lyst,
Bot noyis | he hard, | off no|thing ellis | he wyst.
So blyth | befor | in warld | he had | nocht beyn,
As thair | with sycht, | quhen he | had Wal|lace seyn.

(*d*) James I. (rhyme-royal):

> For wak|it and | for-wal|owit, thus | musing,
>   Wery | forlain | I list|enyt sod|dynlye,
> And sone | I herd | the bell | to ma|tyns ryng,
>   And up | I rase, | no lon|ger wald | I lye :
>   Bot soon, | how trow|e ye ?   Suich | a fan|tasye
> Fell me | to mynd | that ay | me thoght | the bell
> Said to | me, " Tell | on, man, | what the | befell."

(*e*) Henryson (ballad measure ; slight anapæstic substitution):

> Makyne, | the night | is soft | and dry,
>   The wed|*dir is warm* | and fair,
> *And the gre*|nè wuid | richt neir | us by
>   To walk | out on | all quhair :
> Thair ma | na jan|gloor us | espy,
>   That is | to lufe | contrair,
> Thairin, | Makyne, | bath ye | and I
>   Unseen | we ma | repair.

Those who deny the valued *e* in " grenè," as not Scots, may refuse the second instance of trisyllabic feet, but the first will remain.

(*f*) Dunbar (alliterative):

> I saw thre gay ladeis sit in ane grein arbeir,
> All grathit into garlandis of fresche gudelie flouris ;
> So glitterit as the gold wer thair glorius gilt tressis,
> Quhill all the gressis did gleme of the glaid hewis ;
> Kemmit was thair cleir hair, and curiouslie sched
> Attour thair schulderis doun schyre, schyning full bricht.

Dunbar (dimeter iambic quatrains with refrain, and much anapæstic substitution):

Come ne|vir yet May | so fresch|e and grene,
Bot Jan|uar come | als wud and kene—
Wes nev|ir sic drowth | bot anis | come raine,
All erd|ly joy | returnis | in pane.

(*g*) Alexander Scott (stanzas):

It cumis | yow luv|aris to | ·be laill,
Of bo|dy, hairt | and mynd | al haill,
And though | ye with | year la|dyis daill—
    Ressoun ;
Bot and | your faith | and law|ty faill—
    Tressoun !

    .   .   .

Be land | or se,
Quhaur ev|ir I be,
As ye | fynd me,
  So tak | me ;
And gif | I le,
And from | yow fle,
Ay quhill | I de
  Forsaik | me !

(*h*) Montgomerie (*Cherry and Slae* stanza):

About | ane bank | quhair birdis | on bewis
Ten thou|sand tymis | thair notis | renewis
  Ilke houre | into | the day,
The merle | and ma|ueis micht | be sene,
The Prog|ne and | the Phel|omene,
  Quhilk caus|sit me | to stay.
I lay | and leynit | me to | ane bus
  To heir | the bir|dis beir ;
Thair mirth | was sa | melo|dious
  Throw na|ture of | the yeir ;
    Sum sing|ing, ‖ some spring|ing
    With wingis | into | the sky,
    So trim|lie, ‖ and nim|lie,
    Thir birdis | they flew | me by.

XX. Early Elizabethan Period

*Examples of Reformed Metre from Wyatt, Surrey,
and other Poets before Spenser*

(*a*) Wyatt (sonnet)

The long[e] | love that | in my | thought I | harbèr
And in | my heart | doth keep | his re|sidence,

Into | my face | presseth | with bold | pretence,
And there | campèth | display|ing his | bannèr :
She that | me learns | to love | and to | suffèr,
And wills | that my | trust and | lust[e]s neg|ligence
Be rein|ed by rea|son, shame, | and rev|erence,
With his | hardì|ness tak|ès dis|pleasùre,
Wherewith | love to | the hart[e]s | forest | he fleèth,
Leaving | his en|terprise | with pain | and cry,
And there | him hi|deth and | not àp|pearèth. |
What may | I do ? | when my | master | feareth,
But in | the field | with him | to live | and die,
For good | is thè | life | end|ing faithfully.

(I formerly scanned line 9 :

Wherewith | love to | the hart's fo|rest he | fleèth.

But "forèst" is so frequent and makes such a much better rhythm that perhaps it should be preferred. It will, however, emphasise still further the poet's curious uncertainty about the "*-eth*" rhymes—whether he shall arrange them on that syllable only, or take in the penultimate. Besides this point, the student should specially notice the pains taken to get, not merely the feet, but the syllables right at the cost sometimes of pretty strongly "wrenched" accent. On all this see Book II. The final *è*'s are rather a curiosity than important : longè *may* have been sounded, "lust*e*" and "hart*e*" (so printed in Tottel) improbably.)

(*b*) Wyatt (lyric stanza) :

Forget | not yet | the tried | intent
Of such | a truth | as I | have meant,
My great | travail, | so glad|ly spent,
    Forget | not yet !

Forget | not yet | when first | began
The wea|ry life | ye know, | since whan
The suit, | the ser|vice, none | tell can—
    Forget | not yet !

(It will be observed that this rondeau-like motion, with its short lines and frequent repetition, is brought off better than the sonnet, though the French accent sticks in *travail.*)

(*c*) Surrey (sonnet):

> I nev|er saw | my la|dy lay | apart
> Her cor|net black, | in cold | nor yet | in heat,
> Sith first | she knew | my grief | was grown | so great ;
> Which o|ther fan|cies dri|veth from | my heart,
> That to | myself | I do | the thought | reserve,
> The which | unwares | did wound | my woe|ful breast.
> But on | her face | mine eyes | mought ne|ver rest
> Yet, since | she knew | I did | her love, | and serve
> Her gold|en tress|es clad | alway | with black,
> Her smil|ing looks | that hid[es] | thus ev|ermore
> And that | restrains | which I | desire | so sore.
> So doth | this cor|net gov|ern me, | alack !
> In sum|mer sun, | in win|ter's breath, | a frost
> Whereby | the lights | of her | fair looks | I lost.

(Observe how much more surely and lightly the younger poet treads in the uncertain pioneer footsteps of the elder.)

(*d*) Surrey (" poulter's measure "):

> Good la|dies, ye | that have ‖ your pleas|ures in | exile,
> Step in | your foot, | come take | a place | and mourn | with me | a while;
> And such | as by | their lords ‖ do set | but lit|tle price,
> Let them | sit still, | it skills | them not | what chance | come on the dice. |
> But ye | whom love | hath bound ‖ by or|der of | desire
> To love | your lords, | whose good | deserts | none oth|er would | require,
> Come ye | yet once | again ‖ and set | your foot | by mine,
> Whose wo|ful plight | and sor|rows great | no tongue | can even | define.

(Very little to be said for it, except as a school of regular rhythm. Broken up into " short measure " (6, 6, 8, 6) it has been not ineffective in hymns.)

(*e*) Gascoigne (lyric stanza):

> Sing lull|aby, | as wom|en do,
> Wherewith | they bring | their babes | to rest,
> And lull|aby | can I | sing too,
> As wom|anly | as can | the best.
> With lull|aby | they still | the child ;
> And if | I be | not much | beguiled,
> Full ma|ny wan|ton babes | have I
> Which must | be stilled | with lull|aby.

(*f*) Turberville (lyric stanza):

> As I | in this | have done | your will,
>   And mind | to do,
> So I | request | you to | fulfil
>   My fan|cy too,
> A green | and lov|ing heart | to have,
> And this | is all | that I | do crave.

(Observe in both of these the absolute syllabic regularity, and *observance* of foot-rhythm.)

XXI. Spenser[1] at Different Periods

(*a*) *Shep. Kal.* (strict stanza):

> Thou bar|ren ground, | whom win|ter's wrath | has wasted,
> Art made | a mir|ror to | behold | my plight :
> Whilome | thy fresh | spring flower'd, | and af|ter hasted
> Thy sum|mer proud, | with daf|fodil|lies dight ;
> And now | is come | thy win|ter's storm|y state,
> Thy man|tle marr'd | wherein | thou mask|edst late.

(Regular iambs throughout.   One double rhyme.)

(*b*) *Shep. Kal.* (equivalenced octosyllable—*Christabel* or *Genesis and Exodus* metre):

> His harm|ful hat|chet he hent | in hand,
> (Alas ! | that it | so read|y should stand !)
> And to | the field | alone | he speedeth,
> (Aye lit|tle help | to harm | there needeth !)
> Anger | nould let | him speak | to the tree,
> Enaun|ter his rage | mought cool|ed bee ;
> But to | the root bent | his sturd|y stroke,
> And made | many wounds | in the | waste oak.
> The ax|e's edge | did oft turne | again,
> As half | unwill|ing to cut | the grain.
> Seemed | the sense|less ir|on did fear,

---

[1] From Spenser onward the spelling is modern.

$$\smile \ \smile \ -$$

Or to | wrong ho|ly eld | did forbear—
For it | had been | an an|cient tree,

$$\smile \ \smile \ -$$

Sacred | with ma|ny a mys|tery,
And of|ten crossèd | with the pries|tès cruise
And of|ten hal|lowed with ho|ly wa|ter dews.

(Observe that this last is the only distinct, if not the only *possible*, decasyllabic couplet, while it can become an Alexandrine by valuing " hal|lowèd " | ; and that " priestès " is the only attempt at valued Chaucerian *e.*)

(*c*) *Shep. Kal.* (equivalenced stanza) :

$$\smile \ \smile \ -$$

Bring hi|ther the pink | and pur|ple col|umbine,
    With gil|lyflowers ;
Bring cor|ona|tions | and sops | in wine,

$$\smile \smile \ -$$

    Worn of | paramours :
Strow me | the ground | with daf|fadown|dillies,[1]
And cow|slips and | kingcups | and lov|ed lil|liès :
    The pret|ty paunce,
    And the chev|isaunce,
Shall match | with the fair | flow'r delice.

It may be just desirable to remind the student that a final "-ion " is commonly dissyllabic in the sixteenth and earlier seventeenth centuries. " Worn of par|amours " is possible.

(*d*) " Spenserian " stanza (occasional, but mostly slight, equivalence. Pause in ll. 1-8 at discretion ; in 9 usually at middle, but, as in the following, not always) :

So pass|eth, in | the pass|ing of | a day
Of mor|tal life, | the leaf, | the bud, | the flower ;
No more | doth flour|ish af|ter first | decay
That erst | was sought | to deck | both bed | and bower

$$\smile \ \smile - \smile \ \smile \ - \smile \smile \ -$$

Of ma|ny a la|dy and ma|ny a par|amour !

---

[1] Spenser here takes (as he sometimes continued to do even in *F.Q.*) the liberty of shifting the rhyming syllable. There is no doubt that this is not a good liberty. But in struggling out of the fifteenth - century slough Wyatt was constantly driven to it, and it was not till the seventeenth that poets recognised the fact that the easement was more of a disfigurement than it was worth.

Gather, | therefore, | the rose | while yet | is prime,
For soon | comes age | that will | her pride | deflower :
Gather | the rose | of love | whilst yet | is time,
Whilst lov|ing thou | mayst lov|èd be | with e|qual crime.

(*e*) *Mother Hubberd's Tale* (antithetic and stopped heroic couplet) :

Full lit|tle know|est thou | that hast | not tried,
What hell | it is, | in su|ing long | to bide :
To lose | good days | that might | be bet|ter spent ;
To waste | long nights | in pen|sive dis|content ;
To speed | to-day, | to be | put back | to-morrow ;
To feed | on hope, | to pine | with fear | and sorrow ;
To have | thy Prin|ce's grace, | yet want | her Peer's ;
To have | thy ask|ing, yet | wait ma|ny years ;
To fret | thy soul | with cross|es and | with cares ;
To eat | thy heart | through com|fortless | despairs ;
To fawn, | to crouch, | to wait, | to ride, | to run,
To spend, | to give, | to want, | to be | undone.

(*f*) *Epithalamion* (elaborate quasi-Pindaric stanza concerted in different line length, but almost strictly iambic ; "the," etc., before a vowel being probably elided) :

Open | the tem|ple gates | unto | my Love,
Open | them wide | that she | may en|ter in,
And all | the posts | adorn | as doth | behove,
And all | the pil|lars deck | with gar|lands trim,
For to | receive | this Saint | with hon|our due,
That com|eth in | to you.
With trem|bling steps, | and hum|ble rev|erence,
She com|eth in, | before | th' Almight|y's view :
Of her, | ye vir|gins, learn | obe|dience,
When so | ye come, | into | those ho|ly places,
To hum|ble your | proud faces :
Bring her | up to | th' High Al|tar, that | she may
The sa|cred ce|remo|nies there | partake
The which | do end|less ma|trimo|ny make ;
And let | the roar|ing or|gans loud|ly play
The prai|ses of | the Lord | in live|ly notes,
The whiles | with hol|low throats
The cho|risters | the joy|ous an|them sing,
That all | the woods | may an|swer, and | their ech|o ring !

XXII. EXAMPLES OF THE DEVELOPMENT OF BLANK VERSE

(a) *Surrey* (translation of *Aeneid*):

It was | the night ; | the sound | and qui|et sleep
Had through | the earth | the wear|y bod|ies caught,
The woods, | the ra|ging seas, | were fallen | to rest,
When that | the stars | had half | their course | declined.
The fields | whist : beasts | and fowls | of di|vers hue,
And what | so that | in the | broad lakes | remained,
Or yet | among | the bush|y thicks | of briar,
Laid down | to sleep | by sil|ence of | the night,
'Gan swage | their cares, | mindless | of tra|vails past.
Not so | the spirit | of this | Phenic|ian.
Unhappy she | that on | no sleep | could chance,
Nor yet | night's rest | enter | in eye | or breast.
Her cares | redoub|le : love | doth rise | and rage | again,
And ov|erflows | with swell|ing storms | of wrath.

(The interest of the new mode here is manifold. The lines are almost wholly " single-moulded," the author's anxiety to keep himself right without rhyme necessitating this. The cæsura at the fourth syllable is *almost* always kept, according to the tradition of the French line. *Once* (in the penultimate line) he has to overflow ; but into an Alexandrine, not into the next line. Whether by intention or not—" sprite " being possible—he *once* discovers the enormous advantage of the trisyllabic foot.[1] *Once* he makes with " rest " and " breast " the oversight of a " Leonine " rhyme. But, on the whole, the success is remarkable for a beginning ; and there are indications of what has to be done to secure the end.)

(b) First dramatic attempts—*Gorboduc* onwards :

Sackville Your won|ted true | regard | of faith|ful hearts
and Makes me, | O king, | the bold|er to | resume,
Norton. To speak | what I | conceive | within | my breast :
Although | the same | do not | agree | at all
With that | which o|ther here | my lords | have said,
Nor which | yourself | have seem|èd best | to like.
(Gorboduc.)

---

[1] " Fallen " is pretty certainly " fall'n."

Hughes What ! shall | I stand | whiles Ar|thur sheds | my blood ?
and   And must | I yield | my neck | unto | the axe ?
others. Whom fates | constrain | let him | forego | his bliss.
     But he | that need|less yields | unto | his bane
     When he | may shun, | does well | deserve | to lose
     The good | he can|not use. | Who would | sustain
     A ba|ser life | that may | maintain | the best ?
                              (*Misfortunes of Arthur.*)

                          ‿ ‿ −
Peele.   Were ev|ery ship | ten thou|sand on | the seas,
     Manned with | the strength | of all | the eas|tern kings,
     Convey|ing all | the mon|archs of | the world,
          ‿ ‿ −
     To invade | the is|land where | her High|ness reigns—
                                  ‿   ‿   −
     'Twere all | in vain : | for heav|ens and des|tinies
     Attend | and wait | upon | her Maj|esty !
                              (*Battle of Alcazar.*)

                                   ‿ ‿   −
Greene.   Why thinks | King Hen|ry's son | that Mar|garet's love
               ‿ ‿ −
     Hangs in | the uncer|tain bal|ance of | proud time ?
     That death | shall make | a dis|cord of | our thoughts ?
     No ! stab | the earl : | and ere | the morn|ing sun
     Shall vaunt | him thrice | over | the lof|ty east,
     − ‿ ‿
     Margaret | will meet | her Lac|y in | the heavens !
                              (*F. Bacon and F. Bungay.*)

Marlowe. Black is | the beau|ty of | the bright|est day !
     The gol|den ball | of Heav|en's eter|nal fire,
     That danced | with glo|ry on | the sil|ver waves,
     Now wants | the glo|ry that | inflamed | his beams :
     And all | for faint|ness and | for foul | disgrace,
     He binds | his tem|ples with | a frown|ing cloud,
     Ready | to dark|en earth | with end|less night.
                              (*Tamburlaine.*)

(An extreme stiffness and " single-mouldedness " in the
lines; modified in Peele and Greene by trisyllabic feet,
perhaps not intended as such ("heav'n" was pretty
certainly regarded and generally spelt as a monosyllable,
and the pronunciations "ev'ry" and "Margret" are old;
while " t' invade " and " th' uncertain " would be likely), but
virtually so, and inviting, especially in " Margaret," the full
and beautiful value. The *Gorboduc* form, as is natural, is

much the least accomplished. It is indeed what, by an almost incomprehensible inversion of sense and nature, some people call "blank verse *according to the rules* "—ten syllables only, five almost strictly iambic feet (= "accent on the even places "); pause near the middle; stop, metrical, if not grammatical, at every end—in fact, the roughest and most rudimentary form possible.)

(*c*) Early non-dramatic blanks (Gascoigne) :

And on | their backs | they bear | both land | and fee,
Castles | and towers, | reven|ues and | receipts,
Lordships | and ma|nors, fines, |—yea farms|—and all.
" What should | these be?" | (speak you, | my love|ly lord?)
They be | not men : | for why, | they have | no beards.
They be | no boys, | which wear | such side|long gowns.
They be | no gods, | for all | their gal|lant gloss.
They be | no devils, | I trow, | which seem | so saintish.
What be | they? wom|en? mask|ing in | men's weeds
With dutch|kin doub|lets and | with jerk|ins jagged?
With Span|ish spangs, | and ruffs | set out | of France,
With high | copt hats | and feath|ers flaunt-|a-flaunt?
They be, | so sure, | even *woe* | to *men* | indeed.

(It will be noticed that the "single-moulded " character is even more noticeable here than in drama, and is emphasised by the *epanaphora*. There is one redundance —"saintish " ("jagged " is probably "jagg'd "), and, as we know that the author thought the iamb the only English foot, we must not read "rĕvĕnue," but, with "tow'rs," "revènue "—which indeed was, by precisians, regarded as the correct pronunciation not so very long ago.)

(*d*) Perfected "single-mould " :

Peele.   Come, gen|tle Ze|phyr, trick'd | with those | perfùmes
        That erst | in E|den sweet|en'd Ad|am's love,
        And stroke | my bos|om with | thy silk|en fan :
        This shade, | sun-proof, | is yet | no proof | for thee ;
        Thy bo|dy, smooth|er than | this wave|less spring,
        And pu|rer than | the sub|stance of | the same,
        Can creep | through that | his lan|ces can|not pierce :
        Thou, and | thy sis|ter, soft | and sa|cred Air,
        Goddess | of life, | and gov|erness | of health,
        Keep ev|ery fount|ain fresh | and ar|bour sweet ;

No bra|zen gate | her pas|sage can | repulse,
Nor bush|y thick|et bar | thy sub|tle breath :
Then deck | thee with | thy loose | delight|some robes,
And on | thy wings | bring del|icate | perfumes,
To play | the wan|ton with | us through | the leaves.
(David and Bethsabe.)

Marlowe. If all | the pens | that ev|er po|ets held
Had fed | the feel|ing of | their mas|ters' thoughts,
And ev|ery sweet|ness that | inspir'd | their hearts,
Their minds, | and mu|ses, on | admirèd | themes ;
If all | the heav|enly quint|essence | they 'still
From their | immort|al flowers | of po|esy,
Wherein | as in | a mir|ror we | perceive
The high|est reach|es of | a hu|man wit ;
If these | had made | one po|em's per|iod,
And all | combined | in beau|ty's worth|iness,
Yet should | there hov|er in | their rest|less heads
One thought, | one grace, | one won|der at | the least,
Which in|to words | no vir|tue can | digest.
(Tamburlaine.)

(These passages, despite their extreme poetical beauty, are still prosodically immature. Even when, as in the last, there are lines with no technical "stop" at the end, as at "held" and "heads," the grammatical incompleteness does not interfere with the rounding off of the prosodic period or sub-period. Marlowe (*v. inf.*) could enjamb *couplet* beautifully, but not blank verse. Note also that the lines are strictly decasyllabic, the only hints at trisyllabic feet being in words like "Heaven," then regularly a monosyllable, "every," and "flowers.")

(*e*) Shakespeare.

(1) Early single-moulded :

Upon | his blood|y fin|ger he | doth wear
A pre|cious ring, | that light|ens all | the hole,
Which, like | the ta|per in | some mon|ument,
Doth shine | upon | the dead | man's earth|y cheeks,
And shows | the rag|ged en|trails of | the pit.
(Titus Andronicus.)

(Same remarks applying as to the last citation.)

(2) Beginning of perfected stage :

Why art | thou yet | so fair ? | shall I | believe
That un|substan|tial death | is am|orous,
And that | the lean | abhor|rèd mon|ster keeps
Thee here | in dark | to be | his par|amour ?
For fear | of that, | I still | will stay | with thee :
And ne|ver from | this pal|ace of | dim night
Depart | again : | here, here | will I | remain
With worms | that are | thy cham|ber-maids ; O, | here
Will I | set up | my ev|erlast|ing rest,
And shake | the yoke | of in|auspic|ious stars
From this | world-wear|ied flesh.

(Romeo and Juliet.)

(No trisyllabic feet yet, and no redundance : but, by shift of pause and completer juncture of lines, the paragraph effect solidly founded.)

(3) Further process in the same direction :

Nay, ‖ but this dotage of our general's
O'erflows the measure : ‖ those his goodly eyes,
That o'er the files | and musters of the war
Have glowed like plated Mars, ‖ now bend, | now turn,
The office and devotion of their view
Upon a tawny front : ‖ his captain's heart,
Which | in the scuffles of great fights | hath burst
The buckles on his breast, ‖ rene[a]g[u]es all temper,
And is become | the bellows and the fan
To cool a gipsy's lust.

(Antony and Cleopatra.)

(Here the double division marks indicate stronger, and the single lighter, *pauses*—not, as usually in the latter case, *feet*. The variation of the pause for paragraph effect is here consummate ; but the verse, as its conditions require, is of the severer type.)

(4) Perfection in passion :

Blow winds, | and crack | your cheeks ! | rage ! | blow !
You cat|aracts | and hur|rica|noes, spout
Till you | have drench'd | our stee|ples, drown'd | the cocks !
You sul|phurous and | thought-ex|ecut|ing fires,
Vaunt-cour|iers to | oak-cleav|ing thun|derbolts,
Singe my | white head ! | And thou, | all-shak|ing thunder,

Smite flat | the thick | rotund|ity o' | the world !
Crack na|ture's moulds, | all ger⏑mens spill | at once,
That make | ingrate|ful man !

(King Lear.)

(Every extension taken.   Monosyllabic feet either at the
first "blow" and "winds," or the last, and "rage," perhaps
at both (an Alexandrine).   Trisyllabic at "-phurous and,"
"riers to," and "ity o'."   Redundance at "-ing thun⏑der."
Pause fully played upon as above : enjambment at "spout";
parenthetic enjambment at "fires.")

(5) Perfection in quiet :

Our rev|els now | are end|ed.   These | our actors,
As I | foretold | you, were | all spir|its, and
Are melt|ed in|to air, | into | thin air :
And, like | the base|less fab|ric of | this vision,
The cloud-|capped towers, | the gor|geous pal|aces,
The sol|emn tem|ples, the | great globe | itself,
Yea, all | which it | inher|it, shall | dissolve
And, like | this in|substan|tial pa|geant faded,
Leave not | a rack | behind. | We are | such stuff
As dreams | are made | of, and | our lit|tle life
Is round|ed with | a sleep.

(The Tempest.)

(Not much trisyllabic—the dreaminess not requiring it.
A good deal of redundance, and enjambment pushed
nearly to the furthest by taking place at "and."[1])

(*f*) Redundance encroaching.

Beaumont and Fletcher :

"Oh | thou conqu[e]ror,
Thou glo|ry of | the world | once, now | *the pity* :
Thou awe | of na|tions, where|fore didst | *thou fail us ?*
What poor | fate fol|lowed thee, | and plucked | thee on
To trust | thy sa|cred life | to an | *Egyptian ?*
The life | and light | of Rome | to a | *blind stranger,*
That hon|oura|ble war | *ne'er taught* | *a no|bleness*
Nor wor|thy cir|cumstance | show'd what | *a man was ?*

---

[1] For more on Shakespeare's blank verse see the close of this chapter
and the next Book.

That ne|ver heard | thy name | sung but | *in banquets*
And loose | lasciv|ious pleas|ures? to | a boy
That had | no faith | to com|prehend | *thy greatness,*
No stud|y of | thy life | to know | *thy goodness?* . . .
Egyp|*tians, dare* | *you think* | *your high* | *pyra*|*mides*
Built to | out-dure | the sun, | as you | suppose,
Where your | unworth|y kings | lie rak'd | *in ashes,*
Are mon|uments fit | for him! | No, brood | *of Nilus,*
Nothing | can cov|er his | high fame | *but heaven* ;
No pyr|amid | set off | his mem|ories,
But the | eter|nal sub|stance of | *his greatness,*
To which I leave him."

> (*The False One.*)

(Here it will be seen there are two actual Alexandrines (*three* if we allow the full value to "con|queror|") and *twelve* redundant lines to *four* non-redundant! The fire of the poetry fuses this, but cannot always be counted on, as in the next.)

(2) If I | had swelled | the sol|dier, or | *intended*
An act | in per|son lean|ing to | *dishonour,*
As you | would fain | have forced | me, *wit*|*ness Heaven,*
Where clear|est und|erstand|ing of | *all truth is*
(For men | are spite|ful men, | and know | *no pi*[*e*]|*ty*).
When O|lin came, | grim O|lin, when | *his marches,* etc., etc.,
    etc.

> (*The Loyal Subject.*)

(Which, with its repetition of stumbling amphibrachic ends, is rather hideous.)

(*g*) Spread of the infection, and complete decay of blank verse from various causes.

(1) Shirley :

>   I dare,
> With conscience or my pure intent, try what
> Rudeness you find upon my lip, 'tis chaste
> As the desires that breathe upon *my language.*
> I began, Felisarda to *affect thee*
> By seeing thee at prayers ; thy virtue winged
> Love's arrows first, and 'twere a sacrilege
> To choose thee now for sin, that hast a power
> To make | this place | a tem|ple by | thy in|nocence.
> I know thy poverty, and came not to
> Bribe it against thy chastity ; if thou

> Vouchsafe thy fair and honest love, it shall
> Adorn my fortunes which shall stoop to serve it
> In spite of friends or destiny.
>
> (*The Brothers.*)

(Actual *scansion* quite correct, and therefore not marked throughout.   Redundance not excessive ("innocence" may be taken as such, and not as making an Alexandrine, if liked) ; hardly any, and no misused, trisyllabic feet. But enjambment at "what," "to," "thou," and "shall" badly managed.)

(2) Suckling :

> Soft|ly, as death | itself | comes on
> When it | doth steal | away | the sick | man's breath,
> And standers-by perceive it not,
> Have I trod the way unto their lodgings.
> How wisely do those powers
> That give | us hap|piness or|der it !
>
> (*Aglaura.*)

(A hopeless jumble.   The 1st, as a fragment, and 2nd lines are all right, and the 6th could be completed properly.   But 3, 4, and 5—though *3* and *5* *could* come in with other companions—upset any kind of continuous arrangement, and 4 would hardly be good anywhere.)

(3) Davenant :

> Rhodolinda doth become her title
> And her birth.   Since deprived of popular
> Homage, she hath been queen over her great self.
> In this captivity ne'er passionate
> But when she hears me name the king, and then
> Her passions not of anger taste but love :
> Love of her conqueror ; he that in fierce
> Battle (when the cannon's sulphurous breath
> Clouded the day) her noble father slew.
>
> (*Albovine.*)

(More hopeless still, and left unscanned for the student's edification.)

(*h*) The Miltonic Restoration.

Early dramatic experiment.

Comus is evidently written under three different in-

fluences, which may be said to be in the main those of
Marlowe, Shakespeare, and Fletcher.   The poet often uses
Fletcher's heavy trisyllabic endings—

> ⏑ ◡ ◡
> Bore a bright golden flower, but not | in this soil ;

and has not infrequent Alexandrines, the most certain
of which is—

> As to | make this | rela|tion.
>   Care | and ut|most shifts.

But he makes the verse more and more free and
original, as in the following extracts :

> Yea, there | where ve|ry des|ola|tion dwells,
> By grots | and ca|verns shagged | with hor|rid shades,
> She may | pass on | with un|blenched maj|esty,
> Be it | not done | in pride | or in | *presump|tion.*
> Some say | no ev|il thing | that walks | by night,
> In fog | or fire, | by lake | or moor|ish fen,
> Blue mea|gre hag, | or stub|born un|laid ghost,
> That breaks | his mag|ic chains | at cur|few time,
> No gob|lin or | swart fa|ery of | the mine,
> Hath hurt|ful power | o'er true | virgin|ity.
> Do ye | believe | me yet, | or shall | I call
> Anti|quity | from the | old schools | of Greece
> To test|ify | the arms | of chas|tity ?

> Hence had | the hunt|ress Di|an her | dread bow,
> Fair sil|ver-shaft|ed queen | for ev|er chaste,
> Wherewith | she tamed | the brind|ed lioness
> And spot|ted moun|tain-pard, | but set | at nought

> ◡ ◡ ◡
> The fri|volous bolt | of Cu|pid ; gods | and men

>   ◡ ◡ —
> Feared her | stern frown, | and she | was queen | o' the woods.
> .   .   .   .   .   .

>   Methought it was the sound
> Of riot and ill-managed merriment,
> Such as the jocund flute or gamesome pipe
> Stirs up among the loose unlettered hinds,
> When, for their teeming flocks and granges full,
> In wanton dance they praise the bounteous Pan,
> And thank the gods amiss.

(The full comments given on previous passages make

it unnecessary to annotate this much.   The last passage
has the full paragraph combination.[1])

XXIII.   EXAMPLES OF ELIZABETHAN LYRIC

(*a*) Prae-Spenserian :

> Not light | of love, la|dy,
> Though fan|cy do prick | thee,
> Let con|stancy | possess | thy heart :
> Well wor|thy of blam|yng
> They be | and defam|ing,
> From plight|ed troth | which back | do start.
> > Dear dame !
> Then fick|leness ban|ish
> And fol|ly extin|guish,
> Be skil|ful in guid|ing,
> And stay | thee from slid|ing,
> > And stay | thee,
> > > And stay | thee !
> > (*Gorgeous Gallery of Gallant Inventions* (1578).)

(Anapæstic substitution (if not definite anapæstic base)
arising doubtless rather from *tune* than from deliberate
prosodic purpose ; but quite prosodically correct, and sure
to propagate itself.)

(*b*) Post-Spenserian :

> My bon|ny lass, | thine eye,
> > So sly
> Hath made | me sor|row so—
> Thy crim|son cheeks, | my dear,
> > So clear,
> Have so | much wrought | my woe,
> > (*Phœnix Nest* (1593).)

(Pure iambics ; effect produced by short "bob"
rhymes.)

(*c*) Ben Jonson (strict common measure) :

> ‾ ‿
> Drink to | me on|ly with | thine eyes
> And I | will pledge | with mine ;
> Or leave | a kiss | but in | the cup
> And I'll | not look | for wine.

---

[1] For *Paradise Lost, Paradise Regained*, and *Samson Agonistes, v. inf.*
Book II.

> The thirst | that from | the soul | doth rise
> Doth ask | a drink | divine ;
>
> But might | I of | Jove's nec|tar sip,
> I would | not change | for thine.

(As mostly with Ben, strict iambics, save for the opening trochee, and something like a spondee in "Jove's nec-." The wonderful effect which he, or Donne, or the Spirit of the Age, taught to the next two generations is produced entirely by careful choice and fingering of the words and rhymes.)

(*d*) Ben Jonson (anapæstic measure):

> See the cha|riot at hand | here of Love !
> Wherein | my La|dy rid|eth.
> Each that draws | is a swan | or a dove,
> And well | the car | Love guid|eth.
> As she goes, | all hearts | do du|ty
> Unto | her beau|ty ;
> And enam|oured do wish, | so they might
> But enjoy | such a sight,
> That they still | were to run | by her side
> Th[o]rough ponds, | th[o]rough seas, | whither she | would ride.

("Through," as often, is probably to be valued "thorough," and "chariot" was generally "chawyot" or "charret." It will be observed that although this is fine it is slightly laboured. The age was hardly at ease with the anapæst as yet.)

(*e*) Campion (selections):

	English	Follow, | follow,
	anacreontic.	Though with | mischief
		Armed like | whirlwind
		How she | flies still.
(1) Classical	*English*	Constant | to none, | but ev|er false | to me,
	elegiac.	Traitor | still to | love through thy | false desires,
		Not hope | of pit|y now, | nor vain | redress,
		Turns my | grief to | tears and re|newed la|ments.
	English	Rose-|cheeked Lau|ra, come ;
	iambic.	Sing | thou smooth|ly with | thy beauty's
		Sil|ent mu|sic, ei|ther other
		Sweet|ly gracing.

(2) Natural

$$\overline{}\ \cup\ \overline{}\ \cup\ \overline{}\ \cup\ \overline{}\ \cup\ \overline{}\ \cup$$

Follow thy fair sun, unhappy shadow !

$$\cup\ \overline{}\ \cup\ \overline{}\ \cup\ \overline{}$$

Though thou | be black as night,
And she | made all | of light,
Yet fol|low thy | fair sun, | unhap|py shadow !

Break now, | my heart, | and die ! | O no, | she may | relent—
Let my | despair | prevail ! O stay, | hope is | not spent.
Should she | now fix | one smile ! on thee, | where were |
  despair ?
The loss | is but ea|sy which smiles | can repair ;
A stran|ger would please | thee, if she | were as fair.

The student should require little assistance here, odd
as some of the rhythms may seem. But "Rose-cheeked
Laura" ought to be *trochaically* scanned, and will then be
naturally "English." Nothing can make the "English
elegiac" harmonious. Note that line 3 of "Break now"
may be anapæstic like 4 and 5 :

$$\cup\ \overline{}\ \cup\ \overline{}\ \cup\ \overline{}$$

Should she now | fix one smile, etc.[1]

XXIV. Early Continuous Anapæsts

(*a*) Tusser (1st ed. 1557 ; complete, 1573) :

Now leeks | are in sea|son for pot|tage full good,
And spar|eth the milch | cow and purg|eth the blood :
These hav|ing with pea|son for pot|tage in Lent,
Thou spar|est both oat|meal and bread | to be spent.

(Perfectly good, though not very euphonious.)

(*b*) Gifford, H. (1580) :

If I | should write rash|ly what comes | in my train
It might | be such mat|ter as likes | you not best,
And ra|ther I would | great sor|row sustain
Than not | to fulfil | your law|ful request.

(*c*) *Mary Ambree* (*c.* 1584) :

[When] cap|tains coura|geous whom death | could [not] daunt
[Did march | to the siege of] the ci|ty of Gaunt,

---

[1] For scanned examples of Shakespeare's complete prosodic grasp in
lyric, *v. inf.*

> They mus|tered their sol|diers by two | and by three,
> And the fore|most in bat|tle was Ma|ry Ambree.

(Percy patched the bracketed words (his copy being evidently corrupt) in lines 1 and 2. But 3 and 4 are exactly as in the folio; and their anapæstic base is quite clear. At the same time, it is worth remarking that these early lines are apt, frequently though not regularly, to buttress their start on a dissyllabic foot.)

XXV. The Enjambed Heroic Couplet (1580-1660)

(*a*) Spenser.

The very opening of *Mother Hubberd's Tale* (1591), quoted above (p. 62) in its stopped aspect, shows the way to enjambment :

> It was | the month | in which | the right|eous Maid,
> That for | disdain | of sin|ful world's | upbraid,
> Fled back | to heaven.

And we have, further, an instance as shocking to "regular" prosodists as anything in the seventeenth century :

> Whilome, | said she, | before | the world | was civil,
> The Fox | and th' Ape, | *dislik*|*ing of* | *their evil*
> *And hard* | *estate.*

(*b*) Marlowe—as remarkable in *Hero and Leander* for this as for "single-moulding" in blank verse :

> Where the ground
> Was strewed with pearl, and in low coral groves
> Sweet-singing mermaids sported with their loves
> On heaps of heavy gold.

(*c*) Drayton began with fairly separated couplets; but indulged in overrunning later, as in *David and Goliath* :

> Grim vis|age war | more stern|ly doth | awake
> Than it | was wont | and *fur*|*iously* | *doth shake*
> *Her light*|*ning sword.*

(*d*) Browne :

> It chanced one morn, clad in a robe of grey,
> And blushing oft, as rising to betray,

> Enticed this lovely maiden from her bed
> (So when the roses have discoverèd
> Their taintless beauties, flies the early bee
> About the winding alleys merrily)
> Into the wood, and 'twas her usual sport,
> Sitting where most harmonious birds resort,
> To imitate their warbling in April,
> Wrought by the hand of Pan, which she did fill
> Half full of water.

(The actual verse-sentence does not end for another half-dozen lines ; but the scansion is so perfectly regular that it seems unnecessary to mark it. "April" is quite Spenserian, and has both Latin and French justification.)

(*e*) The later seventeenth-century enjambers :

Chalkhill. The rebels, as you heard, being driven hence,
Despairing e'er to expiate their offence
By a too late submission, fled to sea
In such poor barks as they could get, where they
Roamed up and down, which way the winds did please,
Without a chart or compass : the rough seas
Enraged with such a load of wickedness,
Grew big with billows, great was their distress ;
Yet was their courage greater ; desperate men
Grow valianter with suffering : in their ken
Was a small island, thitherward they steer
Their weather-beaten barks, each plies his gear ;
Some row, some pump, some trim the ragged sails,
All were employed and industry prevails.
(*Thealma and Clearchus*, 2203-2216.)

Marmion. When you are landed, and a little past
The Stygian ferry, you your eyes shall cast
And spy some busy at their wheel, and these
Are three old women, called the Destinies.
(*Cupid and Psyche*, iii. 259-262.)

Chamber- But ere the weak Euriolus (for he
layne. This hapless stranger was) again could be
By strength supported, base Amarus, who
Could think no more than priceless thanks was due
For all his dangerous pains, more beastly rude
Than untamed Indians, basely did exclude
That noble guest : which being with sorrow seen
By Ammida, whose prayers and tears had been

His helpless advocates, she gives in charge
To her Ismander—till that time enlarge
Her than restrained desires, he entertain
Her desolate and wandering friend.   Nor vain
Were these commands, his entertainment being
Such as observant love thought best agreeing
To her desires.

(*Pharonnida*, IV. iii. 243-256.)

(The same remark applies here as to Browne.   Some of these poets are indeed great "apostrophators," such things as " t' " for " to," " b' " for " by," and " 's " for " his " being common.   But these uglinesses are generally resorted to in order to attain or keep the strict decasyllable.   Chalkhill (an actual Elizabethan, if he was anything) is less shy of at least apparent trisyllabics, as in " being driv|en," " ex|piate their.|"   The double rhyme of " sea " to " they " and "seas" to "please" is worth noticing; *v. sup.* Rule 34, p. 34.)

XXVI. The Stopped Heroic Couplet (1580-1660)

(*a*) Spenser (*Mother Hubberd's Tale*), *v. sup.* p. 62.

(*b*) Drayton (*Heroical Epistles*, " Suffolk to Margaret ") :

We all do breathe upon this earthly ball,
Likewise one Heav'n encompasseth us all ;
No banishment can be to us assigned
Who doth retain a true resolved mind ;
Man in himself a little world doth bear,
His soul the monarch ever ruling there ;
Wherever then his body doth remain
He is a king that in himself doth reign.

(Here all the characteristics of the eighteenth-century couplet may be found—the central cæsura or split, the balance of the two halves, the completion of sense in the couplet and almost in the line.)

(*c*) Fairfax (end couplets) :

If fictions light I mix with Truth Divine
And fill these lines with other praise than Thine.   (i. 2.)

> We further seek what their offences be :
> Guiltless I quit ; guilty I set them free.   (ii. 5.)

> Thro' love the hazard of fierce war to prove,
> Famous for arms, but famous more for love.   (iii. 40.)

> In fashions wayward, and in love unkind,
> For Cupid deigns not wound a currish mind.   (iv. 46.)

(Observe here the tendency, not merely to balance, but to positive antithesis, in the halves.)

(*d*) Beaumont, Sir John :

> The relish of the Muse consists in rhyme :
> One verse must meet another like a chime.
> Our Saxon shortness hath peculiar grace
> In choice of words fit for the ending-place,
> Which leave impression in the mind as well
> As closing sounds of some delightful bell.

(*e*) Sandys.
Compare the openings of *Job* I. and II. :

> In Hus, a land which near the sun's uprise
> And northern confines of Sabæa lies,
> A great example of perfection reigned,
> His name was Job, his soul with guilt unstained.
>
> .   .   .
>
> Again when all the radiant sons of light
> Before His throne appeared, Whose only sight
> Beatitude infused ; the Inveterate Foe,
> In fogs ascending from the depth below,
> Profaned their blest assembly.

(*f*) Waller :

> With the sweet sound of this harmonious lay
> About the keel delighted dolphins play ;
> Too sure a sign of sea's ensuing rage
> Which must anon this royal troop engage ;
> To whom soft sleep seems more secure and sweet
> Within the town commanded by our fleet.

(*g*) Cowley (*Davideis*) :

> Lo ! with pure hands thy heavenly fire to take,
> My well-chang'd muse I a pure vestal make.
> From Earth's vain joys and Love's soft witchcraft free,
> I consecrate my Magdalene to thee.

> Lo, this great work, a temple to thy praise
> On polish'd pillars of strong verse I raise—
> A temple where if thou vouchsafe to dwell
> It Solomon's and Herod's shall excel.

(It should be observed on these that in Beaumont, Sandys I., Waller, and Cowley the separation of the couplets is strictly maintained; in Sandys II. not. In fact, this passage, but for the rhymes, has almost the run of Miltonic blank verse. Waller once approaches an initial trochee or "inversion of accent" in "With the." Here Cowley is pretty regular. But not far off may be found such a line as—

> Themselves at first against themselves *they excite* ;

where he must either have intended "they-ex-" to be elided or have meant an anapæstic ending of the kind so common in the dramatists his contemporaries. And he constantly uses (explicitly defending it) the Alexandrine, as in—

> Like some | fair pine | o'erlook|ing all | th' igno|bler wood,

or—

> Which runs, | and, as | it runs, | for ev|er shall | run on ;

while he often employs trochees or spondees. He does not use the triplet in the *Davideis*, but does elsewhere, and, after Virgil, he sometimes indulges in half-lines.)

XXVII. Various Forms of Octosyllable-Hepta-syllable (late Sixteenth and Seventeenth Century)

(*a*) Shakespeare (doubtfully ?) :

(1) King Pan|dion | he is | dead,
All thy | friends are | lapped in | lead.

(2) Let | the bird | of loud|est lay
On | the sole | Ara|bian tree.

(These distichs from the *Passionate Pilgrim* will illustrate the two different forms which the heptasyllable—really an octosyllable acephalous or catalectic—can take. The catalectic form (1) becomes trochaic; the acephalous (2), iambic. They can be interchanged, and either can group with the full iambic dimeter ; but, *individually*, it would spoil (1) to scan it as iambic, (2) to scan it as trochaic. Yet on "accentual" scansion there is no difference ; and some advocates of recent fancy "stress"-systems maintain that the rhythms are identical !)

(*b*) Shakespeare (almost certainly) :

> The cat | with eyne | of burn|ing coal
> Now couch|es 'fore | the mou|se's hole,
> And crick|ets sing | at the ov|en's mouth
> As | the : blith|er : from | their : drouth.

(In this famous and eminently Shakespearian passage from *Pericles*, the last line, a heptasyllable, goes perfectly with the rest, or octosyllables, either as acephalous or as catalectic, either as an iambic fellow or a trochaic substitute.)

(*c*) Shakespeare (certainly) :

> And we fairies, that do run
>   By the triple Hecate's team,
> From the presence of the sun
>   Follow:ing | dark:ness | like a dream,
> Now are frolic : not a mouse
> Shall disturb this hallowed house :
> I am sent with broom before,
> To sweep the dust behind the door.

(From *A Midsummer Night's Dream*. Same as last, except that the full octosyllable is only reached at the end, and perhaps in line 4 "Hecat[e]," as often, is dissyllabic.)

(*d*) Browne, W. :

> Be ev|er fresh ! | Let no | man dare
> To spoil | thy fish, | make lock | or wear,
> But on | thy mar|gent still | let dwell,
> Those flowers | which have | the sweet|est smell,
> And let | the dust | upon | thy strand
> Become, | like Ta|gus, gold|en sand.
> Let as | much good | betide | to thee
> As thou | hast fa|vour showed | to me.

(Pure octosyllables. There is a catalectic line now and then elsewhere, but it is an evident exception.)

(*e*) Wither:

> For | in : her | a : grace | there : shines,
> That o'er-daring thoughts confines,
> Making worthless men despair
> To be loved of one so fair.
> Yea, the Destinies agree,
> Some good judgments blind should be,
> And not gain the power of knowing
> Those rare beauties in her growing.

(Pure heptasyllables, taking either cadence, and, when extended, owing the extension mainly, if not wholly, to the double rhyme. The first line gives the alternative scansion; but Wither's run is, on the whole, trochaic, as Browne's is iambic.)

XXVIII. "COMMON," "LONG," AND "IN MEMORIAM" MEASURE (SEVENTEENTH CENTURY)

(*a*) See above, § XXIII., for "Drink to me only."

(*b*) Donne (?), Ayton (?), Anon. (?), (C.M.):

> Thou sent'st | me late | a heart | was crowned,
> I took | it to | be thine;
> But when | I saw | it had | a wound,
> I knew | that heart | was mine.
>
> A boun|ty of | a strange | conceit!
> To send | mine own | to me,
> And send | it in | a worse | estate
> Than when | it came | to thee.

(A capital example of the possibility of rhetorical *addition* to the strict foot-system, as in line 2, "I took it ‖ to be thine."[1] For "conc*ay*t" and "estate" *cf. sup.* § XXV. *sub fin.*)

(*c*) Herrick (C.M.):

> Bid me | to live | and I | will live
> Thy Pro|testant to | be;
> Or bid | me love, | and I | will give
> A lov|ing heart to | thee.

(Strongly flavoured, and greatly improved, by trochaic substitution in first foot.)

---

[1] See Glossary, "Musical and Rhetorical Arrangements."

(*d*) Marvell (L.M.):

> My love | is of | a birth | as rare
> As 'tis | for ob|ject, strange | and high—
> It was | begot|ten of | Despair
> Upon | Impos|sibil|ity.

(*e*) Lord Herbert of Cherbury (*In Memoriam* metre):

> For whose | affec|tion once | is shown,
>   No long|er can | the world | beguile ;
>   Who sees | his pen|ance all | the while
> He holds | a torch | to make | her known.

(Great regularity of feet ; but already the "circular" motion which Tennyson was to perfect.)

XXIX. IMPROVED ANAPÆSTIC MEASURES (DRYDEN, ANON., PRIOR)

(*a*) Dryden (1691 ?):

> While Pan | and fair Sy|rinx are fled | from our shore,
> The Gra|ces are ban|ished, and Love | is no more :
> The soft | god of plea|sure that warmed | our desires
> Has brok|en his bow, | and extin|guished his fires,
> And vows | that himself | and his moth|er will mourn,
> Till Pan | and fair Sy|rinx in tri|umph return.

(These early anapæsts, as noted, are very apt to begin with dissyllabic feet. But it was no rule : in this same piece, "The Beautiful Lady of the May," occurs the line :

> *All the nymphs* | were in white | and the shep|herd in green.

(*b*) Anon. in *Pills to Purge Melancholy* (1719, but contents often much older):

> Let us drink | and be mer|ry, sing, dance, | and rejoice,
> With cla|ret and sher|ry, theor|bo and voice.
> The change|able world | to our joys | is unjust,
> All trea|sure's uncer|tain, then down | with your dust !
> On fro|lics dispose | your pounds, shil|lings, and pence,
> For we | shall be no|thing a hun|dred years hence.

(*c*) Prior (1696):

> While with la|bour assid|uous due plea|sure I mix,
> And in one | day atone | for the bus|iness of six,
> In a lit|tle Dutch chaise | on a Sat|urday night,
> On my left | hand my Hor|ace, a nymph | on my right.

(Observe here in "assid[u]ous" and "bus[i]ness" the liberty of combining adjacent vowels (-*uo*us) and following familiar pronunciation (*biz*ness) which this light verse especially authorises.

XXX. "Pindarics" (Seventeenth Century)

Dryden (complete stanza from "Anne Killigrew" ode):

VI

Born to | the spa|cious em|pire of | the Nine,
One would | have thought | she should | have been | content
To man|age well | that migh|ty gov|ernment ;   90
But what | can young | ambi|tious souls | confine ?
   To the | next realm | she stretched | her sway,
   For Pain|ture near | adjoin|ing lay,
A plen|teous prov|ince, and | allur|ing prey.
A cham|ber of | depen|dencies | was framed,   95
(As con|querors | will nev|er want | pretence,
When armed, | to just|ify | the offence,)
And the | whole fief, | in right | of po|etry, | she claimed.
The coun|try op|en lay | without | defence ;
For po|ets fre|quent in|roads there | had made,   100
   And per|fectly | could rep|resent
   The shape, | the face, | with ev|ery lin|eament,
And all | the large | domains | which the | Dumb Sis|ter swayed ;
   All bowed | beneath | her gov|ernment,
   Received | in tri|umph where|soe'er | she went.   105
Her pen|cil drew | whate'er | her soul | designed,
And oft | the hap|py draught | surpassed | the im|age in | her mind.
   The syl|van scenes | of herds | and flocks,
   And fruit|ful plains | and bar|ren rocks,
   Of shal|low brooks | that flowed | so clear,   110
   The bot|tom did | the top | appear ;
   Of deep|er too | and am|pler floods,
   Which, as | in mir|rors, showed | the woods ;
   Of lof|ty trees, | with sa|cred shades,
   And pèr|spectives | of plea|sant glades,   115
   Where nymphs | of bright|est form | appear,
   And shag|gy sat|yrs stand|ing near,
   Which them | at once | admire | and fear.
   The ru|ins, too, | of some | majes|tic piece,
Boasting | the power | of an|cient Rome | or Greece,   120
Whose sta|tues, frie|zes, col|umns, bro|ken lie,
And, though | defaced, | the won|der of | the eye ;

What na|ture, art, | bold fic|tion, e'er | durst frame,
Her form|ing hand | gave fea|ture to | the name.
So strange | a con|course ne'er | was seen | before,   125
But when | the peo|pled ark | the whole | crea|tion bore.

(88-91, heroics ; 92, 93, octosyllables ; 94-96, heroics ; 97, octosyllable ; 98, Alexandrine ; 99, 100, heroic ; 101, octosyllable ; 102, heroic ; 103, Alexandrine ; 104, octosyllable ; 105, 106, heroics ; 107, fourteener ; 108-118, continuous octosyllables ; 119 - 125, continuous heroics capped and finished off by 126, Alexandrine.   In 97, probably " th' offence.")

XXXI. The Heroic Couplet from Dryden to Crabbe

(*a*) Dryden (early non-dramatic) :

> Our setting sun, from his declining seat,
> Shot beams of kindness on *you*, not of heat ;
> And, when his love was bounded in a few
> That were unhappy, that they might be true,
> Made *you* the favourite of his last sad times,
> That is, a sufferer in his subjects' crimes.
> Thus, those first favours *you* received, were sent,
> Like heaven's rewards, in earthly punishment :
> Yet fortune, conscious of *your* destiny,
> E'en then took care to lay *you* softly by,
> And wrapped *your* fate among her precious things,
> Kept fresh to be unfolded with *your* king's.

(Note recurrent *you* and *your* employed like pauses to vary verse.   Otherwise strictly "regular.")

(*b*) Dryden (" heroic "-dramatic type at best) :

> Fair though you are
> As summer mornings, | and your eyes more bright
> Than stars that twinkle : in a winter's night ;
> Though you have eloquence to warm and move
> Cold age : and praying hermits : into love ;
> Though Almahide with scorn : rewards my care,—
> Yet, | than to change, | 'tis nobler to despair.
> My love's my soul ; | and that from fate is free ;
> 'Tis that unchanged and deathless part of me.

> (*Conquest of Granada* II., III. iii.)

(Observe how the alternation of central pause, strongly
(|) and weakly (:) or hardly at all (no mark) emphasised,
knits and shades the verse; and how, in the first line,
there is positive enjambment. Yet there is still no trisyllabic substitution. This type is continued and perfected
in the great satires and didactic pieces for argument and
attack, and in the *Fables* for narrative. It admits, to
relieve monotony, the Alexandrine (*Hind and Panther*,
i. 23, 24))—

> Their corps[e] to perish, but their kind to last,
> So much | the death|less plant | the dy|ing fruit | surpassed ;

the triplet (*ibid.* a little further)—

> Can I believe eternal God could lie
> Disguised in mortal mould and infancy,
> That the great Maker of the world could die?

both combined (*Palamon and Arcite*, ii. 560-562)—

> There saw I how the secret felon wrought,
> And treason labouring in the traitor's thought,
> And mid|wife time | the ri|pened plot | to mur|der brought ;

and sometimes the fourteener (*Medal*, 94)—

> Thou leapst o'er all eternal truths in thy Pindaric way.

(*c*) Passages from Garth, (1), and Pope, (2) and (3), to
illustrate the mechanical character of the eighteenth-century
couplet, the ease with which it can be shifted from
decasyllabic to octosyllabic, and its peculiar construction
of ridge-backed antithetic pause :

> (1) With ~~breathing~~ fire his pitchy nostrils blow,
> As from his sides he shakes the ~~fleecy~~ snow.
> Around this ~~hoary~~ prince from wat'ry beds
> His subject islands raise their ~~verdant~~ heads.
>
> .   .   .   .   .
>
> Eternal spring with ~~smiling~~ verdure here
> Warms the mild air and crowns the ~~youthful~~ year.
>
> .   .   .   .   .
>
> The vine undressed her ~~swelling~~ clusters bears,
> The labouring hind the ~~mellow~~ olive cheers.
>
> (*The Dispensary.*)

(Read, omitting the interlined epithets, and you get perfectly fluent octosyllables.)

> (2) First in these fields, I try the *sylvan* strains,
> Nor blush to sport on Windsor's *blissful* plains.
> Fair Thames, flow gently from thy *sacred* spring,
> While on thy banks *Sicilian* Muses sing ;
> Let *vernal* airs thro' *trembling* osiers play
> And Albion's cliffs resound the *rural* lay.

(Windsor Forest.)

Now this, in the same way, by the omission of some of the italicised *gradus* epithets, becomes—

> First in these fields I try the strains,
> Nor blush to sport on Windsor's plains.
> Fair Thames, flow gently from thy spring,
> While on thy banks [the] Muses sing ;
> Let vernal airs through osiers play
> And Albion's cliffs resound the lay.

> (3) Not with more glories in th' *ethereal* plain
> The sun first rises o'er the *purpled* main,
> Than issuing forth the rival of his beams
> Launch'd on the bosom of the *silver* Thames.
> Fair nymphs and well-drest youths around her shone,
> But ev'ry eye was fix'd on her alone.
> On her *white* breast a *sparkling* cross she wore,
> Which *Jews* might kiss and *Infidels* adore.
> Her *lively* looks a *sprightly* mind disclose,
> Quick as her eyes and as unfixed as those.
> *Favours* to none to all she *smiles* extends,
> *Oft* she rejects but never *once* offends.
> Bright as the sun her eyes the gazers strike,
> And like the sun they shine on all alike.
> Yet graceful ease and sweetness void of pride
> Might hide her faults if Belles had faults to hide.
> If to her share some female errors fall,
> Look in her face and you'll forget them all.

(The Rape of the Lock.)

Of course Pope,[1] in the close of the *Dunciad* and elsewhere, has passages of the utmost dignity ; and the antithetic arrangement is good for satire. But perhaps

[1] For more on the differences of his couplet and Dryden's, see next Book.

the finest passages of this class of couplet—certainly the finest *with* the *Dunciad* close—are the following, from

(*d*) Johnson (*Vanity of Human Wishes*—end) :

> Where then shall Hope and Fear their objects find ?
> Must dull suspense corrupt the stagnant mind ?
> Must helpless man, in ignorance sedate,
> Roll darkling down the torrent of his fate ?
> Must no dislike alarm, no wishes rise,
> No cries invoke the mercies of the skies ?
> . . . . . .
> Yet, when the sense of sacred presence fires
> And strong devotion to the skies aspires,
> Pour forth thy favours for a healthful mind,
> Obedient passions, and a will resigned ;
> For love which scarce collective man can fill ;
> For patience sovereign o'er transmuted ill ;
> For faith that, panting for a happier seat,
> Counts death kind nature's signal of retreat.
> These goods for man the laws of Heaven ordain,
> These goods He grants who grants the power to gain ;
> With these celestial Wisdom calms the mind,
> And makes the happiness she does not find.

and

(*e*) Crabbe ("Delay brings Danger "—end) :

> Early he rose, and looked with many a sigh
> On the red light that filled the eastern sky ;
> Oft had he stood before, alert and gay,
> To hail the glories of the new-born day :
> But now dejected, languid, listless, low,
> He saw the wind upon the water blow,
> And the cold stream curled onward as the gale
> From the pine hill blew harshly down the dale ;
> On the right side the youth a wood surveyed,
> With all its dark intensity of shade ;
> Where the rough wind alone was heard to move,
> In this, the pause of nature and of love,
> When now the young are reared, and when the old,
> Lost to the tie, grow negligent and cold—
> Far to the left he saw the huts of men,
> Half hid in mist, that hung upon the fen ;
> Before him swallows gathering for the sea,
> Took their short flights and twittered on the lea ;
> And near the bean-sheaf stood, the harvest done,
> And slowly blackened in the sickly sun ;

> All these were sad in nature, or they took
> Sadness from him, the likeness of his look
> And of his mind—he pondered for a while,
> Then met his Fanny with a borrowed smile.

(Observe, besides the other points mentioned, that trisyllabic feet practically never occur in Garth, Pope, and Johnson—"wat'ry for watery," and words like "ether(ea)l," " celest(ia)l," " happ(ie)r," being *intended* to take the benefit of elision, though, as a matter of fact, they *give* that of extension.   Only Crabbe, in " gathering," may perhaps not have meant " gath'ring.")

XXXII. Eighteenth-Century Blank Verse

(*a*) Thomson :

> First the flaming red
> Sprung vivid forth ; the tawny orange next ;
> And next delicious yellow ; by whose side
> Fell the kind beams of all-refreshing green.
> Then the pure blue that swells autumnal skies,
> Etherial played, and then of sadder hue
> Emerged the deepened indigo (as when
> The heavy-skirted evening droops with frost),
> While the last gleamings of refracted light
> Died in the fainting violet away.

(This, from the poem on Newton, is Thomson at his very best in blank verse, or nearly so.   He was, however, too apt to emphasise his phrases into full stops, producing what Johnson justly called "broken style," as thus :

> On he walks
> Graceful, and crows defiance.   In the pond
> The finely-chequered duck, before her train,
> Rows garrulous.   The stately sailing swan, etc.)

The trick was pushed to a pitch of absurdity by

(*b*) Glover :

> Mindful of their charge,
> The chiefs depart.   Leonidas provides
> His various armour.   Agis close attends,
> His best assistant.   First a breastplate arms
> The spacious chest ;

and is somewhat noteworthy in Young and others. The reason probably was a sort of nervous fear lest, in the absence of rhyme, the versification should not be sufficiently marked. But at length the proper flow was recovered by

(*c*) Cowper :

      ‒   ‒   ‒ ◡

Time made | thee what | thou wast, | king of | the woods,
And time hath made thee what thou art—a cave
For owls to roost in. Once thy spreading boughs
                            ◡ ◡
O'erhung the champaign ; and the nu|merous flocks
That grazed it stood beneath that ample cope
Uncrowded, yet safe-sheltered from the storm.
No flock frequents thee now. Thou hast outlived
Thy popularity, and art become
(Unless verse rescue thee awhile) a thing
Forgotten, as the foliage of thy youth.
                           (*Yardley Oak.*)

         ‒   ‒   ‒ ◡
(The spondee " Time made " and trochee " king of " are certainly intentional, whether consciously as such or not.

        ◡ ◡   ‒
The anapæst " -merous flocks " may not have been *meant*, for Cowper had not cleared his mind up about " elision," but is one in fact.)

XXXIII. The Regularised Pindaric Ode

Analysis of Gray's *Bard* (the second and third divisions coincide to the minutest degree) :

I. i.

1.   " Ruin seize thee, ruthless King !
2.   Confusion on thy banners wait ;
3. Tho' fanned by Conquest's crimson wing
4.   They mock the air with idle state.
5. Helm, nor hauberk's twisted mail,
6. Nor e'en thy virtues, Tyrant, shall avail
7. To save thy secret soul from nightly fears,
8. From Cambria's curse, from Cambria's tears ! "
9. —Such were the sounds that o'er the crested pride
10.   Of the first Edward scatter'd wild dismay,

11. As down the steep of Snowdon's shaggy side
12.   He wound with toilsome march his long array :—
13. Stout Glo'ster stood aghast in speechless trance ;
14. "To arms !" cried Mortimer, and couch'd his quivering lance.

I. i. (*Strophe*)

1. Troch. dim. cat. $-\cup-\cup-\cup-$.
2. Iamb. dim. acat. $\cup-\cup-\cup-\cup-$.
3.   ,,   ,,   ,,
4.   ,,   ,,   ,,
5 as 1.
6 and 7. Heroics nearly pure, $\cup-\cup-\cup-\cup-\cup-$.
8 as 2 to 4.
9 to 13. Heroics
14. Alexandrine $\cup-\cup-\cup-\cup-\cup-\cup-$. " Quiv'ring," probably.

I. ii.

1.   On a rock, whose haughty brow
2. Frowns o'er old Conway's foaming flood,
3.   Robed in the sable garb of woe
4. With haggard eyes the Poet stood
5. (Loose his beard and hoary hair
6. Stream'd like a meteor to the troubled air),
7. And with a master's hand and prophet's fire
8. Struck the deep sorrows of his lyre :
9.   " Hark, how each giant-oak and desert-cave
10. Sighs to the torrent's awful voice beneath :
11. O'er thee, oh King ! their hundred arms they wave,
12.   Revenge on thee in hoarser murmurs breathe ;
13. Vocal no more, since Cambria's fatal day,
14. To high-born Hoel's harp, or soft Llewellyn's lay.

I. ii. (*Antistrophe*)

Identical.

I. iii.

1.   "Cold is Cadwallo's tongue,
2.   That hush'd the stormy main :
3. Brave Urien sleeps upon his craggy bed :
4.   Mountains, ye mourn in vain
5.   Modred, whose magic song
6. Made hugh Plinlimmon bow his cloud-topt head.
7.   On dreary Arvon's shore they lie
8. Smear'd with gore and ghastly pale :
9. Far, far aloof the affrighted ravens sail ;
10.   The famish'd eagle screams, and passes by.

11. Dear lost companions of my tuneful art,
12.   Dear as the light that visits these sad eyes,
13. Dear as the ruddy drops that warm my heart,
14.   Ye died amidst your dying country's cries—
15. No more I weep ; They do not sleep ;
16.   On yonder cliffs, a griesly band,
17. I see them sit ; They linger yet,
18.   Avengers of their native land :
19. With me in dreadful harmony they join,
20. And weave with bloody hands the tissue of thy line.

I. iii. (*Epode*)

1. Iamb. dim. brachycat. ⌣ — ⌣ — ⌣ —.
2.   „   „   „
3. Heroic.
4, 5, as 1, 2, with trochee substituted in first place.
6 as 3.
7. Iamb. dim. acat.
8. Troch. dim. cat.
9 to 14. Heroics : the last 4 in quatrain.
15 to 18. Iamb. dims. arranged in stanza quatrain ; internal rhymes
    only in lines 15 and 17.
19. Heroic.
20. Alexandrine.

Rhyme scheme of Strophe and Antistrophe.	Rhyme scheme of Epode.
a	*a*
b	*b*
a	*c*
b	*b*
c	*a*
c	*c*
d	*d*
d	*e*
e	*e*
f	*d*
e	*f*
f	*g*
g	*f*
g	*g*
	o[1]
	h
	o[1]
	h
	i
	i

[1] Unrhymed termination as far as end-syllable goes.

XXXIV. Lighter Eighteenth-Century Lyric

(*a*) Gay:

> The school|boy's desire | is a play-|day,
> The school|master's joy | is to flog,
> The milk|maid's delight | is on May-|day,
> But mine | is on sweet | Molly Mog.

(Remarkable for the improvement, by the redundant syllable in the odd lines, on the plain anapæstic three-foot quatrain used later by Shenstone and Cowper, as well as for its leading up to the more obvious successes of Praed and Mr. Swinburne; *v. inf.* § XLIV.)

(*b*) Gray:

> 'Twas on a lofty vase's side
> Where China's gayest art had dyed
>   The azure flowers that blow—
> Demurest of the tabby kind,
> The pensive Selima reclined,
>   Gazed on the lake below.

(Eleventh - century poets employed the old romance-six, or *rime couée*, almost more largely than any other metre for general lyrical purposes.)

(*c*) (D. Lewis ?):

> And when with envy Time, transport|ed,
>   Shall think to rob us of our joys,
> You'll in your girls again be court|ed,
>   And I'll go wooing in my boys.

(Another instance of the refreshing and alterative effect of redundance—in this case on the old "long measure." But even in its stricter form the century managed "L.M." better than "C.M.," which, till Blake, was almost always sing-song.)

XXXV. The Revival of Equivalence
(Chatterton and Blake)

Percy's *Reliques*, however, taught it something better; though Percy's own imitations and those of others were often as described above.   Yet soon we find in (*a*) Chatterton, such adaptations of ballad metre as—

> I ken | Syr Ro|ger from | afar
> Trippynge | over | the lea,
> Ich ask | whie | the lov|erd's son
> Is moe | than mee?

and such equivalenced octosyllabic couplet and stanza as—

> ˘ − ˘˘ − ˘ ˘ − ˘ − − −
> Sir Bo|telier then | having con|quer'd his twayne,
> ˘ − ˘ ˘ − ˘ ˘ − − −
> Rode con|queror off | the tour|neying playne,
> ˘ − ˘ − ˘ ˘ − ˘˘ −
> Receiv|ing a gar|land from Al|ice's hand,
> ˘ − ˘ − ˘ − ˘ −
> The fair|est la|dye in | the lande.

But the real Columbus here was

(*b*) Blake, who from 1780 onwards wrote such things as—

> ˘ − ˘̄
> The wild | winds weep
> ˘ ˘ − ˘˘ −
> And the night | is a-cold ;
> ˘ − ˘ −
> Come hi|ther, Sleep,
> ˘ ˘ − ˘ −
> And my griefs | unfold.
> ˘ − ˘ − ˘ −
> But lo ! | the morn|ing peeps
> − ˘ ˘ − ˘̄ −
> Over | the east|ern steeps,
> ˘ ˘ − ˘ − ˘ −
> And the rust|ling beds | of dawn
> ˘ − ˘ −
> The earth | do scorn.

> − ˘˘ −
> Lo ! | to the vault
> ˘ − ˘ −
> Of pa|vèd heaven,
> ˘ − ˘ −
> With sor|row fraught,
> ˘ − ˘̄ −
> My notes | are driven.
> ˘ − ˘ − ˘ −
> They strike | the ear | of night,
> − − − −
> Make weep | the eyes | of day ;

They make mad | the roar|ing winds,

And with tem | pests play.

Like a fiend | in a cloud,

With howl|ing woe

After night | I do crowd

And with night | will go ;

I turn | my back | to the East,

From whence com|forts have | increased,

For light | doth seize | my brain

With fran|tic pain.

(This cannot be studied too carefully, and is almost a typical example of sound prosody, orderly without monotony and free without licence. Every substitution is justified, both on the general principles expounded throughout this book, and to the ear in each individual case.)

XXXVI. Rhymeless Attempts (Collins to Shelley)

(a) Collins (*Ode to Evening*):

If aught | of oat|en stop | or pas|toral song
May hope, | O pen|sive Eve, | to soothe | thine ear
Like thy | own sol|emn springs,
Thy springs | and dy|ing gales.

(Perfectly regular heroics and sixes ; "pastoral" most probably intended to be "past'ral.")

(b) Sayers (Choruses of *Moina*) :

I.

Hail to | her whom | Frea | loves,
Moina | hail !
When first | thine in|fant eyes | beheld
The beam | of day,

Frea | from Val|halla's | groves
Mark'd thy | birth in | silent | joy ;
Frea, | sweetly | smiling | saw
The swift-|wing'd mes|senger | of love
Bearing | in her | rosy | hand
The gold-|tipt horn | of gods.

(This—which is fairly but not wholly free from the fault noted in II.—is ordinary iambic and trochaic mixture.)

II.

Dark, dark | is Moi|na's bed,
On earth's | hard lap | she lies.
[Where is | the beau|teous form
That he|roes loved ?]
[Where is | the beam|ing eye,
The rud|dy cheek ?]
Cold, cold | is Moi|na's bed,
And shall | no lay | of death
[With pleas|ing mur|mur soothe
Her part|ed soul ?]
[Shall no | tear wet | the grave
Where Moi|na lies ?]
The bards | shall raise | the lay | of death,
The bards | shall soothe | her part|ed soul,
[And drop | the tear | of grief
On Moi|na's grave.]

(It will be observed that each of the couplets enclosed in square brackets is simply a blank-verse line, arbitrarily split. This is probably the result of the effort at rhymeless *stanza*. Observe the unbroken iambic rhythm—another danger.)

(*c*) Southey (*Thalaba*) :

How beau|tiful | is Night !
A dew|y fresh|ness fills | the si|lent air :
No mist | obscures, | nor cloud | nor speck | nor stain
Breaks the | serene | of heaven :
In full-|orbed glo|ry yon|der moon | divine
Rolls through | the dark | blue depths.
Beneath | her stead|y ray
The des|ert-cir|cle spreads,

$$- \; \smile \quad - \quad -$$

Like the | round o|cean, gir|dled with | the sky.
How beau|tiful | is Night !

(Iambic lines of various lengths with trochaic and spondaic but no other substitution (there are anapæsts elsewhere). The couplet - six, or split Alexandrine, is intentional, but Southey expressly avoids split heroics.)

(*d*) Shelley (*Queen Mab*) :

> How wonderful is Death,
> Death and his brother Sleep !
> One, pale as yonder waning moon
> With lips of lurid blue ;
> The other, rosy as the morn
> When throned on ocean's wave
> It blushes o'er the world :
> Yet both so passing wonderful !

XXXVII. THE REVISED BALLAD (PERCY TO COLERIDGE)

(*a*) Percy's imitation of equivalence and extension of scheme (*Sir Cawline*) :

> Then she | held forth | her lil|y-white hand
> Towards | that knight | so free ;
> He gave | to it | one gen|til kiss,
> His heart | was brought | from bale | to bliss,
> The tears | sterte from | his ee.

(Not bad; might have been improved by "*And* the tears|.")

(*b*) Goldsmith (regularised sing-song) :

> Turn An|geli|na, ev|er dear,
> My charm|er, turn | to see
> Thy own, | thy long-|lost Ed|win here
> Restored | to love | and thee !

(*c*) Southey (quite sound in principle, and not bad in effect ; but a little more poetic powder wanted) :

> They laid | her where | these four | roads meet
> Here in | this ver|y place—
> The earth | upon | her corpse | was pressed,
> This post | was driv|en into | her breast,
> And a stone | is on | her face.

(*d*) Coleridge (the real thing in simpler and more complex form):

> It is | an an|cient ma|riner,
> And he stop|peth one | of three—
> " By thy long | grey beard | and glit|tering eye,
> Now where|fore stop'st | thou me ? "
>
> . . . .
>
> Her lips | were red, | her looks | were free,
> Her locks | were yel|low as gold ;
> Her skin | was as white | as lep|rosy—
> The night|mare Life-|in-Death | was she,
> Who thicks | man's blood | with cold.
>
> . . . .
>
> We list|ened and | looked side|ways up !
> Fear at | my heart, | as at | a cup,
> My life-|blood seemed | to sip!
> The stars | were dim | and thick | the night,
> The steers|man's face | by his lamp | gleamed white ;
> From the sails | the dew | did drip—
> Till clomb | above | the east|ern bar
> The horn|èd moon, | with one | bright star
> Within | the neth|er tip.

(The presence and absence of anapæstic substitution here, with its effect in each case, should be carefully studied.)

XXXVIII

Specimens of *Christabel*, with note on the application of the system to later lyric. (Some have said that in *Christabel* "the consideration of feet is dropped altogether," and others, that it "cannot be analysed," or can only be so by the rough process of counting accents. Let us go and do it.)

> 'Tis the mid|dle of night | by the cas|tle clock,
>
> And the owls | have awa|kened the crow|ing cock,
>
> Tu—-whit—tu whoo !
>
> And hark, | again ! | the crow|ing cock,
>
> How drow|sily | it crew. |

(A five-lined ballad stanza, freely but regularly equivalenced with anapæsts. Line 3 may be four monosyllabic
feet, or an iambic monometer—two feet,—according to the
value put on the first note of the owl's cry.) The rest of
the piece is *not* in ballad stanza, but in octosyllabic couplet,
again more or less freely but regularly equivalenced, and
allowing itself occasional licences of rhyme-order, line-length,
etc. Thus the succeeding lines are in two batches, where
the anapæstic substitution dwindles, disappears, and reappears (with trochaic and spondaic)—monosyllabic feet
being also *ad libitum* :

> Sir Le|oline, | the Ba|ron rich,
>
> Hath | a tooth|less mas|tiff, bitch ;
>
> From | her ken|nel beneath | the rock
>
> Ma|keth an|swer to | the clock,
>
> Four | for the quar|ters and twelve | for the hour ;
>
> Ev|er and aye, | by shine | and shower,
>
> Sixteen | short howls | not o|ver loud ;
>
> Some say, | she sees | my la|dy's shroud.
>
>
> Is | the night | chilly | and dark ?
>
> The night | is chil|ly, but | not dark.
>
> The thin | gray cloud | is spread | on high,
>
> It cov|ers but | not hides | the sky.
>
> The moon | is behind, | and at | the full ;
>
> And yet | she looks | both small | and dull.
>
> The night | is chill, | the cloud | is gray :
>
> 'Tis a month | before | the month | of May,
>
> And the spring | comes slow|ly up | this way.

The whole of the rest follows suit, with occasional variations (*not*, save in one case perhaps, "irregularities"), as, for instance—

      ˘
And ‖ in : si|lence : pray|eth : she.

From ‖ the : love|ly : la|dy's : cheek,

where a triple scansion might appear possible : (1) mono-syllabic beginnings indicated by ‖; (2) three-foot lines with anapæstic opening (|); and (3) the trochaic variation common in seventeenth-century poets (:). A famous third line—

    ‒ ˘ ˘ ˘ ‒ ˘ ‒
    Beau|tiful | exceed|ingly,|

decides in favour of (1), for (2) and (3) would exceedingly spoil its beauty. There is sometimes almost *complete* anapæstic substitution—

   ˘ ‒ ˘ ˘ ‒ ˘ ˘ ‒ ˘ ‒
Save the boss | of the shield | of Sir Le|oline tall,
   ˘ ‒ ˘ ˘ ‒ ˘ ˘ ‒ ˘ ˘ ‒
Which hung | in a mur|ky old niche | in the wall;

which is still further developed in the spell of Geraldine—

   ˘ ˘ ‒ ˘ ˘ ‒ ˘ ˘ ˘ ‒
In the touch | of this bo|som there work|eth a spell.

(This, in couplet, is a little dangerous.)

Note on the Application of the " Christabel" System to Nineteenth-Century Lyric generally.

It is most remarkable, but suggestive to a further extent of the fact that Coleridge did not entirely understand what he was doing, that *Christabel*, especially its opening stanza, supplies a complete key to the later nineteenth-century lyrical scansion which (*v. sup.* p. 27) he and others failed to understand in Tennyson. That opening stanza, placed side by side with the "Hollyhock Song" (see above again), will completely interpret it to any one who has eye and ear enough to mutate the *mutanda.* And when the connection and the interpretation have once been seized, there is nothing, from Shelley's apparently impulsive and instinctive harmonies to the most complicated experiments of Browning and Swinburne, which will not yield to the master keys of equivalent substitution and varying of line-length, subject to the general law of rhythmical uniformity, or at least symphonised change.   It has been said, for instance, by the latest and most painful French student of English prosody, M. Verrier, that in Shelley's *Cloud* "traditional metric renounces the attempt" to divide it into feet.   Here is the division, made without its being necessary to think twice—hardly to think once—about a single article of it :

> I bring | fresh showers | for the thirst|ing flowers,
>   From the seas | and the streams ;
> I bear | light shade | for the leaves | when laid
>   In their noon|day dreams.
> From my wings | are shaken | the dews | that waken
>   The sweet | buds ev|ery one,
> When rocked | to rest | on their mo|ther's breast,
>   As she dan|ces about | the sun.
> I wield | the flail | of the lash|ing hail,
>   And whi|ten the green | plains un|der,
> And then | again | I dissolve | it in rain,
>   And laugh | as I pass | in thun|der.

(Base anapæstic, and normal length dimeter ;   but shortened to three and two feet, thus—424243434343. The two last three-foot lines catalectic dimeter, or, to put the same thing in another way, the first threes plain, the last redundanced.   Substitution of iamb or spondee for anapæst perfectly regular, and (to keep the anapæstic base specially marked against the iambic) not very much indulged in. "Showers" and "flowers" as well as probably "shaken" and "waken" used in their shortened or practically monosyllabic value.   Nothing in the least incalculable, eccentric, or even difficult, on the foot system.)

XXXIX. NINETEENTH-CENTURY COUPLET (LEIGH HUNT TO MR. SWINBURNE)

(The examples given will be found to be all more or less of the enjambed variety. Not only has the other been much less practised, owing to reaction from the over-fondness of the eighteenth century for it, but that century, including the period of throwing back to Dryden,[1] practically found out all its considerable but limited possibilities.)

(*a*) Leigh Hunt (*Story of Rimini*):

> — ◡
> All the | sweet range-wood, flowerbed, grassy plot
> Francesca loved, but most of all this spot.
> Whenever she walk'd forth, wherever went
> About the grounds, to this at last she bent :
>
> — ◡
> Here she had brought a lute | and a | few books.
>
> — ◡
> Here would she lie for hours, | often | with looks
> More sorrowful by far, yet sweeter too ;
> Sometimes with firmer comfort, where she drew
>
> ◡ ◡ —
> From sense of in|jury's self | and truth sustained,
> Sometimes with rarest indignation gained,
> From meek, self-pitying mixtures of extremes,
>
>   ◡̆ —
> Of hope, and soft despair, and child|like dreams,
> And all that promising calm smile we see
> In Nature's face when we look patiently.

(Various substitutions marked, as also in the following.)

(*b*) Keats (*Endymion*):

> At this, from every side they hurried in,
> Rubbing their sleepy eyes with lazy wrists,
> And doubling over head their little fists
> In backward yawns.   But all were soon alive :
> For as delicious wine doth, sparkling, dive
> In nectar'd clouds and curls through water fair,
> So from the arbour roof down swell'd an air
> ◡̆ ◡̆
> Odor|ous and | enli|vening ; mak|ing all
> To laugh, and play, and sing, and loudly call

---

[1] See next Book.

> For their sweet queen : when lo ! the wreathed green
> Disparted, and far upward could be seen
> Blue heaven, and a silver car, air-borne,
> Whose silent wheels, fresh wet from clouds of morn,
> Spun off a drizzling dew,—which falling chill
> On soft Adonis' shoulders, made him still
> Nestle and turn uneasily about.

(As in the seventeenth-century patterns, not much equivalence :—the paragraph effect, produced by enjambment and varied pause, being chiefly relied on to prevent monotony. Later, in *Lamia*, Keats tried, after study of Dryden, a less fluent pattern, with stop as well as enjambment, Alexandrine, and triplet.)

(*c*) Browning (*Sordello*):

> As, shall I say, some Ethiop, past pursuit
> Of all enslavers, dips a shackled foot,
> Burnt to the blood, into the drowsy black
> Enormous watercourse which guides him back
> To his own tribe again, where he is king ;
> And laughs because he guesses, numbering
> The yellower poison-wattles on the pouch
> Of the first lizard wrested from its couch
> Under the slime (whose skin, the while, he strips
> To cure his nostril with, and festered lips,
> And eyeballs bloodshot through the desert-blast),
> That he has reached its boundary, at last
> May breathe ;—thinks o'er enchantments of the South
> Sovereign to plague his enemies, their mouth,
> Eyes, nails, and hair ; but, these enchantments tried
> In fancy, puts them soberly aside
> For truth, projects a cool return with friends,
> The likelihood of winning more amends
> Ere long ; thinks that, takes comfort silently,
> Then, from the river's brink, his wrongs and he,
> Hugging revenge close to their hearts, are soon
> Off-striding for the Mountains of the Moon.

(Practically a long blank-verse paragraph with the addition of rhyme, which sometimes almost escapes notice.)

(*d*) M. Arnold (*Tristram and Iseult*):

> The young surviving Iseult, one bright day,
> Had wander'd forth. Her children were at play

> In a green cir|cular hol|low in the heath
> Which borders the sea-shore—a country path
> Creeps over it from the till'd fields behind.
> The hollow's grassy banks are soft-inclined,
> And to one standing on them, far and near
> The lone unbroken view spreads bright and clear
> Over the waste.   This cirque of open ground
>   —   —
>
> Is light and green ; the heather, which all round
> Creeps thickly, grows not here ; but the pale grass
> Is strewn with rocks, and many a shiver'd mass
> Of vein'd white-gleaming quartz, and here and there
>   — ◡
> Dotted with holly-trees and juniper.

(An admirable following of Keats's model ; the rhymes not too much kept out of view, and suggestions of trochaic and spondaic as well as trisyllabic substitution deftly used. For some strange reason he never returned to it, but left it for William Morris to develop, completely and most effectively, in *Jason* and *The Earthly Paradise*.)

(*e*) Tennyson very seldom tried the couplet, but when he did, as in "The Vision of Sin," he achieved it magnificently :

> I had a vision when the night was late :
> A youth came riding toward a palace gate.
> He rode a horse with wings, that would have flown
> But that his heavy rider kept him down.
> And from the palace came a child of sin,
> And took him by the curls and led him in,
> Where sat a company with heated eyes,
> Expecting when a fountain should arise :
> A sleepy light upon their brows and lips—
> As when the sun, a crescent of eclipse,
> Dreams over lake and lawn, and isles and capes—
> Suffused them, sitting, lying, languid shapes,
> By heaps of gourds, and skins of wine, and piles of grapes.

(Observe how fine this couplet is, and how *personal*. We have seen how Keats studied Dryden : this is as if Dryden had studied Keats.)

(*f*) Mr. Swinburne (*Tristram of Lyonesse*) :

> Love, that is first and last of all things made,
> The light that has the living world for shade,

The spirit that for tem|poral veil | has on
The souls of all men, wo|ven in un|ison,
One fi|ery rai|ment with all lives inwrought
And lights of sun|ny and star|ry deed and thought.

(In this splendid metre the characteristics of stopped
and enjambed couplet are to a great extent combined.
Considerable anapæstic substitution to gain speed.)

XL. Nineteenth-Century Blank Verse
(Wordsworth to Mr. Swinburne)

(*a*) Wordsworth (" Yew Trees ") :

Beneath whose sable roof
Of boughs, as if for festal purpose, decked
With unrejoicing berries—ghostly shapes
May meet at noontide ; Fear and trembling Hope,
        — ◡
Silence | and Foresight, Death the Skeleton
And Time the Shadow ;—there to celebrate,
As in a na|tural tem|ple scattered o'er
With altars undisturbed of mossy stone,
United worship ; or in mute repose
To lie, and listen to the mountain flood
Murmuring | from Glaramara's inmost caves.

(The student should notice the difference, slight but
distinctly perceptible, from the Miltonic model.)

(*b*) Shelley (*Alastor*) :

Soft mossy lawns
Beneath these canopies extend their swells,
Fragrant with perfumed herbs, and eyed with blooms
Minute yet beautiful.   One darkest glen
Sends from its woods of musk-rose, twined with jas|mine,
A soul-dissolving odour, to invite
To some more lovely mys|tery.   Through | the dell,
Silence and Twilight here, twin-sisters, keep
Their noonday watch, and sail among the shades,
Like va|porous shapes | half seen ; beyond, a well,
Dark, gleaming, and of most translucent wave,
Images all the woven boughs above,
And each depending leaf, and every speck
Of azure sky, darting between their chasms,

(There are actually seven lines more before the paragraph comes at once to a line-end and a full stop in punctuation. Note also the Thomsonian mid-stops; the Wordsworthian atmosphere (cf. citation above); the actual or suggested trisyllabics; the actual redundance in "jas|mine," and the suggested one in "chas|m.")

(*c*) Browning—early (*Pauline*):

> Sun-treader!—life and light be thine for ever!
> Thou art gone from us; years go by, and spring
> Gladdens, and the young earth is beautiful,
> Yet thy songs come not, other bards arise,
> But none like thee: they stand, thy majesties,
> Like mighty works which tell some spirit there
> Hath sat regardless of neglect and scorn,
> Till, its long task completed, it hath risen
> And left us, never to return, and all
> Rush in to peer and praise when all in vain.
> The air seems bright with thy past presence yet,
> But thou art still for me as thou hast been
> When I have stood with thee as on a throne
> With all thy dim creations gathered round
> Like mountains, and I felt of mould like them,
> And with them creatures of my own were mixed,
> Like things half-lived, catching and giving life.

(Wordsworthian-Shelleyan, but with a greater touch of dramatic soliloquy in it. Redundance, but no trisyllabics.)

(*d*) Browning—later (*Mr. Sludge, " The Medium "*):

> O|ver the way
> Holds Captain Sparks his court :| is it bet|ter there?
> Have you not hunting-stories, scalping-scenes,
> And Mex|ican War | exploits to swallow plump
> If you'd be free | o' the stove-|side, rocking-chair.
> And tri|o of af|fable daugh|ters? Doubt succumbs!
>
> .   .   .   .   .
>
> Yet screwed him into henceforth gulling you
> To the top | o' your bent,|—all out of one half-lie!

(This unhesitating trisyllabic substitution sometimes reaches the very dangerous adjustment of trochee-anapæst, as in—

> Guilty | for the whim's | sake! Guil|ty he some|how thinks.
> *The Ring and the Book.*)

(*e*) Tennyson—early (*Lover's Tale*) :

    — ◡
Gleams of the water-circles as they broke,

  — ◡
Flickered | like doubtful smiles about her lips,

  — ◡
Quivered | a flying glory in her hair,

   — ◡
Leapt like | a passing thought across her eyes.
And mine, with one that will not pass till earth
And heaven pass too, dwell on *my* heaven—a face
Most starry fair, but kindled from within
As 'twere with dawn.

(Substitution trochaic only, except for "heaven "—always ambiguous in value.)

(*f*) Tennyson—standard middle (*Ulysses*) :

There lies the port ; the vessel puffs her sail :
There gloom the dark broad seas.   My mariners,
Souls that have toil'd, and wrought, and thought with me—
That ever with a frolic welcome took
The thunder and the sunshine, and opposed
Free hearts, free foreheads—you and I are old ;
Old age hath yet his honour and his toil ;
Death closes all : but something ere the end,
Some work of noble note, may yet be done,
Not unbecoming men that strove with Gods.
The lights begin to twinkle from the rocks :
The long day wanes : the slow moon climbs : the deep
Moans round with many voices.   Come, my friends,
'Tis not too late to seek a newer world.
Push off, and sitting well in order smite
The sounding furrows ; for my purpose holds
To sail beyond the sunset, and the baths
Of all the western stars, until I die.
It may be that the gulfs will wash us down :
It may be we shall touch the Happy Isles,
And see the great Achilles, whom we knew.
Tho' much is taken, much abides ; and tho'
We are not now that strength which in old days
Moved earth and heaven ; that which we are, we are ;
One equal temper of heroic hearts,
Made weak by time and fate, but strong in will
To strive, to seek, to find, and not to yield.

(Verse-paragraph completely achieved by variation of

pause and different weighting of line, with, again, little
or no trisyllabic substitution.)

Tennyson—later (*The Holy Grail*) :

" There rose a hill that none but man could climb,
Scarr'd with a hundred wintry wa|tercourses—
Storm at the top, and when we gain'd it, storm
Round us and death ; for ev|ery mo|ment glanced
His silver arms and gloom'd : so quick and thick
The lightnings here and there to left and right
Struck, till the dry old trunks about us, dead,
Yea, rotten with a hundred years of death,
Sprang into fi|re : and at | the base we found
On either hand, as far as eye could see,
A great black swamp and of an evil smell,
Part black, part whiten'd with the bones of men,
Not to be crost, save that some ancient king
Had built a way, where, link'd with many a bridge,
A thousand piers ran into the great Sea.
And Ga|lahad fled | along them bridge by bridge,
And ev|ery bridge | as quickly as he crost
Sprang into fire and vanish'd, tho' I yearn'd
To fol|low ; and thrice | above him all the heavens
Open'd and blazed with thunder such as seem'd
Shoutings of all the sons of God : and first
At once I saw him far on the great Sea,
In silver-shining armour starry-clear ;
And o'er his head the Holy Vessel hung
Clothed in white samite or a lu|minous cloud.
And with exceeding swiftness ran the boat,
If boat it were—I saw not whence it came.
And when the heavens o|pen'd and blazed | again
Roaring, I saw him like a silver star—
And had he set the sail, or had the boat
Become a living creature clad with wings?
And o'er his head the Holy Vessel hung
Redder than any rose, a joy to me,
For now I knew the veil had been withdrawn.
Then in a moment when they blazed again
Opening, I saw the least of little stars
Down on the waste, and straight beyond the star
I saw | the spiri|tual cit|y and all | her spires
And gateways in a glory like one pearl—
No larger, tho' the goal of all the saints—
Strike from the sea ; and from the star there shot
A rose-red sparkle to the cit|y, and there

> Dwelt, and I knew it was the Holy Grail,
> Which never eyes on earth again shall see."

(Paragraph still more ambitious and elaborate, with much trisyllabic substitution and some redundance.)

XLI. The Non-Equivalenced Octosyllable of Keats and Morris

(*a*) Keats (*Eve of St. Mark*) :

> Upon a Sabbath day it fell ;
> Twice holy was the Sabbath-bell,
> That called the folk to evening-prayer ;
> The city streets were clean and fair
> From wholesome drench of April rains ;
> And on the western window-panes
> The chilly sunset faintly told
> Of unmatured green valleys cold,
> Of the green thorny bloomless hedge,
> Of rivers new with spring-tide sedge,
> Of primroses by sheltered rills,
> And daisies on the aguish hills.
> Twice holy was the Sabbath-bell :
> The silent streets were crowded well
> With staid and pious companies,
> Warm from their fire-side orat'ries,
> And moving, with demurest air,
> To even-song and vesper prayer.
> Each archèd porch, and entry low,
> Was filled with patient folk and slow,
> With whispers hush, and shuffling feet,
> While played the organ loud and sweet.

(*b*) Morris (*The Ring given to Venus*) :

> By then his eyes were opened wide.
> Already up the grey hillside
> The backs of two were turned to him :
> One, like a young man tall and slim,
> Whose heels with rosy wings were dight ;
> One like a woman clad in white,
> With glittering wings of many a hue,
> Still changing, and whose shape none knew.
> In aftertime would Laurence say
> That though the moonshine, cold and grey,
> Flooded the lonely earth that night,

> These creatures in the moon's despite
> Were coloured clear, as though the sun
> Shone through the earth to light each one—
> And terrible was that to see.

(Here the effect is entirely achieved by dividing the couplets, with full stops or strong pauses at the end of the first line, and running the sense of the second into the first of the next ; by considerable variations of internal pause, and by placing emphatic or brightly coloured words at different spots.   Equivalence is practically limited to such things as "glittering," "aguish," " many a," etc., where it is at minimum strength.)

XLII.   THE CONTINUOUS ALEXANDRINE (DRAYTON AND BROWNING)

(*a*) Drayton (*Polyolbion*):

> Whenas the pliant Muse, with fair and even flight,
> Betwixt her silver wings is wafted to the Wight,—
> That Isle, which jutting out into the sea so far,
> Her offspring traineth up in exercise of war ;
> Those pirates to put back, that oft purloin her trade,
> Or Spaniards or the French attempting to invade.
> Of all the southern isles she holds the highest place,
> And evermore hath been the great'st in Britain's grace.
> Not one of all her nymphs her sovereign fav'reth thus,
> Embracèd in the arms of old Oceanus.
> For none of her account so near her bosom stand,
> 'Twixt Penwith's furthest point and Goodwin's queachy sand.

(*b*) Browning (*Fifine at the Fair*):

> O trip and skip, Elvire !   Link arm in arm with me !
> Like husband and like wife,   together let us see
> The tumbling troop arrayed,   the strollers on their stage,
> Drawn up and under arms,   and ready to engage.

(Printing of lines disjoined to show the *extra* stress which Browning lays on the middle pause, and which, though not universal, is general throughout the poem.   The case is rather the other way with Drayton.   He *observes* the pause, which is indeed the law of the line ; but he does not seem to avail himself of it much as a prosodic or rhetorical instrument.)

XLIII

The Dying Swan of Tennyson, scanned entirely through to show the application of the system. (It brings out a scheme of *dimeters* wholly iambic at the lowest rate of substitution, wholly anapæstic at the highest, mixed between. A few instances occur of the other usual and regular licences—trochaic and spondaic substitution, monosyllabic feet (*or* catalexis) and one or two of brachycatalexis, three feet instead of four. And it is to be specially noted that the poet uses these, not at random, but so as to swell and raise his rhythm, proportionately and progressively, from the slow motion and scanty syllabising of the opening scene-stanza to the "flood of eddying song" at the close. This process is entirely unaccounted for on the bare "four-stress" system.)

I.

The plain | was grass|y, wild | and bare,

Wide, wild, | and o|pen to | the air,

Which | had built | up ev|erywhere

An un|der-roof | of dole|ful gray.

With an in|ner voice | the riv|er ran,

Adown | it float|ed a dy|ing swan, |

And loud|ly did | lament.

It was | the mid|dle of | the day.

Ever | the wea|ry wind | went on,

And took | the reed-|tops as | it went.

II.

⏑   ⏑   —   ⏑   ⏑   —   ⏑   —
Some : blue | peaks : in | the dis|tance rose,

⏑   —   ⏑   —   ⏑   —   ⏑   —
And white | against | the cold-|white sky,

⏑   —   ⏑   —   ⏑   —
Shone out | their crown|ing snows.

⏑   —   ⏑   —   ⏑   ⏑   —   ⏑
One wil|low o|ver the riv|er wept,

⏑   —   ⏑   —   ⏑   —   ⏑   —
And shook | the wave | as the wind | did sigh ;

⏑   —   ⏑   —   ⏑   ⏑   —
Above | in the wind | was the swal|low,

—   ⏑   —   ⏑   ⏑   —   ⏑
Chas:ing | itself | at its own | wild will,

⏑   —   ⏑   —   ⏑   —   ⏑   —
And far | thro' the mar|ish green | and still |

⏑   —   ⏑   —   ⏑   —   ⏑   —
The tan|gled wa|ter-cour|ses slept,

⏑   —   ⏑   —   ⏑   —   ⏑   —   ⏑
Shot o|ver with pur|ple and green, | and yel|low.

III.

⏑   —   ⏑   —   ⏑   —   ⏑
The wild | swan's death-|hymn took | the soul

⏑   —   ⏑   —   ⏑   —
Of that | waste place | with joy

—   ⏑   —   ⏑   —   ⏑   —
Hidden | in sor|row : at first | to the ear

⏑   —   ⏑   —   ⏑   —   ⏑   —
The war|ble was low, | and full | and clear ;

⏑   —   ⏑   ⏑—   ⏑   —   ⏑   —
And float|ing about | the un|der-sky,

⏑   —   ⏑   —   ⏑   ⏑   —   ⏑⏑
Prevail|ing in weak|ness, the cor|onach stole

—   ⏑   —   ⏑   —   ⏑   —
Some|times afar, | and some|times anear ;

⏑   ⏑—   ⏑   —   ⏑   —   ⏑   —
But anon | her aw|ful ju|bilant voice,

⏑   ⏑—   ⏑   —   ⏑   —   ⏑   —
With a mu|sic strange | and man|ifold,

—   —   ⏑   ⏑   —   ⏑   —   ⏑   —
Flow'd forth | on a car|ol free | and bold ;

⏑   —   ⏑   —   ⏑   ⏑   —   ⏑   —
As when | a might|y peo|ple rejoice

⏑   —   ⏑   —   ⏑   —   ⏑   —   ⏑   —
With shawms, | and with cym|bals, and harps | of gold,

And the tu|mult of their | acclaim | is roll'd

Thro' the o|pen gates | of the ci|ty afar,

To the shep|herd who watch|eth the e|vening star.

And the creep|ing moss|es and clam|bering weeds,

And the wil|low-bran|ches hoar | and dank,

And the wa|vy swell | of the sough|ing reeds,

And the wave-|worn horns | of the ech|oing bank,

And the sil|very mar|ish-flowers | that throng

The de|solate creeks | and pools | among,

Were flood|ed o|ver with ed|dying song.

This piece, with the "Hollyhock" (*v. sup.* p. 27), Blake's "Mad Song" (§ XXXV.), Shelley's "Cloud" (note, p. 100), and the *Christabel* selections (§ XXXVIII.), will almost completely exemplify substitution in lyric. But the germ is far older—in Shakespeare, in "E.I.O.,", and even in pieces earlier still.

XLIV. The Stages of the Metre of "Dolores" and the Dedication of "Poems and Ballads"

This remarkable measure illustrates, with especial appositeness, the natural history of metrical evolution, and so may be dealt with more fully as a specimen. There can be little doubt that its original, or the earliest form to which it can be traced, is the split Alexandrine or three-foot iambic, which appears in the French of Philippe de Thaun, and in several English poems, such as the *Bestiary*, translated from Philippe's—

> After | him he | filleth,
> Drageth | dust with | his stert,

and as even *King Horn*. But this gives far too little room

in English ; and the rhymes, when rhyme is introduced,
come too quick. Substitution of trisyllabic feet remedies
both faults ; while the actual six, with *interchanged* rhyme,
gives beautiful work, though the lines are still rather short :

> With lon|gyng y | am lad,
> On mol|de I wax|e mad;
>   a maid|e mar|reth me ;
> Y grede, | y grone, | un-glad,
> For sel|den y | am sad
>   that sem|ly for | te se ;
>   Levedi, | thou rew|e me,
> To rou|the thou havest | me rad ;
> Be bote | of that | y bad,
>   My lyf | is long | on the.
>   (Wright's *Specimens of Lyric Poetry*, No. vii.)

This shortness kept it back, more especially when the
fear of *mainly* trisyllabic measures came in after the
fifteenth - century anarchy.   But as soon as that fear
disappeared, and the anapæst forced itself into general
use, logic, assisted by tune, suggested a cutting down of
the popular dimeter or four-foot anapæstic line to three.
This, for a long time, maintained itself in strict literature
without much variety of structure, as, at different times,
is shown by Shenstone in the well-known—

> Since Phyl|lis vouchsafed | me a look,
>   I nev|er once dreamt | of my vine ;
> May I lose | both my pipe | and my crook,
>   If I know | of a kid | that is mine ;

and by Cowper in the still better known "Alexander
Selkirk " lines—

> I am mon|arch of all | I survey,
>   My right | there is none | to dispute :
> From the cen|tre all round | to the sea
>   I am lord | of the fowl | and the brute ;

and in " Catherina "—

> She came— | she is gone— | we have met,
>   And meet | perhaps nev|er again :
> The sun | of that mo|ment is set
>   And seems | to have ris|en in vain.

Now, though these lines are pretty, they are exposed to the charge of being pretty sing-song, and monotonous jingle. But this had, long before Cowper, been to a great extent remedied, though for comic purposes only or mainly, in such things as Gay's "Molly Mog," quoted above, and Chesterfield-Pulteney's

> Had I Hanover, Bremen, and Ver|den,
>   And likewise the Duchy of Zell,
> I would part with them all for a far|thing,
>   To have my dear Molly Lepell !

(Pronounce "Verden" with the proper English value of *er*, and give "farthing" its then correct form of "farden," and the rhyme will be spotless.)

What it was that made Byron take this up for a serious purpose in the lines to Haidee (before *Don Juan*) is not, I believe, known :

> I en|ter thy gar|den of ro|ses,
>   Belov|ed and fair | Haidee,
> Each morn|ing where Flo|ra repo|ses,
>   For sure|ly I see | her in thee.

The gain here, from the redundant syllable and double rhyme in the odd lines, and from a rather more frequent use of *dissyllabic* feet to prevent monotony, is immense. Praed adopted the measure, and improved it still further, in his admirable "Letter of Advice" :

> Remem|ber the thrill|ing roman|ces
>   We read | on the bank | in the glen ;
> Remem|ber the suit|ors our fan|cies
>   Would pic|ture for both | of us then.
> They wore | the red cross | on their shoul|der,
>   They had van|quished and par|doned their foe—
> Sweet friend, | are you wi|ser or cold|er ?
>   My own | Aramin|ta, say "No !"

And then Mr. Swinburne had the probably final inspiration of shortening the last line to two feet (or an anapæstic monometer), with an astonishing result of added and finished music :

> Though the ma|ny lights dwin|dle to one | light,
> There is help | if the heav|en has one,
> Though the skies | be discrowned | of the sun|light,
> And the earth | dispossessed | of the sun,
> They have moon|light and sleep | for repay|ment
> When, refreshed | as a bride | and set free,
> With stars | and sea-winds | in her rai|ment,
> Night sinks | on the sea.

XLV. Long Metres of Tennyson, Browning, Morris, and Swinburne

(*a*) Tennyson (*The Lotos-Eaters*):

For they | lie be|side their | nectar, | and the | bolts are | hurl'd

Far be|low them | in the | valleys, | and the | clouds are | lightly | curl'd

Round their golden houses, girdled with the gleaming world,

Where they smile in secret, looking over wasted lands,

Blight and famine, plague and earthquake, roaring deeps and fiery sands,

Clanging fights, and flaming towns, and sinking ships, and praying hands.

(Trochaic six- and seven-foot lines, always hypercatalectic, or, in stricter language, trochaic trimeters hypercatalectic and tetrameters catalectic.)

At the close the poet avails himself of the iambic alternative which is so effective, and has a pure fourteener:

O rest | ye, bro|ther ma|riners, | we will | not wan|der more. |

(There is no trisyllabic substitution.)

(*b*) Tennyson (*Maud*):

Cold and clear-cut face, why come you so cruelly meek,

Breaking a slumber in which all spleenful folly was drown'd,

Pale with the golden beam of an eyelash dead on the cheek,

Passionless, pale, cold face, star-sweet on a gloom profound ;

Womanlike, taking revenge too deep for a transient wrong

Done but in thought to your beauty, and ever as pale as before

Growing and fading and growing upon me without a sound,

Luminous, gemlike, ghostlike, deathlike, half the night long
Growing and fading and growing, till I could bear it no more,
‿ ‿ –
But arose, and all by myself in my own dark garden ground,
Listening now to the tide in its broad-flung shipwrecking roar,
Now to the scream of a madden'd beach dragg'd down by the wave,
Walk'd in a wintry wind by a ghastly glimmer, and found
‿ –
The shining daffodil dead, and Orion low in his grave.

(A rather deceptive metre ; for which reason foot-division has been postponed above.)   It may look at first sight like a trochaic run, but this will be found not to fit.   Then hexameters of the *Evangeline* type, with a syllable cut off at the end, suggest themselves ; but it will be seen that some openings make this very bad.   It is really a six-foot anapæst with the usual allowance of iambic substitution and of monosyllabic (" anacrustic ") beginning, as thus :

Cold | and clear-|cut face, | why come | you so cru|elly meek,

But arose, | and all. | by myself | in my own | dark gar|den ground,

The shin|ing daf|fodil dead, | and Ori|on low | in his grave.

(c) Tennyson (*Voyage of Maeldune*) :

And we came | to the Isle | of Flowers :| their breath | met us out | on
    the seas,
For the Spring | and the mid|dle Sum|mer sat each | on the lap | of
    the breeze ;
And the red | passion-flower | to the cliffs, | and the dark-|blue
    clem|atis, clung,
And starr'd | with a myr|iad blos|som the long | convol|vulus hung.

(Same metre, but almost purely anapæstic ; the central pause frequently strong.)

(d) Tennyson (*Kapiolani*)

When : from the | terrors of | Na:ture a | peo:ple have | fash:ioned
    and | wor:ship a | spir:it of | E:vil.

(Apparently intended for a dactylic *octometer*.   Like all these things in English, it probably goes better as anapæstic with anacrusis and hypercatalexis.   See dotted scansion.)

(*e*) Browning (*Abt Vogler*) :

Would : that the | struc:ture | brave, : the | man:ifold | mu:sic I | build, :
Bid:ding my | or:gan o|bey, :|| call:ing its | keys : to their | work,
Claim:ing each | slave : of the | sound : at a | touch, : as when |
   So:lomon | willed
Ar:mies of | an:gels that | soar, :|| le:gions of | de:mons that | lurk.

Man, brute, :| reptile, :| fly, :|| alien : of | end : and of | aim,
   Ad:verse | each : from the | oth:er, | hea:ven-high | hell-:deep
   re|moved,—
Should rush : into sight : at once : as he named : the ineff:able name,
And pile : him a pal:ace straight, : to plea:sure the prin:cess he loved.

(Note the alliteration.)

At first, as you read this, you can, if your ears are
accustomed to classical metres, have no doubt about the
scheme. It is simply the regular elegiac couplet "accentu-
ally" rendered in English, with the abscission of the last
syllable of the hexameter—a catalectic hexameter and a
pentameter acatalectic. For the first four lines of the first
octave there is no doubt at all. But when you get on to
the second half you are pulled up. In the fifth and sixth
lines the pentameter seems to have got to the first place,
and the seventh is no more hexameter than the eighth is
its proper companion. For a moment you may fancy that
this was intended—that the poet meant octaves of two
different parts. But when you look at the other stanzas
you will find that this is by no means the case. Truncated
elegiac cadence appears, reappears, disappears in the most
bewildering fashion, till you recognise—sooner or later
according to your prosodic experience—that it was only
simulated cadence after all, a sort of leaf-insect rhythm,
and that the whole thing (as marked by the dotted scansion
lines) is in six-foot anapæsts equivalenced daringly, but
quite legitimately, with monosyllabic and dissyllabic feet.

(*f*) W. Morris ("The Wind") :

Ah ! | no, no, | it is no|thing, sure|ly no|thing, at all,
On|ly the wild-|going wind | round | by the gar|den wall,
For the dawn | just now | is break|ing, the wind | begin|ning to fall.
   Wind, wind, | *thou art* | *sad, art* | *thou kind?*
   Wind, | *wind,* | *unhap|py !* *thou* | *art blind,*
   Yet still | *thou wan|derest* | *the lil|y-seed* | *to find.*

(First three lines six-foot (trimeter) anapæsts with full substitution. Refrain a graded "wheel" of four, four *or* five, and six iambic feet.)

(*g*) Morris (*Love is Enough*):

Such words shall my ghost see the chronicler writing
In the days that shall be—ah!—what would'st more, my fosterling?
Knowest thou not how words fail us awaking,
That we seemed to hear plain amid sleep and its sweetness.

(Intentionally irregular "accentual" lines, but with an anapæstic or amphibrachic "under-hum." There is a good deal of alliteration elsewhere, and some here.

(*h*) Morris (*Sigurd* metre, but the actual example from *The House of the Wolfings*):

Thou sayest it, I am outcast : ‖ for a God that lacketh mirth
Hath no more place in God-home ‖ and never a place on earth.
A man grieves, and he gladdens, ‖ or he dies and his grief is gone ;
But what of the grief of the Gods ? and ‖ the sorrow never undone ?
Yea, verily, I am the outcast. ‖ When first in thine arms I lay,
On the blossoms of the woodland ‖ my godhead passed away ;
Thenceforth unto thee I was looking ‖ for the light and the glory of life,
And the Gods' doors shut behind me ‖ till the day of the uttermost strife.
And now thou hast taken my soul, thou ‖ wilt cast it into the night,
And cover thine head with the darkness ‖ and cover thine eyes from the light.
Thou would'st go to the empty country ‖ where never a seed is sown,
And never a deed is fashioned ‖ and the place where each is alone ;
But I thy thrall shall follow, ‖ I shall come where thou seem'st to lie,
I shall sit on the howe that hides thee, ‖ and thou so dear and nigh !
A few bones white in their war-gear, ‖ that have no help or thought,
Shall be Thiodolf the Mighty, ‖ so nigh, so dear—and nought !

(A splendid construction from older and newer examples. Strongly stressed, strictly middle-paused, but perfectly regular anapæstic sixes, with substitution *and a hyper-catalectic syllable or half foot at the pause.*)

(*i*) Mr. Swinburne (*Hesperia* and *Evening on the Broads*).

The first line of *Hesperia* is practically a Kingsleyan hexameter (*v. inf.*) of the very best kind—

Out | of the gold|en remote | wild west | where the sea | without
    shore | is ;

while the second—

    Full of the sadness and sad : if at : all with the fulness of joy,

is a pentameter of similar mould, with the centre gap
cunningly filled in by the two short stitches " if at,"
capable, as you see below in

    Thee I beheld as bird : borne : in with the wind from the west,

of being duly equivalenced with one long stitch, like
"borne." Yet the second line is capable also of being
scanned exactly as the first—anacrusis and five anapæsts
—but without the final redundance or hypercatalexis ;
and in other long lines you will find that the principle of
equivalence is preserved throughout—that two shorts, as in

    ◡ ◡
As a wind | blows in | from the au|tumn that blows | from the re|gion
    of stories,

defeat the hexametrical movement, and pull off the mask at
the beginning, though it returns at the end. The metre
is really anapæstic throughout. And in *Evening on the
Broads* the poet has carried this further still, providing in
some cases regular apparent elegiacs :

O|ver the : sha|dowless : wa|ters a:drift | as a : pin|nace : in per|il,
    Hangs | as in : hea|vy sus:pense ‖ charged | with ir:re|solute : light.

(*j*) Mr. Swinburne (*Choriambics*) :

    — ◡   ◡ ◡   —   ◡ ◡   —   — ◡ ◡
Love, what | ailed thee to leave | life that was made | lovely we
    —   ◡   —
thought | with love ?—

(*k*) Mr. Swinburne (other long anapæstic and trochaic
measures) :

If again | from the night | or the twi|light of a|ges Aris|tophanes | had
    ari|sen.

That the sea | was not love|lier than here | was the land, nor the
    night | than the day, | nor the day | than the night.

Night is | utmost | noon, for|lorn and | strong, with | heart a|thirst
and | fasting.

Till the dark|ling desire | of delight | shall be far, | as a fawn | that is
free | from the fangs | that pursue | her.

(These are respectively seven-foot anapæsts with redundance (anapæstic tetrameter catalectic); ditto eight-foot
(tetrameter acatalectic); trochaic tetrameter acatalectic;
and anapæstic tetrameter hypercatalectic (eight feet and
a half).)

XLVI. The Later Sonnet

(To illustrate the strict octave and sextet pattern with
final rhymes adjusted on the Italian pattern.)
Dante Rossetti:

Under the arch of Life, where love and death,
Terror | and mys|tery, guard | her shrine, I saw
Beauty enthroned ; and though her gaze struck awe,
I drew it in as simply as my breath.
Hers are the eyes which, over and beneath
The sky and sea, bend o'er thee—which can draw
By sea, or sky, or woman, to one law
The allot|ted burden of her palm and wreath.

This is that Lady Beauty, in whose praise
Thy voice and hand shake still—long known to thee
By flying hair and flut|tering hem|—the beat
Following | her daily of thy heart and feet.
How pas|sionately | and irretrievably
In what fond flight, how many ways and days !

XLVII. The Various Attempts at " Hexameters "
in English

(a) Earlier (Elizabethan):

All travel|lers do | gladly re|port great | praise of U|lysses,

For that he | knew many | men's man|ners and | saw many | cities.
(Watson, ap. Asch. *Schoolmaster*, p. 73, ed. Arber.)

But the | Queene in | meane while | carks quan|dare deepe | anguisht,
Her wound | fed by Ve|nus, with | firebayt | smoldred is | hooked :
Thee wights | doughtye man|hood, leagd | with gen|tilytye | nobil,
His woords | fitlye | placed, with his | heunly | phisnomye | pleasing,
March throgh her | hert mas|tring, all in | her breste | deepelye she |
      printeth.
                    (Stanyhurst, *Æn.* iv. 1-5, ed. Arber, p. 94.)

What might I | call this | tree ? A | Laurell ? | O bonny | Laurell.
Needes to thy | bowes will I | bow this | knee and | vayle my bo|netto.
                    (Harvey in letter to Spenser, *Eliz. Crit. Essays,*
                              ed. Gregory Smith, i. 106.)

See yee the | blindefold|ed pretie | god, that | feathered | archer

Of lo|vers mise|ries ‖ which maketh | his bloodie | game.
                    (Spenser in letter to Harvey, *ibid.* i. 99.)

(All these tried to *accommodate* — though sometimes
rather roughly — English pronunciation to such of the rules
of Latin quantity, by " nature " and " position," as could
be applied.   Some of them even tried to make general
rules for English quantity.   But the wiser, from Ascham
to Campion, admitted that dactylic rhythm was difficult, if
not impossible, to keep up in our language.)

(*b*) Later Georgian and Victorian.

(1) Coleridge (Specimen *c.* 1799 ?) :

In : the hex|am:eter | ri:ses the | foun:tain's | sil:very | col:umn ;
In : the pen|ta:meter | aye ‖ fall:ing in | mel:ody | back.

(A very fair attempt, but already showing the natural
tendency of the lines, when *poetically* rhythmed, to anapæstic
— the dotted — scansion.)

(2) Southey (*Vision of Judgment*) :

'Twas at that | sober | hour when the | light of | day is re|ceding
And from sur|rounding | things the | hues wherewith | day has a|dorned
      them
Fade like the | hopes of | youth, till the | beauty of | each has de|parted.

(Anapæstic run avoided with some skill, save now and
then ; but at the cost of weak beginnings, frequent, and

admitted, substitution of trochaic for spondaic effect, and, above all, as in line 1, an ugly rocking-horse division into *three* batches of two feet each instead of the proper $2\frac{1}{2} + 3\frac{1}{2}$ or $3\frac{1}{2} + 2\frac{1}{2}$.)

(3) Longfellow (*Evangeline*) :

Long with|in had been | spread the | snow - white | cloth on the | table ;
There stood the | wheaten | loaf, and the | honey | fragrant with | wild flowers ;
There stood the | tankard of | ale and the | cheese fresh | brought | from the | dairy ;
And at the | head of the | board the | great arm-|chair of the | farmer.
Thus did Ev|angeline | wait at her | father's | door as the | sunset
Threw the long | shadows of | trees o'er the | broad am|brosial | meadows.
Ah ! on her | spirit with|in a | deeper | shadow had | fallèn.

(A popular, tunable sort of rhythm, obtained by a very large proportion of dactyls—often really giving (and always when really good) the anapæstic effect,— unhesitating adoption of trochees and even pyrrhics for spondees, and not seldom the Southeyan split at feet 2 and 4. An essentially *rickety* measure.)

(4) Clough—earlier (in the *Bothie of Tober-na-Vuolich— Evangeline* type, but with more spondees and spondaic endings) :

I was quite | right last | night, it | is too | sōon, tōo | sudden.

(5) Later he attempted English "quantitative" things of this kind :

To the pal|ate grate|ful ; more | luscious | were not in | Eden ;
and

Unto the | sweet flut|ing, girls, of a swarthy shepherd.

This deliberate *neglect* of pronunciation ("palate" for "palate," "shepherd" for "shepherd.") has, in the last half-century or so, developed itself into a still more deliberate crusade *against* pronunciation ; it being supposed that a conflict of accent and quantity has something attractive about it. Thus the late Mr. Stone wrote as a hexameter :

Is my | weary tra|vail [1] end|ed ? Much | further is | in store.

(6) On the other hand, Kingsley's *Andromeda*—the best poem of some length intended for English hexameters— is clearly, though not consciously, anapæstic, as thus :

O|ver the moun|tain aloft | ran a rush | and a roll | and a roar | ing
Down|ward the breeze | came malig|nant and leapt | with a howl | to the wa|ter,
Roar|ing in cran|ny and crag | till the pil|lars and clefts | of the ba|salt
Rang | like a god-|swept lyre.

And Mr. Swinburne did the same thing (see above) consciously.

XLVIII. Minor Imitations of Classical Metres

(*a*) Sapphics (Watts) :

When the | fierce North-|wind with his | airy | forces
Bears up | the Bal|tic to a | foaming | fury,
And the | red light|ning with a | storm of | hail comes
Rushing a|main down.

This illustrates—as do the pieces which it, beyond all doubt, patterned, though in succession rather than directly (Cowper's "Hatred and Vengeance," Southey's "Cold was the Night Wind," and Canning's triumphant parody of this latter, the "Needy Knifegrinder")—the unyoke-ableness of classical metres — when not merely iambic, trochaic, or anapæstic—to English rhythm. The proper run of the Sapphic line is—

$$\text{tumti-tumtum-tumtity-tumti-tum} \begin{cases} \text{-ti} \\ \text{-tum} \end{cases} ;$$

---

[1] I regret that in my larger *History* (iii. 430-431) I did not notice the misprint of "travel" ; metrically, however, it makes no real difference.

but this constantly in English, though not so much in the first line as elsewhere, changes itself into

$$\text{tumtity-tum} \begin{cases} \text{-tum} \\ \text{-ti} \end{cases} \| \text{ tumtiti-titumty.}$$

Mr. Swinburne has got it right, but only as a *tour de force*, and, as in line 2, not always quite certainly.

> Saw the | white im|placable | Aphro|dite,
> Saw the | hair un|bound and the | feet un|sandalled
> Shine as | fire of | sunset on | western | waters,
>   Saw the re|luctant.

But Southey and Canning always suggest the wrong:

>   – ‿ ‿   –   ‿   –   ‿ ‿   ‿ –   ‿
> She had no : home, the : world was all : before her,

and

>   – ‿ ‿   –   ‿   – ‿   ‿   ‿ –   ‿
> Story, sir ? : Bless you ! : I have none : to tell you ;

    (*b*) Alcaics (Tennyson):

> O migh|ty- mouthed | in|ventor of | harmonies,
> O skilled | to sing | of | Time or E|ternity,
> God-gift|ed or|gan-voice | of Eng|land,
>   Milton, a | name to re|sound for | ages.

(Correct, but not natural.)

    (*c*) Hendecasyllabics (Coleridge):

> Hear, my be|loved, an | old Mi|lesian | story !—
> High, and em|bosom'd in | congre|gated | laurels,
> Glimmer'd a temple upon a breezy headland ;
> In the dim distance, amid the skiey billows,
> Rose a fair island ; the god of flocks had blest it.

(These very pretty lines exhibit a most curious instance of the unconscious force of the prosodic genius of a language. Coleridge was a good classical scholar, and quite enough of a mathematician to know the difference between 11 and 12. Yet every one of these *hendeca*-syllabics will be found to be a *dodeca*syllabic ; the poet having substituted (as in English prosody is quite allowable) an initial dactyl for the dissyllabic foot of the original metre. Once more this shows the English *impatience* of classical form.)

(*d*) Hendecasyllabics (Tennyson) :

> O you chorus of indolent reviewers,
> Irresponsible, indolent reviewers,
> Look, I come to the test, a tiny poem
> All composed in a metre of Catullus.
>
> .　　　.　　　.　　　.
>
> Hard, hard, hard is it, only not to tumble,
> So fantastical is the dainty metre.

A triumph, but a criticism as well, as its own ending shows :

> As some rare little rose, a piece of inmost
> Horticultural art—

or " *versi*cultural " rather.

(*e*) Galliambics.

These have been tried splendidly by Tennyson in *Boadicea*, interestingly by Mr. George Meredith in *Phaethon*, unsuccessfully by the late Mr. Grant Allen in his version of the *Atys* of Catullus. But the metre is not quite plain sailing even in Greek and Latin, and it is therefore better to leave it alone here and return to it in Glossary.

XLIX. Imitations of Artificial French Forms

(*a*) Triolet :

> Rose kissed | me to-day.
> 　Will she kiss | me to-mor|row ?
> Let it be | as it may,
> Rose kissed | me to-day.
> But the plea|sure gives way
> 　To a sa|vour of sor|row ;—
> Rose kissed | me to-day,—
> 　*Will* she kiss | me to-morrow ?

(*b*) Rondeau :

> With pipe and flute the rustic Pan
> Of old made music sweet for man ;
> 　And wonder hushed the warbling bird,
> 　And closer drew the calm-eyed herd,—
> The rolling river slowlier ran.

> Ah ! would,—ah ! would, a little span,
> Some air of Arcady could fan
> This age of ours, too seldom stirred
> With pipe and flute !
>
> But now for gold we plot and plan ;
> And from Beersheba unto Dan,
> Apollo's self might pass unheard,
> Or find the night-jar's note preferred ;—
> Not so it fared, when time began,
> With pipe and flute !

(The number of lines in a rondeau is not immutable, nor is it in a rondel, where the principle is the return of whole lines as in the triolet, but, since the poem is longer, giving room for more *not* repeated matter.)

(*c*) Ballade :

> Ship, to the roadstead rolled,
> What dost thou ?—O, once more
> Regain the port.   Behold !
> Thy sides are bare of oar,
> Thy tall mast wounded sore
> Of Africus, and see,
> What shall thy spars restore ?—
> Tempt not the tyrant sea !
>
> What cable now will hold
> When all drag out from shore ?
> What god canst thou, too bold,
> In time of need implore ?
> Look ! for thy sails flap o'er,
> Thy stiff shrouds part and flee,
> Fast—fast thy seams outpour,—
> Tempt not the tyrant sea !
>
> What though thy ribs of old
> The pines of Pontus bore !
> Not now to stern of gold
> Men trust, or painted prore !
> Thou, or thou count'st it store
> A toy of winds to be,
> Shun thou the Cyclads' roar,—
> Tempt not the tyrant sea !

ENVOY.

Ship of the State, before
A care, and now to me
A hope in my heart's core,—
Tempt not the tyrant sea !

(All these examples are Mr. Austin Dobson's, and inserted here by his kind permission. It will be observed that the *lines* follow general English prosodic rules. It is only the stanza that is borrowed.)

L. LATER RHYMELESSNESS

(*a*) M. Arnold (*The Strayed Reveller*. Words printed exactly as original, except the added " *and* "; the also added brackets show the unconscious decasyllabism):

[Ever new magic !
Hast thou then lured hither,]
[Wonderful Goddess, by thy art,
The young], [languid-eyed Ampelus,
Iacchus' darling—]

.   .   .   .

[They see the Indian
Drifting, knife in hand,]
[His frail boat moor'd to
A floating isle thick-matted]
[With large-leaved [*and*] low-creeping melon-leaves,]
[*x*]   And the dark cucumber.
[He reaps, and stows them,
Drifting—drifting ;—round him,
[Round his green harvest-plot,
Flow the cool lake-waves,]
[*y*]   The mountains ring them.

(Here the first piece is three pure decasyllables, with redundance, cut into five. The second requires only the addition of the italicised " and " to make it a complete blank-verse passage with two shortened lines or half-lines, *x* and *y*, of the kind common in Shakespeare. The poem is crammed with shorter stanza-pieces of the same kind.)

(*b*) Mr. Henley ("Speed." Printed as original and as prose):

Roads where the stalwart
Soldier of Cæsar
Put by his bread
And his garlic, and girding
[His conquering sword
To his unconquered thigh,]
Lay down in his armour,
And went to his Gods
By the way that he'd made.

Roads where the stalwart soldier of Cæsar put by his bread and his garlic, and girding [his conquering sword to his unconquered thigh,] lay down in his armour, and went to his Gods by the way he had made.

(The decasyllable is not quite avoided even here, as in the bracketed phrase. But the main point is that the thing reads perfectly well as prose, with no obvious suggestion of metre at all.)

LI. SOME "UNUSUAL" METRES AND DISPUTED SCANSIONS

Some measures of recent poets have been objected, or at least proposed, as offering difficulties in respect of the system of this book. It has therefore seemed well to scan them here.

(*a*) Frederic Myers (*St. Paul*):

Yes, with|out : cheer | of : sis|ter : or | of : daugh|ter—

Yes, with|out : stay | of : fa|ther : or | of : son—

Lone on | the land | and home|less on | the water

Pass I | in pa|tience till | the work | be done.

(There is nothing very peculiar or at all original in this, though it was probably now first used continuously for a poem of some length. It is only decasyllabic quatrain with uniform redundance in the first and third lines, and a strong inclination to trochaic opening, which in its turn suggests a primary dactyl and trochees to follow, as an alternative (see dotted scansion). Examples of it anterior

to Myers may be found—commented on in the larger
History (vol. iii. 481)—in *Zophiel,* very likely known to
Myers, as he was much connected by family friendship with
the Lake School; in the famous poem

> From the lone sheiling on the misty island,

the authorship of which has been so much contested;
and in Emily Bronte's *Remembrance* (see again vol. iii. of
Hist. Pros. p. 378), of which he cannot possibly have been
ignorant.[1] His own share in the matter would seem to
have been limited to the persevering adoption of it in an
unvaried form. Whether this be an advantage or not is a
question of taste : the prosodic description of the metre is
clear and in no way recondite.)

(*b*) Ernest Dowson (*Cynara*) [*Non sum qualis eram,* etc.]:

> Last night, | ah ! yes|ter night | betwixt | her lips | and mine
> There fell | thy sha|dow, Cy|nara ! | thy breath | was shed
> Upon | my soul | between | the kiss|es and | the wine,
> And I | was de|solate, | and sick | of an | old passion ;
> Yea, I | was de|solate | and bowed | my head.
> I have | been faith|ful to | thee, Cy|nara, in | my fashion.

(Sextet of Alexandrines with decasyllable (or brachycatalexis) in the 5th line, and with hypercatalexis, redundance, or double rhyme in the 4th and 6th. An
original collocation, so far as I know, but nothing new
or strange in principle. The actual poem is a rather
beautiful one ; but how much is contributed to the beauty
by the special metre is another question. At any rate,
once more, it has no difficulties for foot-scansion.)

(*c*) The universally known passage in *Macbeth*—

> To-morrow and to-morrow and to-morrow,

with the following lines, has also been proposed as a *crux*.
But this must have been a not very brilliant joke ; and it
would be an insult to the student to scan the passage. It

---

[1] In fact, there are even much older examples, as in Cleveland's *Mark
Antony* and some things of Dryden's, on one of their possible scansions,
see *Hist. Pros.* III. chap. iii.

is one of the finest specimens of Shakespearian equivalence and " fingered " blank verse, but offers no more difficulties, on the system of this book, than any couplet of Pope or any verse of the " Old Hundredth." On the other hand, many passages of Shakespeare may not illegitimately puzzle the student if he does not realise that, although (it is be-lieved) every line which is not corrupt can be scanned on our system, every line is by no means an exact five-foot. In accordance with the best English practice, older and newer, Shakespeare does not scruple to *extend* his lines to Alexandrines, and even to fourteeners, while the exigencies of drama entitle him to use lines of *less* than five full feet. *But all these—the fragments as well as the extended lines— obey the general law of iambic arrangement with substitution in individual feet.* Thus in Lady Macbeth's invocation of the Spirits of Evil (I. v. 49)—

> And take | my milk | for gall, | you mur|dering min|isters,

is a regular Alexandrine. Her husband's hallucination—

> I see thee yet, in form as palpable
> As this | which now | I draw,

stops in the second line at the third foot. Different lines of the ghost's great speech in *Hamlet* (I. v. 42-91) show the Alexandrine—

> O, hor|rible ! | O, hor|rible ! | most hor|rible !

and a fragment of two feet and a half—

> All my | smooth bo|dy.

If studied in this way, even the scenes where short speeches of the conversational kind form the staple will be found to piece themselves together perfectly well in continuous scansion.

BOOK II

HISTORICAL SKETCH OF ENGLISH PROSODY

CHAPTER I

FROM THE ORIGINS TO CHAUCER——THE CONSTITUTION OF ENGLISH VERSE [1]

THE main fact, at once central and fundamental——a pivot whereon the whole structure at once rests and turns,—— which it is necessary to understand in order to understand English prosody, is connected with——is indeed one side or case of——the other fact of the history of English language and English literature.   So far as is known to the present writer, no other language and no other literature stand in precisely the same condition, as regards the relation of their technically "Old," "Middle," and "New" or "Modern" forms.   The relation of what is called "Old" French to Modern is not that of "Old" English to Modern, but rather that of "Middle," if not a closer one still.   And though "High" and "Low" German have had their various stages separated for philological purposes, the Continental Teutonic dialects have never undergone anything like the process of modification by Romance influence, older and younger, popular and literary, which turned Anglo-Saxon into English between the eleventh and the thirteenth centuries.   This process was one not so much——if indeed it was one at all——of conscious borrowing : it was one not so much of deliberate imitation (though

(marginal note) Relations of "Old" to "Middle" and "New" English

[1] Running illustrations of the following chapters will be found in the preceding Scanned Conspectus, but additional ones will be supplied in notes when necessary.   It may not be superfluous to call the student's special attention to this chapter.   All correct appreciation of English prosody depends upon the facts contained in it ; and while the ignoring or mistaking of these facts is fatal, it has unfortunately been too common.

generally,
there was much of that in a way) as one of actual physical impregnation, fertilising, blending, which resulted in a true and permanent " cross " or " hybrid perpetual," possessing and exercising the faculties of self-development and self-propagation.

In perhaps no way were these faculties more strikingly and remarkably exercised and illustrated than in regard to prosody; and it must, unluckily, be added that in no instance has their exercise been more frequently and more fatally misconstrued. The present writer begins a fresh attempt to set forth what really happened with the following encouragement—in the way of a reviewer's sentence on

and in prosody.
his earlier and larger effort—before his eyes : " Mr. S.'s contention is that A.S. prosody died out, and that English prosody is entirely drawn from the Latin, with the aid of French and Provençal." Now the "contention" of the *History of English Prosody* is as directly and deliberately bent *against* this doctrine as against Dr. Guest's theory, that the principles of Anglo-Saxon prosody have governed English throughout its course. These "falsehoods of extremes" appear to have more lives than a cat, if not as many heads as a hydra; and their main principle of vitality no doubt is that it is possible to put them in plump plain-looking phraseology "which the Beaver can well understand." What did actually happen was far less simple; but the attempt to explain it must once more be made.

Anglo-Saxon prosody itself.
As to what Anglo-Saxon prosody itself was, although, as in all these matters, there are minor dissidences among the authorities, the main arrangement is sun-clear. There is practically only one line; though (and the fact is of inestimable importance, and when once really understood will carry the understander through to the very present day) the syllabic lengths of that line may differ largely even in normal cases, and to an at first sight almost irrational degree in what are called the "extended" varieties.

This normal line in its most normal condition—neither

cut short nor drawn out—consists usually of about nine
or ten syllables. These are not arranged so as to produce
a definite foot-rhythm, though there is a general suggestion
of the trochee. And attempts (not to be spoken of with anything but encouragement and wishes for their success, if
with some doubt as to its attainment) have been made
to assign, in all cases, definite division into associations of
syllables which might be called "feet." Other features
are unmistakable and incontestable. There is always a
sharp middle division—so strong that the lines may be,
and often are, printed as halves. There are always more
or fewer (most frequently two in the first half and one
in the second) *alliterated* syllables (one consonant or any
vowel). And these syllables, with occasionally another or
so, are usually *accented*, but divided from each other by
a certain or uncertain number of *unaccented* ones. The
proportion and arrangement of these fall into the contro-
verted things ; and the *extension* of the normal line is a
point only of indirect importance, though of very great
importance indirectly, here. The attempts which have
been made to trace ballad metre, nursery-rhyme metre, etc.,
to A.S. originals are also outside our limits. To the
present writer they appear to be hopelessly vitiated by two
absolutely certain facts : (1) that we do not know how
Anglo-Saxon was pronounced ; (2) that its pronunciation,
whatever it was, must have been radically affected by the
changes which made it into Middle English. But four
cardinal points remain, of such importance that they cannot
be too attentively studied or too constantly remembered.
They are these : that the oldest English prosody rested
on (1) a system of hard and fast middle pause ; (2)
alliteration, distributed over the whole line ; (3) accented
and unaccented syllables, the former usually knit to the
alliteration in some kind of sub-combination ; but (4) that
the laws of this combination, and the principle on which
the sub-combinations could be substituted, omitted, or
multiplied, were of the freest description. It is said, and
it can well be believed, that they forbade some things.

It is certain that they permitted very many, combining the freest *substitution* in the same line, of the kind observable in the Latin and Greek hexameter or trimeter, with an apparent variety of lengths, in different lines, hardly inferior to that of a Greek chorus or ode.

This prosody governed English verse from a time certainly anterior to the existence of any "English" nationality to about 1000 A.D., the great bulk of the production resulting under it being considerably older than the last-named date. At or about that date, certainly before the "Conquest," it began to be subjected to devitalising and disintegrating influences, not necessary to be discussed in detail here. The important fact is that from *c.* 1000 to *c.* 1200 the existing amount of Old English verse is very small indeed; and that, even in the few existing probably dated examples, singular changes begin to exhibit themselves. In the "Rhyming Poem" (before 1000?) the introduction of the element indicated in the title completely revolutionises the system.[1] In the "Grave Poem" (*c.* 1100?) a new element of rhythm appears, the tendency being, here and henceforth, to substitute iambic, varied by anapæstic, cadence for the general trochaic run, and to associate two lines or four halves in a kind of quatrain.[2] In the remarkable fragments of St. Godric (1150?) rhyme, which does not appear in the "Grave Poem," assists the rhythmical tendency of this latter to make a new music;[3] and the well-known "Canute Song"[4] chimes in. While if the "Paternoster" be really of the twelfth century, as some have said, there

Prosody of the Transition to Middle English

---

[1] Werig winneth : widsith onginneth
Sar ne sinneth : sorgum cinnith
Blæd his blumith : blisse linnath
Listum linneth : lastum ne linneth.

[2] *V. sup.* Scanned Survey II.
[3] *V. sup.* Scanned Survey III.

[4] Merie sungen the muneches binnen Ely
Tha Cnut ching rew therby.
(Roweth cnihtes neer the land
And here we thes muneches sang.

are in it iambic dimeter couplets [1] of a kind which never, by any chance, suggests itself in the whole corpus of Anglo-Saxon poetry proper.

This couplet is neither more nor less than a pair of iambic dimeters or "four-accent ['-beat'] lines in rising stress," shortened occasionally to seven syllables instead of eight, probably from the first also admitting extension, *not* by addition of feet, but by substitution of them.   Two couplets, or two batches of short (half) lines, from Layamon will show the difference at once and unmistakably to any one who possesses an ear : Contrast in Layamon.

> Eorles : ther com:en ||
> riche : and wel : idone. |
>
>   .   .   .
> ∪ − ∪ − ∪ − ∪ −
> Tha an|swere|de Vor|tiger
> ∪ − ∪ − ∪ − −
> Of el|chen vu|el he | wes wer.

The first distich, it will be observed, is a loose and broken-down one on the schemes of perfect O.E. verse. There is hardly any real alliteration, and the accented syllables are clumsily placed and valued.   But the thing does retain, and that pretty sufficiently, the strong centre pause, and the folding-back swing of the two halves, like those of a flail or a pair of lemon-squeezers, which are the real characteristics of O.E. or A.S. verse.   It is not itself "riche" versification ; it is not "wel idone"; but you cannot mistake it for anything but what it is.

With the other you have got into a new world.   There *is* alliteration here ; but it has nothing on earth to do with the construction and run of the verse.   There is what you may call accent if you insist upon it ; but it is quite dif-

---

[1] Vre feder thet in heouene is,
That is al soothful iwis.
Wee moten to theos weordes iseon
Thet to liue and to saule gode beon.
Thet weo beon swa his sunes iborene
Thet he beo feder and we him icorene
Thet we don alle his ibeden
And his wille for to reden.

ferently and much more regularly arranged, constituting, moreover, a rhythm perfectly distinct to the ear. There are two halves ; but the second half is not so much a completion as a repetition. And instead of the strong middle break—a break and nothing else—the halves are tipped with *rhyme*—a division which, if they were printed straight on, you would not notice till you got to the end of the second, and which requires very little (hardly any) stop of the voice, while the breach of the old couplet insists on this.

Now the question legitimately suggests itself, "Why is this strange contrast present ? "—a contrast which, it should be added, is not only present but *omnipresent* in this great poem of 30,000 (half) lines in all forms, from something quite near the old A.S. line, through things farther from it, to imperfect forms of the new couplet and so to perfect ones. One answer is as follows : " This couplet was already established in *French* literature—in fact in the very French literature (Wace) which formed part of Layamon's originals. Moreover, it exists also in *Latin*—the Latin of the hymns with which the priest Layamon must have been perfectly familiar. When, therefore, it appears, he is simply imitating it with more or less success." Now the facts of this answer, as far as they go, are indisputable. The octosyllabic couplet, though not so old as the decasyllabic *line* in O.F., is very old, and by Layamon's time had been written very largely indeed. Octosyllabic lines, both of iambic and trochaic cadence, form the very staple of the Latin hymns ; and both in Latin (earlier far) and in French, after a period of assonance, rhyme had thoroughly established itself.

[margin note] Examinations of it— Insufficient.

So far, so good ; but it is to be hoped that intelligent minds will perceive an occurring difficulty. If this selection of metre is an elaborate attempt to imitate French or Latin, or both, why are its results so extraordinarily *sporadic*? One could understand the presence of many imperfect lines and couplets ; it might even be surprising that in a first attempt there should be such good ones as that above quoted. But how could the man, in an actual

majority of cases, produce stuff like the other distich
quoted, and many more unrhythmical still, which are not
even *attempts* at the iambic couplet—which have no connection whatever with it?

No; an explanation at once more subtle and more
natural is wanted; for it is a great mistake to think that
the subtler is necessarily the less natural. Does not this Sufficient.
immense mass of apparently confused experiment suggest
that the language itself has passed into a new rhythmical
atmosphere?—that two different metrical systems, one
dropping and dying off ever fainter to the ear, the other
becoming clearer and clearer to it, were sounding in
Layamon's brain? Sometimes he writes under one influence; sometimes under the other; more frequently
under confused echoes of both. Such a set of causes
would produce exactly such a set of results.

Nor is it of the slightest relevance, as an objection, to
say that the total number of new Romance *words* in
Layamon is very small—a couple of hundred perhaps in
both forms of the poem taken together. You do not
necessarily require one Romance word to fashion the
most complicated metres of Tennyson and Mr. Swinburne.
The point is, "What was the general *rhythm*, and what
were the means of obtaining it, which sounded most grate-
fully in English ears at the opening of the thirteenth
century and onwards?"

The facts, if they, as they too seldom have been, are
carefully arranged and impartially considered, answer this
further question as clearly as any reasonable person can
desire.

We possess a relatively considerable number of poems
composed probably between 1200 and 1250. The most
important of these are, besides Layamon's *Brut* itself, the
Ormulum, the *Poema Morale* or *Moral Ode*, the *Orison of
Our Lady*, a *Bestiary*, the *Proverbs of Alfred* and of
Hendyng, the *Love-Rune* and other minor pieces, the
Middle English *Genesis and Exodus*, and *The Owl and the
Nightingale*.

Other
documents.
Hardly two of these are in the same metre, at least in the same form of the same metre, and none of them exhibits exactly the same curious blend of old and new as that which appears in the *Brut*. But, for that very reason, they enforce the same general lesson—for they do enforce it—in the most striking and conclusive way possible. That lesson is, as we saw, that the new *language* of English was seeking in every possible way for a new *prosody* of English, and was finding it under several and special forms of experiment, but in the same general spirit.

The
Ormulum.
Orm—evidently, from his punctilio about spelling,[1] a man curious and particular about details—adopts the French principle of absolute syllabic uniformity; though he does not accept any of the actually existing French metres, and rejects—possibly to save trouble, possibly as thinking them unsuitable to his sacred subject—both assonance and rhyme. He writes—in the strictest and most humdrum iambic cadence, as of the least-inspired French or Latin poetry—"fifteeners" or combinations of eights and *sevens*. Of the old long-lined stave he has kept no positive quality but its centre pause, and hardly any important negative one save its rhymelessness. Of the new metre, he has aimed at—he has certainly reached—nothing but its foot-division and consequent rhythm. But he has got these in the most pronounced, if hardly in the most attractive, form. Except for the odd syllable, we are here already in full presence of the jog-trot ballad and hymn "common measure" of the seventeenth and eighteenth centuries. Nay, this odd syllable itself is of great interest, for it reappears in the *sung* "breath" or "grunt"—"a":

> Your sad one tires in a mile-a, etc.

The *Moral
Ode* and the
*Orison of
Our Lady*.
Opinions may differ slightly on the question whether this *fif*teener is actually the same as the *four*teener which later became so common, and which directly engendered the common measure itself; or whether the two were independent attempts to *metricise* the old long line. It is

---

[1] In doubling the consonant after a short vowel-sound.

of course clear that, as final *e*'s dropped off, fifteen would become fourteen in any case.   But in two of the poems mentioned above, the *Moral Ode* and the *Orison of Our Lady*, although the first-named has many fifteeners, and the last is highly irregular, the set towards iambic seven-foot rhythm is well marked.   And there are two still more interesting things about these two poems.   We have several versions of the *Poema Morale* which have been arranged—*not* on prosodic grounds—in order of chronological sequence.   And it is in the highest degree noteworthy that the latest of these forms, like the later version of Layamon, exhibits remarkable touches of prosodic *melioration*.   It is still more important that among the irregular and experimental varieties of the *Orison* actual iambic *decasyllables*, and, what is more, something like the decasyllabic couplet, make their appearance nearly two centuries before Chaucer.[1]

These remarkable lessons in comparison are repeated, with the usual and invaluable confirmation of variety, in the curious documents called respectively the *Proverbs of Alfred* and the *Proverbs of Hendyng.*   The relation, in point of matter, of the latter to the former, and of the former itself to a possible A.S. collection made by the king, or under his auspices, need not concern us.   It is enough that our existing *Proverbs of Alfred* are M.E. in language and early thirteenth century in date ; while those of " Hendyng " are perhaps half a century younger. These latter are slightly more modern in language ; but this is accompanied by, and no doubt not a little directly connected with, still greater modernisation of form. The earlier rehandler (or some of the rehandlers, for the work is pretty certainly not of one only) evidently stuck as near as he could to his original—words and all.   But he was, or they were, in Layamon's state—only more so. Rhyme appears fitfully ; regular iambic and trochaic rhythm more fitfully ; alliteration most fitfully of all.   The

The
Proverbs of Alfred and *Hendyng.*

---

[1] Examples of all this will be found in the Scanned Survey and in the Glossaries and Form-lists of Book IV.

various sections are stanza-bundles of short lines or half lines, which, taken singly and printed straight on, might tempt no very hasty, ill-informed, or unintelligent reader to regard them as sheer prose, with an irregular sing-song and jingle here and there. On the other hand, the *Proverbs of Hendyng* are unmistakable English verse, the stanza called in French *rime couée*, from the Latin *versus caudatus* (afterwards common and famous as the six-line stanza in which a very large proportion, if not the majority, of our romances are written). It is a combination of eight- and six-syllabled lines arranged 8, 8, 6, 8, 8, 6, and rhymed *aabccb*; the rhythm being regularly iambic, and the whole differing in no respect from similar verse of the nineteenth century, and in only one respect from such as Gray's "Cat" ode in the eighteenth. And that one is priceless, for it is the appearance of substitution— the great English characteristic which separates our verse from its French patterns—if patterns they were—which the seventeenth and eighteenth centuries unwisely gave up, for which Shenstone pleaded,[1] and which Chatterton, and Blake, and Southey, and Coleridge restored. Monosyllabic and trisyllabic feet, as shown in the examples,[2] are freely employed; and the result is that a double advantage is secured. The actual shapelessness of one direct parent, the broken-down A.S. versicle, is effectu-

---

[1] For more on all this see Scanned Conspectus and next Book.

[2] Thus queth Alured.
Wis childe is fader blisse.
If hit so bi-tideth
that thu bern ibidest,
the hwile hit is lutel
ler him mon-thewes
than hit is wexynde ;

hit schal wende thar to.
the betere hit schal iwurthe
euer buuen eorthe,
ac if thu him lest welde
werende on worlde
lude and stille
his owene wille.

Mon that wol of wysdam heren,
At wyse Hendyng he may lernen,
   That wes Marcolues sone ;
Gode thonkes and monie thewes
Forte teche fele shrewes ;
   For that wes ever is wone.

Wis mon halt is wordes ynne,
For he nul no gle begynne
   Er he have tempred is pype.
Sot is sot, and that is sene,
For he wol speke wordes grene
   Er then hue buen rype,
   "Sottes bolt is sone shote,"
Quoth Hendyng.

ally cured : there is no possibility of mistaking *this* composition for prose.   The possible monotony and sing-song of the other—the regular syllabic French model, long afterwards parodied and exposed immortally in Chaucer's *Sir Thopas*—is avoided likewise.   There is a little assonance, but for the most part quite regular and satisfactory rhyme. There is effective correspondent rhythm, resulting from feet clearly marked, but, as has been said, boldly handled in the English, not the French or Low Latin manner. The stanza is well kept, though the substitution prevents its being a mere mechanic reproduction.   In short, there is freedom, and there is order.

Not less worthy of study is the *Bestiary*.[1]   Here the direct origins are fortunately known and are of the utmost importance.   The ultimate one is the Latin of Thetbaldus in "Leonine" hexameters—that is to say, hexameters with, in this case not very complete or regular, but still unmistakable, rhyme at the cæsura and the end.   This gives something of a ready - made correspondence to the old A.S. line with its middle break, and, at the same time, suggests rhyming halves.   But there was also at hand a *French* bestiary by Philippe de Thaun, where the writer, taking the other already established hexameter-trimeter of his own literature, the Alexandrine, breaks *it* into regular

The Bestiary.

---

[1] *Latin.*   Nam leo stans fortis super alta cacumina montis,
            Qualicunque via vallis descendit ad ima,
            Si venatorem per notum sentit odorem,
            Cauda cuncta linit quae pes vestigia figit.

French.
Uncore dit Escripture	Desfait sa trace en terre,
Leuns ad tele nature,	Que hom ne l' sace querre ;
Quant l'om le vait chazant,	Ceo est grant signefiance,
De sa cue en fuiant	Aiez en remembrance.

English.
The leun stant on hille,	After him he filleth,
And he man hunten here,	Drageth dust with his stert
Other thurg his nese smel	Ther he [dun] steppeth,
Smake that he negge,	Other dust other deu,
Bi wilc weie so he wile	That he ne cunne is finden,
To dele nither wenden,	Driueth dun to his den
Alle hise fet-steppes	Thar he him bergen wille.

six-syllabled couplets. The Englishman, whoever he was, endeavours to follow this arrangement, and perhaps something more. He has got the six-syllable line and couplet in his ear; he has got even a sort of notion of stanza in addition, and he now and then hears rhyme. But he is a very rough verse-smith, in the *Proverbs of Alfred* stage or near it, and he is perpetually hitting and missing cadences and constructions which were not to be perfected for long, but half developed—queer creatures rearing themselves from the earth like those in the old woodcuts of the Creation. He has more variety than Layamon, and sometimes more music than the *Alfred* man; but with them he provides the great museum of examples of English verse in the first stage of making.

Every now and then, too, he provides us with something that is not rough at all, as in the passage appended,[1] which is perfect modern English rhythm and goes to a well-known carol tune. And of this more perfect craftsmanship, in forms precise enough to bring out the qualities and capacities of the new prosody, the minor and miscellaneous poems of the thirteenth century supply ample and varied

Minor poems. instances. There is Romance-six, probably earlier than the *Proverbs of Hendyng*; "fourteener" metre, more polished than that of the *Moral Ode*; and, best of all, the beginning, in the *Love-Rune*,[2] of the great alternately rhymed octosyllabic quatrain, the "long measure" ("common," or the split fourteener, was to be a little later) of a myriad hymns and secular pieces since. This long measure is in some ways more advanced than almost anything of the seventeenth and eighteenth centuries, displaying equivalence,

---

[1] All is man so is this erne [eagle],
    Would[è] ye now listen,
    Old in his[è] sinn[e]s derne [dark],
    Or he becometh Christen.

The spelling is designedly modernised, but very slightly.

[2] Maid[è] here thou mightst behold
    This world[è]s love is but o res [a race],
    And is beset so fele-vold [manifoldly],
    Fick|le and frack|le [frail] and wok | and les [weak and false].

admitting internal rhyme[1]—prophesying, through Chatterton and Blake, the Great Instauration of Coleridge, Southey, and Scott.

But we must complete this group by what are perhaps its most important, though not its earliest members, the two great examples of the octosyllabic line itself in its simplest couplet form.   It may almost be said that *Genesis and Exodus* (the M.E. not the A.S. paraphrase) and *The Owl and the Nightingale* are sufficient between them to teach all the main secrets of English prosody.   They are certainly sufficient to show what it is and what it is not.

We have seen how this couplet emerges in the *Brut* of Layamon, and how it there presents itself as a " transient and embarrassed " alternative to mostly broken-down and shapeless pairs of something like the old half-line.   In the two poems just mentioned it is not transient, but abides ; nor is it in the least embarrassed.   It has quite shaken off its dilapidated companions, and abides in its own house. But that house is a house of two wings or two fronts.   The one which the author of *The Owl and the Nightingale* prefers approximates in its verse-building to the French system of architecture, and is, if not rigidly uniform in syllabic arrangement (and especially patient as the metre always has been since of limitation to *seven* with a consequent hint of trochaic rhythm), yet almost rigidly iambic *or* trochaic in run.   The other, of which *Genesis and Exodus* is the main occupant, admits, with the utmost freedom, that principle of trisyllabic (if not also monosyllabic) equivalence into which the old liberty of Anglo-Saxon had transformed itself under the sufficient but not tyrannical pressure of the new foot-prosody.   And it presents an almost perfect specimen of the metre which Spenser (whether intentionally or not) employed in parts of the *Shepherd's Calendar*, and which Coleridge, more than 500 years later, believed himself to have invented, and explained in a very insufficient manner.

It is upon the understanding which the student attains

The Owl and the Nightingale and *Genesis and Exodus.*

---

[1] Und|er mould | they li|eth [plural] cold
[grow yellow] And fal|loweth as | doth mead|ow grass.

of and upon the interpretation which he makes or accepts of the group of pieces from the *Brut* to *Genesis and Exodus*, which have just been discussed, that this student's whole conception of English prosody will depend. Unfortunately, he will not find such authorities as have delivered themselves on the subject by any means unanimous; more unfortunately still, it must be said here, he will find most of them inadequate, and not a few positively wrong. In another part of this book some account of the more usual theories is given. It is enough to say here, that neither the system which regards this verse as consisting of a certain number of "stressed" syllables and a certain or uncertain number of "unstressed," nor that which would regard some of it as following old English, some new French models, appears to fit the actual facts or explain their actual consequences. To assign the "equivalenced" varieties to a northern, the "unequivalenced" to a southern origin, may or may not be in accordance with historical and geographical fact, but is prosodically irrelevant. To be content with discovering actual or possible *particular* foreign models for each metre may not be useless (something on the subject will again be found elsewhere in this volume), but will be inadequate, and may be misleading, if the *general* phenomena are not examined or if their lesson is not learnt.

It should not be hard to learn for any one who will patiently consider the facts narrated in this chapter, the dates (as far as they are known or guessed), and the scanned examples given in the text, the notes, and the general survey. It will be strange if he does not perceive that there is here something much more than a mere regularising of accentual verse with the addition of rhyme, something much more than a mere imitation of French and Latin models, like the frequent attempts at English hexameters, or those at English ballades and rondeaux which were revived some thirty years ago; above all, something not in the least adequately described by the phrases "adopting the French principles of prosody," "following the rhythm of the foreigner," and so forth. If, as he should,[1] he possesses some knowledge of Latin verse, classical and mediæval, some of French, a little (the more the better) of Old English, and as much as possible of Modern ; if he will allow this knowledge to settle and clarify his observation of this Middle English verse of the latest twelfth and the first half of the thirteenth century, without allowing arbitrary theories of any kind to interfere, it seems almost impossible that he can fail to see what.was going on.   The prosody of English was changing from accent and alliteration to feet and rhyme ; but it was not following French, or the general run of mediæval Latin, in adopting syllabic uniformity as a rule ; and it was, in a large number, if not the majority of instances, allowing the substitution of equivalent feet (especially anapæsts for iambs) exactly as some, but not all, classical metre had allowed it.

Another point with which the student cannot familiarise himself too early, and one which he will find rarely or never insisted on in works dealing with English prosody, is that this apparent irregularity of foot arrangement brings out the existence, the importance, and, so to speak, the *personality* of the feet themselves, in a way impossible of achievement when a uniform number of syllables is insisted on in a line, and when "accent," "stress," or whatever the emphasising agent be called or considered, is restricted wholly or as much as possible to exactly corresponding places in that line.   This monotony may sometimes seem to soothe, but in reality only deadens the susceptibility of the ear, and that ear comes to recognise only, if not only to demand, such coarser stimulus as that given by strong and more or less uniform centre-pause, as the sharp snap or clang of the concluding rhyme, and as rhetorical, not strictly poetical, emphasis placed on special points, especially by the aid of antithesis.   On the other hand, the

[1] It is sometimes asked by persons who should know better, "What has *English* prosody to do with these mostly un-English things?" The answer is simple—that these un-English things went largely, and essentially, to the making of English prosody.

slight effort necessary to recognise the unity of the equivalent feet, under their diversity of substitution, demands and begets an active sensitiveness, which very soon yields positive, keen, and varied delight. No modern poetry can vie with English in the possession and provision of this, and those who neglect it deprive themselves of one of the greatest privileges of an Englishman.

But it is, of course, not contended that perfection in so difficult and exquisite an accomplishment was, or could have been, attained at once. The prosody, like the language, had to " make itself," to " grow," and, even more than the language, it had not merely to grow like a vegetable, but to make itself by animated, if often unconscious, efforts. Had things been otherwise it would have been far less interesting. As it is, there is not one of the imperfect efforts which have been briefly reviewed here that is not a "document in the case," a step in the progress, a fresh attempt of the bird to chip the shell and get clear of the fragments.

The later thirteenth century and the fourteenth.

These documents, speaking approximately, have brought us to, and perhaps a little beyond, the middle of the thirteenth century. Philologists and palæographers do not give us much as dating from the latter part of that century, or at least from the third quarter of it. But towards the close, and onwards to the supposed birth date of Chaucer (1340), we have an ever-increasing mass of interesting material continuing the demonstration just given. At an uncertain period (not impossibly close to that birth itself) we find also a new phenomenon of a general kind and of first-rate importance; and in the last half or, say, the last third of the century we come, not only to Chaucer himself, but to two other poets, lesser than himself as masters of form, but by no means small in that respect, and contrasted with him in it after a really marvellous fashion.

We can give less individual attention to the first-named group of documents; but as a matter of fact they require less, and sub-group themselves. At the close of the thirteenth century we have a body of verse, the

whole of it sometimes ascribed by guess-work, part of it
ascribed with certainty, and yet more not without probability, to Robert of Gloucester.   This work, consisting of   Robert of
a *Chronicle* and of many *Saints' Lives*, is entirely written   Gloucester.
in fourteener (or, when there is a final *e*, fifteener) couplets
of the same general stamp as those which we have seen
in the *Moral Poem*, but differentiated from those of the
Ormulum by the admission of equivalence.   They are,
however, much more advanced than even the latest
version of the *Poema Morale*; and the writer, or writers,
can make them into a capital narrative vehicle, distinctly
indicating, if not freely expressing, the further resolution
into the ballad metre of eight and six.

But this craving for narrative in verse did not confine
itself to a single vehicle; indeed, in probably a very great
majority of instances, it preferred another, or two others,
with which we are also acquainted, and further varieties still
which we have not yet seen, but which show, unmistakably,
the advance in prosodic aptitude.   The great body of
narrative verse, known as "the Romances," begins to date
from the end of the thirteenth century — a few, such
as *Havelok* and *Horn*, are certainly earlier than the
fourteenth; by the end of the first third, if not of the
first quarter, of this latter, a very large number were
as certainly in existence.

Now probably the whole of these Romances were more   The
or less directly imitated from French originals, nearly all   Romances.
of which we actually possess; but it is extremely remarkable that they by no means always followed the metre of
those originals, and that when they did they took considerable liberties with it.   That metre was almost invariably
Alexandrine or decasyllabic, in long batches not couplets,
or octosyllabic in couplet.   Of the two probably oldest
of ours, *Havelok* and *Horn*, the first does attempt this
octosyllabic couplet, but treats it in a very rough and
independent fashion, something in the *Genesis and
Exodus* line, while *King Horn* seems to favour something like what we observe in part of the English *Bestiary*

and the whole of the French one—a split Alexandrine or six-syllabled couplet. Very soon the *rime couée* or Romance-six (which had not been a staple romance-metre in French) appears, and occasionally more elaborate stanzas still, such as the complicated arrangement of *Sir Tristrem.* Those writers who prefer couplet improve upon *Horn* and *Havelok*, but they follow *Genesis and Exodus* much more than *The Owl and the Nightingale.*

Indeed, some of them develop this couplet in a manner possessing almost infinite "future." They not merely follow the writer of *Genesis and Exodus* in substituting trisyllabic, if not also monosyllabic, feet for dissyllabic to the number of *four*, but some of them develop hints, which may be found in that composition, by extending the actual foot-length of the line to *five*, and sometimes repeating this in an actual "heroic" pair. Whether this was in some, or even at first in all, cases accidental, does not really matter. The decasyllable or five-foot line was already existent in great masses of French poetry, though not in single couplets; it was natural that, occasionally, more room should be wanted than the octosyllable provides; and there is the undoubted fact that, in more than one other European language, ten, or according to the structure of the particular tongue, eleven syllables were suggesting themselves as the most convenient size. The fourteener was so long as to suggest breaking up quite early; the Alexandrine has never naturalised itself for continuous use in English; and the octosyllable, though its early appearance, the wealth of models for it, and its ease, fostered and sustained it, had the already mentioned drawback of lack of *content.* It was certain that, in a language which was showing itself so fortunately free from hide-bound qualities, the decasyllable would establish itself. It has been usual to say that, in couplet at any rate, Chaucer "took it from the French." As a matter of actual practice he may have done so; but in the order of nature and thought it was not in the least necessary for him to do it. Indeed, it would be almost

literally true[1] to say that English had decasyllabic couplet
before French—that it was an English invention.

For the time, however, the octosyllable was the staple Lyrics.
for narrative, varied to no mean extent by the stanzas
already described; while these stanzas, often of the most
elaborate and complicated descriptions, were adopted from
French (and perhaps Provençal) or extemporised by the
taste and fancy of the writers.   One famous collection[2]
indicates the school of which our poets were scholars by
alternating French poems with English.   But this very
collection shows amply that these same writers refused
to undergo the syllabic constraints of French, and held
to what were to be always the real, if frequently the
unrecognised and sometimes the denied, principles of the
New English in verse—that is to say, the constitution of
the line by feet, *not* syllables—and the consequent possibility of obtaining equivalent lines by the substitution of
feet, varying in syllabic constituence, but interchangeable
in metrical value.   Some examples of all these things will
be found in the Scanned Conspectus; the student should
search the books named in the notes for more, which he
will find in the fullest abundance.   What is important is
that by this study he may and should discover the real
and too commonly misunderstood relation of Chaucer to
precedent English verse.

There is, however, another fact of the fourteenth
century which it is not less important for him to
recognise, and which also has been too often misunderstood, or at least not put in its proper place.   This is the
revival of alliterative-accentual verse.

As there are few things, in treating prosody, of greater The
alliterative
revival.
weight than to keep carefully before the student the dif-
ference between controversial and uncontroversial points,
it should be said at once that "revival" is not quite one
of the latter.   There have been some who have taken it

---

[1] The poem commonly reputed as the oldest in French, *St. Eulalia*, is
in something very like it, but was not followed up.

[2] MS. Harl. 2253.   Published by Thomas Wright for the Percy Society
(London, 1847) as *Specimens of Lyric Poetry*.

for granted that the alliterative-accentual form *never* ceased
out of the land. It may be so; there is even a sort of
antecedent plausibility about the notion. But the important historical fact is that no such verse apparently
exists of a probable date between about 1250 (the later
form of Layamon itself, much further encroached upon by
metre and rhyme) and about 1350. Somewhere about
this latter time it does reappear; and before very long
has its chief pure representative in Langland, at the same
time as metre has *its* chief pure representative in Chaucer.

But this reappearance is conditioned and qualified by
a very remarkable fact. There is, as has just been said,
pure alliterative verse. It is not, indeed, an exact repre-
sentation of the old A.S. line. It is somewhat longer
than the shorter forms of that line, and very much shorter
than the "extended" variety. In some cases, especially
in the later examples, the alliteration is richer, extending
to four, five, or even six syllables. Most noteworthy of
all is the substitution, in the general rhythmical run, of
anapæstic-iambic for trochaic basis—a fact the importance
of which, in the general history of the morphology of
English poetry and of the change from A.S. to M.E.,
cannot be exaggerated.

But it is also worthy of the most careful remark that,
in a relatively large number of instances, the alliterative-
accentual system is apparently unable to rely upon itself.
It is tempted or driven to borrow metre, or rhyme, or
both. Of the two best pieces in the alliterative division,
outside *Piers Plowman*, *Gawain and the Green Knight*
combines, with an unrhymed body or *tirade*, a rhymed
"bob and wheel" in every stanza; while *The Pearl*,
though alliterated almost to the highest possible strength,
is strictly metrical and strictly rhymed throughout. Others
form their stanzas of lines roughly rhythmed but fairly
well rhymed.

The later fourteenth century. By the last quarter of the fourteenth century, therefore,
there were in England two contrasted and in a way rival,
but, as has been said, overlapping, systems of versification:

one a sort of atavistic revival, the other the result of a process—*two* centuries old to a certainty, and probably nearer *four*—of blending the characteristics of Low Latin and French prosody with those of Old English.

In the three chief poets of the later fourteenth century (Chaucer, Gower, and Langland) we have three object lessons as to the results of this process, which could not have been improved if the course of events had been exclusively devoted to the task of making these results, and the process itself, clear to the student. They had best be taken in reverse order.

Langland represents, in the greatest perfection that can reasonably be expected, the attempt to preserve, or revert to, verse arranged without rhyme, without metre in the strict sense, and depending for its separation from prose upon alliteration, accent, and strong middle pause. In spite of himself, and in consequence of the state of the language, actually metrical lines — decasyllables, Alexandrines, and fourteeners—do appear ; but, as a rule, he avoids them either with singular skill or with remarkable luck, and on the whole achieves a consistent medium, not so much dominated as permeated by a sort of anapæstic underhum of rhythm, but otherwise maintaining its independence. Being possessed of great literary and even distinctly poetical genius, he makes it a by no means unsuitable vehicle for his tangle of apocalyptic dreams, and no ill one for the occasional passages of a more mundane description which he interlards. But it is deficient in beauty, if not in vigour ; it is clearly unsuited for many of the subjects of poetry ; and to any one acquainted with metre and rhyme it constantly suggests the question and complaint, " *Why* are we to be deprived of these already-won beauties and conveniences, and cut off with this rough makeshift ? " Langland.

As Langland represents the purely accentual division or phase of English prosody at this time, so does Gower represent the almost purely syllabic. He uses, with insignificant exceptions,[1] the old octosyllabic couplet ; but he Gower.

[1] The rhyme-royal decasyllables of the " Supplication," or " Letter to

comes closer than any other English writer of the Middle English period to the strict French model. He does not, like his forerunners, and like even Chaucer, allow himself the seven-syllable line as a variation ; and though he does, by the admission of those who are opposed to the system of this book, occasionally admit an "extrametrical syllable," and, according to that system, much oftener a trisyllabic foot, this interferes little with the general uniformity of his verse-run. Almost the only variations that he relies upon are frequent initial trochees an occasional balanced arrangement of the halves of the line—

> The cloth was laid, the board was set—

contrasted with less strongly marked pauses, and especially a device whereby a full stop comes at the first line of two couplets separated by another, so that a sort of *In Memoriam* quatrain effect, with first and last lines blank, is obtained, as thus :

> Hew down this tree and let it fall,
> The leavès let defoul in haste,
> And do the fruit destroy and waste,
> And let offshredden every branch.

To this the present writer would add distinct trisyllabic feet where others see slur, as in—

> The weath|er was mer|ry and fair | enough.

The result, especially with syncopation of these trisyllables, is what some call "pre-eminent smoothness" of metre, others dominant monotony. The metre had proved itself of old well suited for actual narrative, and, as Gower can tell a story, when he has a good one to tell, the effect, as in the passages about Nebuchadnezzar, Medea, Ceyx and Alcyone, Rosiphelè, the "Trump of Death," and other persons and things, is quite excellent. But in the didactic and conversational parts it is often terribly tedious and lamentably limp.

Venus and Cupid," at the close of the *Confessio*, and of the poem "In Praise of Peace."

Thus Langland, from yet another point of view, represents the rejection of the new English prosody altogether or as far as possible, and Gower, the timid imitation of French.   Chaucer, on the other hand, despite his undoubted attention to French and Italian models, is in the direct line which we have been tracing, and represents, if not completely, yet to a very large extent, at once the development and the perfecting of the processes which we have described.   It has indeed been urged by some that Chaucer probably knew nothing, or very little, of *English* poetry before his own day.   But while, on the one hand, this is quite unproven, and not a little improbable, those who urge it do not seem to see that, even if it were so, it is comparatively irrelevant.   It is not in the least necessary to suppose that Chaucer must have borrowed the Vernon MS. or another like it, taken it home to the rooms above Aldgate, "stirred the fire and taken a drink" as Henryson did later with his own *Troilus*, and then, after discussing to himself principles of versification, have decided that this was to be followed, that to be avoided, that again to be perfected and carried further.   The main and undoubted facts remain that Chaucer was an Englishman of 1340(?)-1400 ; that he was the greatest Englishman of letters of his time ; that he spoke and wrote the English language, and that thus, by what he would himself have called "the law of kind," he entered into the inheritance of all that had been done in this English matter by Englishmen for generations beforehand.   As a matter of fact, there is plenty of evidence destructive of the contention referred to.   He had read the Romances, or he could not have written *Sir Thopas* ; he knew the alliterative poems, or he could not have made the famous reference to *rum ram ruf* in the Prologue to the *Parson's Tale*, which Gascoigne caught up. It is odd if he had not heard (even if he had not read) the plays that folk like his own Absolon played "upon a scaffold high."   But, as has been said, it does not matter.

For his work is there, and it is incontestably—whatever

His perfect-
ing of M.E.
verse. its author had read or not read—the logical and biological continuation and perfecting of all that had gone before from Godric and the *Paternoster*. He begins with the fluent octosyllable and the melodious and usefully stringent rhyme - royal, as well as other more or less elaborate stanzas. He communicates to the couplet[1] a greater combination of order and variety than it had ever known in English ; he makes of the stanza,[2] in the case of rhyme-royal, the most perfect formal arrangement of verse that English had yet seen. Later he takes up,[3] very probably because he had written so many separate examples of it in rhyme - royal itself at the close of each stanza, the *decasyllabic* couplet, and makes of that something greater still—a metrical instrument or vehicle escaping at once the scanty content and slightly insignificant bearing of the octosyllable, the elaborateness and rather melancholy quality of rhyme-royal. In doing this it is inevitable that, as Spenser did in parallel case afterwards, he should lean rather towards precision than towards great laxity and luxuriance of form ; for things needed order. But he sets the example of that variation of pause in rhyme-royal which was fortunately taken as a rule, and which preserved for English one of the very greatest means of metrical achievement. In the octosyllable he reproduced knowingly, and with definite apology, that "failing of a syllable" which gives acephalous or trochaic alternation, and which all the greatest masters of the metre, except (following Gower) William Morris, have imitated. And he broke up the lines very largely by conversation-fragments, by putting full stops at the end of the first line of a couplet, and by making a whole paragraph end at the same place.

But next to his provision of a perfectly finished stanza— in other words, of a complete, and *pro tanto* final, prosodic

---

[1] In the disputed *Romance of the Rose*, and the undisputed *Death of Blanche*, and the somewhat later *House of Fame*.

[2] The *Parliament of Fowls*, *Troilus and Criseyde*, etc.

[3] First in the *Legend of Good Women* and then in the *Canterbury Tales*.

result — in rhyme-royal, the most important thing done Details of
his prosody.
by Chaucer in this department was the arranging and
setting on foot of the decasyllabic couplet, which he began
well in the *Legend of Good Women,* but carried on much
better in the *Canterbury Tales.* Not half of his actual
achievement here, and a very much smaller part of his
promise and stimulus for the future, can be perceived by
those who limit him to the decasyllable as such by devices
of elision and syncope ; still less by those who would
have his varieties of line exactly to represent variations
of the French decasyllable. The former proceeding is
inadequate and defacing ; the latter practically impossible,
except as a bare and barren matter of arithmetic. You
cannot imitate the prosodic effect of one language in
another, even though you take the exact number of
syllables and (as far as you can) divide the words, arrange
the accents, etc., with the most slavish copying. The
result will laugh at you prosodically; and while it is
very unlikely to give you anything similar, it is nearly
certain to give you something quite different.[1]

When Chaucer's verse in "heroic" or "riding rhyme"
is examined, simply on its own merits and without regard to
arbitrary theories of pronunciation, but with all necessary
remembrance of the value of the final *e,* etc., it is seen to
follow, in every respect, the general principles which we
have seen evolving themselves in all English poetry
hitherto, subject only to the general reforming or
regimenting tendency which has been noticed. The
normal line is beyond all question five-foot iambic, or
decasyllabic with short and long syllable alternately.
But there are a few instances[2] of so-called acephalous
lines where the first syllable seems to have been missed—
where, at any rate, there are only nine to account for,

---

[1] These words are written, not merely on general principles, but from
long and extensive knowledge of French fourteenth-century poetry.

[2] Such as the well-known

Twen|ty: bok|ès: clad | in: black | or: red

of the Oxford clerk.

and where you consequently have to choose between a monosyllabic foot in the first place or trochaic cadence throughout. There is little doubt in the mind of the present writer that if these lines (which, after all, are very few) were deliberately written and meànt to be kept, the reason of their existence was a false analogy with the octosyllable, where, as we have said, such acephalous lines, trochaic and heptasyllabic, do occur, and where they produce not only no ill, but a positively good effect. Unluckily the cutting down does *not* produce a good effect in the larger couplet ; and if trochaic rhythm is permitted—in other words, if the missing syllable is shifted from the beginning to the end—it produces a very bad one. But they are, as has been said, in very small proportion, though there are too many of them to be simply "mended" out of existence.

Proceeding, we find, in a far larger number of instances, not a defect but an excess of syllables. As far as these syllables are found at the end of the line (in great measure caused by the final *e*) there is no difficulty and no dispute about them. They are allowed by everybody; and they come under that general law of almost (not quite) all prosodies which makes the final place of a line one of liberty. But it is different with those which come *within* the line, and with apparent extensions beyond the eleventh syllable. Many, perhaps most, prosodists would shut their eyes to the latter, regarding them as mere extra-redundances, and explain away those which occur within the line by elision before a vowel, by syncope or crasis or the like (see Glossary) when they come before a consonant.

To the present writer these devices and shifts appear unnecessary, discordant, the reverse of natural, and alike the consequence and the cause of prosodic error. With regard to *hiatus* (*i.e.* the actual contact of vowels) it has to be fully admitted that there is a strong tendency in MSS. to sink one of them and to write not merely "tharray" for "the array," but even "in thalyghte" for "in thee alyghte." The habit continued for a long time, and we find even in Surrey and Wyatt "tembrace" for "to embrace" and so forth. But it is important to observe first that this habit is not constant, as we should expect it to be if it represented a definite and reasoned wish always to reduce two such syllables to one ; and further, that it will not affect the other cases of syllables, such as the last of "Heaven" (which, however, pretty certainly *was* monosyllabic at this time and later), "ever," the *-eth* of the third person singular and plural, *y* in "many a," *i-* in scores of words, and the like.

To the present writer, once more, it is certain, and even indisputable, that whether Chaucer deliberately used trisyllabic feet or not, there are trisyllabic feet by nature and poetic right in Chaucer, for any one who chooses them. And he is of opinion, though not so strongly, that Chaucer allowed himself an occasional Alexandrine or twelve-syllabled line,[1] just as preceding writers had allowed themselves occasional ten-syllabled lines in octosyllabics. What is once more certain, and almost indisputable, is that his lines can be so scanned with euphonious effect, and that similar phenomena manifest themselves all the way up to his time.

Of his rhymes nothing necessarily need be said here. He often avails himself for rhyme, as well as for rhythm, of the choice between Teutonic and Romance accent— the former always seeking the beginning of the word, the latter generally the end. This was hardly even a licence at his period.

One much-vexed point it is, however, impossible to omit, though far more, in every sense, has been made of it than it is worth. It occurred many years ago to a distinguished scholar, the late Mr. Bradshaw of Cambridge, to make a

---

[1] Westward | right swich, | ano|ther in | the op|posite.
        (*Knight's Tale*, 1036.)

And said, | O deer|e hous|bond:e, *be|nedici|tee* !
        (*Wife of Bath's Tale*, 231.)

Doth so | his ce|rimo|nies and | obei|saunces,
And ke|peth in | semblant | all his | obser|vaunces.
        (*Squire's Tale*, 515, 516.)

test out of the rhyme of *y* and *ye*, which, he thought (despite a famous example in *Sir Thopas* [1]), never occurs in the work unquestionably Chaucer's. To the present writer the occurrence of the rhyme in *Sir Thopas* closes the question, and he would have much to say against the establishment of the test, even if *Sir Thopas* were acknowledged as not Chaucerian. But from the strict point of view of this book the whole thing is really irrelevant. It does not matter to us *who* wrote certain pieces of English poetry, but what the characteristics of those and other pieces of English poetry are. The student of prosody may and should note that in some pieces of this period the rhyme of *y* and *ye* certainly does occur, that in others it apparently does not; but beyond this he need not, and, as a student of prosody, should not, go.

[1] "Sir Guy," which cannot have an *e*, and "chivalrye," which must have one.

CHAPTER II

FROM CHAUCER TO SPENSER—DISORGANISATION AND RECONSTRUCTION

IT might be supposed, especially in face of the unquestion- able reputation which Chaucer had attained before his death—and which he maintained undisturbed, and hardly approached, for the entire period until Spenser's birth,— that his prosodic work, once done, would have been done once for all; that in points of form, though individual inferiority of poetic gift might show itself, there could be no great technical falling off. To think this, however, would be to ignore—as, in fact, men too usually do ignore, and have ignored—the necessary and intricate connection between language and prosody. Chaucer had raised the state of English versification to the highest point possible in his time; in fact, there are reasons for saying that he had screwed it up beyond the level possible to ordinary men. To mention nothing else, the exactness, and at the same time the rhythmical variety of his verse, depend on two special points—the valuing of the final *e* and the optional but carefully selected shift from French to English ac- centuation.[1] We know that, even in the mouths and on the pens of his own contemporaries, the *e* was breaking down, and that it "went" more and more during the fifteenth century; and we know likewise, though less certainly, that though, even at the close of the period with

Causes of decay in Southern English prosody.

---

[1] These are certain and incontestable. The present writer would add the sprinkling of trisyllabic feet, Alexandrines, etc.—even more difficult for clumsy followers to imitate successfully.

which we are dealing, French accentuation was still permissible to poets, an English standard was gradually establishing itself, violation of which was disapproved.[1] Moreover, the fact remains undeniable that the poetic quality of the followers of Chaucer, in Southern English of the literary kind, was low to a point unprecedented, and never yet again reached since.

The progress of prosody between Chaucer and Spenser divides itself, sharply but unequally in point of time, between a longer space (about a century and a quarter) from Chaucer to poets like Hawes, Skelton, and Barclay; a shorter (of about half a century or less) from Wyatt to Spenser. In the first division a subdivision—of matter, not time—has to be made between the literary poets in Southern English, the Scottish Chaucerians from James the First to Douglas or Lyndsay (if not even to Montgomerie, who died later than Spenser himself), and the ballad, carol, and other folk-song writers of the fifteenth century.

The history of the first division is the history of the breakdown just referred to. Except in the so-called *Chauceriana*—pieces such as " The Cuckoo and the Nightingale," " The Flower and the Leaf," " The Court of Love," etc., once attributed to Chaucer himself, but cast out on various kinds of evidence ranging from practically conclusive to very doubtful—and sometimes even in these Lydgate, . poets from Lydgate and Occleve, who for no very small Occleve, etc. portion of their lives were Chaucer's own contemporaries, downwards, seem to be struck with metrical palsy or metrical blindness. Examples, given in the Scanned Conspectus above, will show the way in which they confuse different metres, vary the lengths of their lines not by intentional substitution but by sheer muddlement, violate rhythm and cadence—turn, in fact, the perfect harmony of their master into a cacophony which is not even prosaic. Sometimes, especially in Occleve, by rigid counting of syllables, they escape worse blunders, though they seldom

---

[1] As by Gascoigne (*v. inf.*).

make real music. Generally, even this resource fails them, and there is no worse chaos than in Hawes, one of the latest and not one of the least of them ; while Skelton, perhaps the acutest intelligence of all, takes refuge in frank, *not* clumsy, and intentional doggerel.

To this spectacle of disorganisation and decay the Scottish followers of Chaucer (who, generally with acknow- The Scottish poets. ledgment as eager and hearty as that of their English comrades, take him for their master) present what may at first sight seem an astonishing and almost unintelligible contrast. With final *e*'s allowed for (or in case of necessity touched in), the *Kingis Quair*, traditionally ascribed, and never with solid reason denied, to James the First, is a piece of rhyme-royal as soundly constructed, and as well fitted and polished, as if it were Chaucer's own. Henryson, in his following of Chaucer's *Troilus*, and in his other poems, never breaks down in metre, but handles every form that he touches with equal precision and charm. Even more may be said of Dunbar, whose lyrics possess the peculiar grace only given by metrical accomplishment, who can manage alliterative metre more smoothly than Langland and with not less vigour, and who, if he wrote the "Friars of Berwick," is, next to Chaucer himself, the greatest master of the early (Middle English) heroic couplet. Of the verse-chroniclers, Wyntoun, though not very poetical, uses octosyllabic couplet, with not infrequent equivalence, effectively enough, and Blind Harry writes very strict decasyllabic couplet with cæsura at the fourth syllable, after the French model. The earlier sixteenth-century writers, Douglas and Lyndsay, if not perhaps quite impeccable, appear so beside Hawes and his fellows ; while the two latest strictly Scots poets, Scott and Montgomerie, manage most complicated measures— reminding us of early French and Provençal, or of those of the English fourteenth century in lyric and drama—with unerring accuracy and finished grace. Of this strange contrast the simple fact of writing in a different dialect, requiring more care in imitation, may supply some explanation ; the other fact, that this dialect was more of a literary convention than a vernacular speech, some more; and the higher quality of individual genius, more still; but a margin of surprise remains.

Ballad, etc. It is difficult to say whether that margin is reduced or widened by the fact that a contrast, almost as striking, is found between the English literary poetry of the period and the "folk-song," sacred and profane. It is probable that the bulk of our older ballads date from the earliest fifteenth century or the very close of the fourteenth. The latter would seem to be true of the "Robin Hood" ballads; the former is pretty certainly true of "Chevy Chase." We have also from the fifteenth century a large body of carols, or sacred poems for singing.

Now in these, though they naturally vary much in poetic merit and in prosodic accomplishment, it is remarkable that this latter scarcely ever falls to the level of the worst literary poetry, and never falls in exactly the same way. The ballad-writers invariably, and the carol- and hymn-writers very commonly, preserve the English licence of equivalence in the fullest fashion; and this seems to relieve their motion of the staggering and fatal cramp which rests on their superiors in formal literary rank. They sing naturally: they do not aim at, and break down in, a falsetto. Although it would be impossible to have anything in a worse condition, as far as copying goes, than our oldest version of "Chevy Chase," its natural ballad motion carries it safe through all the corruptions and defacements; the sacred song of "E.I.O." is admirable metre; the Carol of the Virgin, "I sing of a maiden," is matchless in quiet metrical movement; and the famous "Nut-brown Maid," which is certainly not later than this century, deserves the same praise in more rapid melody.

These compositions, however, though they did a precious office in preserving the true principles of English prosody, could not exercise immediate influence; and the disorganising of literary versification was no doubt partly cause and partly consequence of the continuance of the

alliterative revolt which did not die till after Flodden—
indeed, not till after Musselburgh (Pinkie). But, indirectly,
this revolt encouraged fresh developments of English metre
itself. The old fourteener had taken new and lively form
in such pieces as *Gamelyn* [1] (late fourteenth century) and
Beryn (middle fifteenth), and through it and other things
—the musical adaptations of songs and hymns and the
like—there was arising, in dramatic literature especially,
a disorderly, imperfect, but very important notion of
wholly " triple-timed " or anapæstic metre. In fact, it is
not excessive to regard the English fifteenth century as a
period when all elements of prosody were thrown into a
sort of cauldron, sack, sieve, or lucky-bag, in which, as
according to the different metaphors suiting these objects,
they were to be boiled down, shaken together, sifted out,
and taken as fortune would have it, to supply the stock
of a new venture in more orderly and polished verse-manu-
facture when actual speech had settled itself once more.

At what period, in what manner, and by what persons Dissatisfac-
exactly, conscious discontent with this confusion and tion and
reform.
dilapidation was made manifest, is not known. That it

[1] Litheth and lesteneth · and herkeneth aright,
And ye schulle here a talking · of a doughty knight ;
Sire Johan of Boundys · was his righte name,
He cowde of norture enough · and mochil of game.
Thre sones the knight hadde · that with his body he wan ;
The eldest was a moche shrewe · and sone he bigan.
His bretheren loved wel here fader · and of him were agast,
The eldest deserved his father's curse · and had it at the last.
The goode knight his fader · livede so yore,
That deth was comen him to and handled him full sore.
The goode knight cared sore · syk ther he lay,
How his children scholde · liven after his day.
He hadde ben wyde-wher · but no housband he was,
Al the lond that he hadde · it was verrey purchas.
Fayn he wolde it were · dressed among hem alle,
That ech of hem hadde his part · as it might falle.
                                    (*Gamelyn*, 1-16.)

(Here l. 8, with the almost certain *crasis* of " theldest," is a pure
iambic fourteener.   Elsewhere there are monosyllabic beginnings, con-
tractions of whole or half feet, and great apparent " irregularity," but at the
same time nearer and nearer approach to the anapæstic dimeter, which
was to become so popular.)

was felt consciously about the middle of the sixteenth century we do know positively from a passage in the *Mirror for Magistrates*; and later still we find the precepts of Gascoigne virtually, if not always expressly, directed against it.   But, as has been hinted, even Skeltonic evinces an earlier attempt to escape from it in practice as far back as the first quarter of the century; while, at an uncertain time for first efforts, during the second, and then ever increasingly during the third, till the death of Gascoigne himself, poetical practice proclaims the fact, even more emphatically than any preceptist rules of criticism could do.   Indeed, there has hardly ever been any mistake, and it is difficult to think that by persons possessed of ears and eyes any could be made, about the surprising revolution manifest in the verse of Sir Thomas Wyatt, and of his younger disciple, Henry Howard, known by his courtesy title as the Earl of Surrey.   Instead of the weltering and staggering discords of the poets from Lydgate onward, we come back to verse almost as clear, regular, and harmonious as Chaucer's, though with a much more modern pronunciation and accent, to which it occasionally seems to have some difficulty in reconciling itself.   The final *e* has in most cases disappeared, though it is probably there in a few cases, and in a few others has settled itself into *y*.[1]   The inordinate variety of syllables in the line, not explicable by any trisyllabic foot, is reformed.   Indeed, the need of the reform is so strongly felt that the poets run into the opposite error—salutary for the time—of excessive syllabic uniformity.

Wyatt and Surrey.   There can be no question that Wyatt, and, through or after him, Surrey, were enormously helped, if not originally stimulated to reform, by the existence of new, exact, and attractive foreign models derived, at any rate originally, from a new language.   French had hitherto been almost the only source of such models, and it had lost its virtue—

---

[1] *I.e.* forms like " hugy" (Sackville), " bleaky" (Dryden), and "paly" (Coleridge).   These forms somehow identified themselves with the artificial poetic diction of the eighteenth century, and have, since the early part of the nineteenth, been rather eschewed by poets.

not least perhaps because *ballades* and other formal devices, though excellent in themselves, had been practised all through the period of disorganisation. Italian supplied, in the sonnet, *terza rima*, and blank verse, fresh models, in the attempt to imitate which precision of syllabic and rhythmical arrangement almost inevitably enjoined itself. To write either sonnet or *terza* in shuffling doggerel would destroy the particular form ; to write blank verse in such a way (as was actually shown a hundred years afterward by the later " Elizabethan " dramatists) is to lose *all* form ; so that the instinct of preservation kept the new experimenters right. Precisely why they adopted another form which is not Italian at all — the poulter's measure of alternate Alexandrine and fourteener—is not so easy to decide ; but it may very reasonably be taken to be an attempt to regularise two of the shapes to which the doggerel of the time and its predecessor most nearly approximated. It is not a very good form (though when it splits up into " short measure " it has some merits), and even in the hands of two such poets as Wyatt and Surrey it is terribly sing-song. But this very sing-song carried regularity with it. Of the imported measures *terza* has never suited English very well, though numerous attempts have been made at it by poets sometimes of supreme quality. On the other hand, the sonnet — not the commonest Italian form at first, but that also later— has made itself thoroughly at home ; and blank verse— not much more of a success in Italian itself than *terza* in English—has, in English, grown to be one of the greatest metres in the world's prosodic history.

It should be at once seen that these processes of reform involved an almost inevitable—a certainly very natural—" drawing-in of the horns " of verse, which was positively beneficial in practice, but which led to rather disastrous mistakes in theory. On the one hand, so far as Italian admits of foot-distribution, it is distributable only into dissyllabic feet in the metres affected.[1] On the other,

[1] Or, rather, as any one may see from different editions of Dante,

the utter disorganisation of English verse which had pre-
vailed might well seem to have been caused by the neglect
to observe accurate division into such feet—a division
which, in our language, will always chiefly favour the
iamb, or foot with the first syllable short and the second
long. Accordingly we find that in Wyatt and Surrey
themselves; in their companions when (long after the
death of the first, and nearly a decade after that of the
second) their work came to be published in *Tottel's
Miscellany*; in the huge rubbish-heap of the *Mirror for
Magistrates* with its one pearl of price in Sackville's
contributions; and in the poets of the third quarter of
the sixteenth century—George Turberville and Gascoigne
himself—this iambic rhythm is omnipresent, though the
line-length and other combinations may be largely variable.
There is, it is true, one remarkable exception in the
Georgic poet Tusser, who uses frequent and accurate
anapæst; but the nature of his subject, the homeliness
of his diction, and the character of his intended readers,
may have been thought to put him out of strictly poetical
consideration. When Gascoigne—merely as narrating and
regretting a fact, *not* announcing, as some have erroneously
thought, a principle—stated the limitation, his fact was
for the most part a fact, and had been so for more than
a generation.

Their
followers. It would, however, be a gross mistake in criticism, as
well as a piece of unpardonable ingratitude, to find fault
with these poets for their prosodic limitation. It was
their business to limit and be limited—to substitute, at
whatever cost of temporary restriction of freedom, order
for the abominable disorder of the preceding century,
rhythm for its limping or staggering movement, harmonious
and well-concerted metrical arrangement for its hubbub of
halting verse or scarcely more than even half-doggerelised
prose. And they did this. When, as in the cases of Wyatt,
Surrey, and Sackville, they were men of real and genuine

the trisyllables which do occur are almost always capable of being
"slurred up."

poetic gift they did much more; though the two first were still hampered by the uncertainty of pronunciation. From this Sackville is comparatively free; though the deliberate archaism in him no doubt assists this freedom, and may have suggested something similar to Spenser. Even Turberville and Gascoigne, though their strictly poetic powers are less, manage to produce, by no means seldom, sweet and harmonious measures. And all do the inestimable work of drilling, regimenting, and preparing the raw and demoralised state of English prosody so that it may be ready to the hands of a real master and commander.

Such a master and commander duly presented himself in Spenser. Naturally enough—and even commendably enough on the principle of proving all things and holding fast that which is good—he spent a little time on classical "versing"; only to give it up so completely that (as is not the case with his friend Sidney) no single example of it, or of any approach to it, occurs in his actual poetical works. He must have spent much more on experiments in English verse proper, before the ever-famous and admirable *Shepherd's Calendar* appeared in the winter of 1579-80. Spenser.

For poetical excellence, combined with prosodic regularity, there had been nothing like this since Chaucer; for poetical excellence combined with prosodic variety it may be questioned whether Chaucer himself—his whole work being set against this novice's essay—can show anything equal. Spenser had not yet ventured to publish (though it is more than probable that he had sketched it out[1]) his immortal stanza, and he did not issue till later any exact and complete followings of Chaucer's riding rhyme. But he uses (the exact order is for special reasons not followed) a very fine six-line stanza (decasyllables rhymed *ababcc*); slightly altered Romance-six with fresh substitution and redundance in the short lines; various stanzas much "cuttit and broken" (*i.e.* of very varied line-length and rhyme - order); the Chaucerian octave; common ballad The *Shepherd's Calendar.*

[1] The scheme of the *Faerie Queene* was sent to Harvey soon afterwards.

measure; and another metre, much discussed and not universally agreed upon, but, on the more probable interpretation of it, one of the most interesting in the whole history of English poetry.

This arrangement, which is found in the "February," "May," and "September" pieces, but most characteristically in the part of "February" devoted to the tale of "The Oak and the Brere" (Briar), has been thought by some to be evidence that Spenser misunderstood Chaucer's "riding rhyme" owing to the disuse of the final valued *e* and other changes, these pieces presenting the result of the misconception. Unfortunately for this notion, the pieces themselves contain large numbers of consecutive decasyllabics perfectly well filled and rhythmed; while Spenser later wrote another piece, *Mother Hubberd's Tale*, which is in impeccable "riding rhyme" from first to last. He is also, not merely in his later work, but in the other nine-twelfths of the *Calendar* itself, an equally impeccable master of every rhythm and metre that he tries, so that it is practically inconceivable that he should here have been stumbling blindfold, or wandering aimlessly, between perfect decasyllabic couplets, perfect octosyllabic couplets, and doggerel anapæstic lines inconsistent with both. On the other hand, there had been in English, as we have seen, from *Genesis and Exodus* downwards, a variety of octosyllabic couplet which had admitted anapæstic equivalence freely, which reappeared in the Romances, and which, though not favoured by Chaucer or Gower or their immediate followers, had persevered in various places down to Spenser's own time. It seems to the present writer, as it did to Gray a hundred and fifty years ago, and has to many others since *Christabel*, though Coleridge himself strangely did not notice it, that Spenser here followed his elders, and anticipated Coleridge himself, in choosing equivalenced octosyllable to vary his non-equivalenced decasyllable. And on this theory we have in *Genesis and Exodus*, the *Shepherd's Calendar*, and *Christabel*, the three main piers of a great bridge which unites the earliest and the latest ages of

English prosody, and which carries that prosody's most vital and differential principle.

The result, however, of Spenser's experiments was that, for his great poem the *Faerie Queene*, he chose none of the metres in which he had thus experimented, nor any which had been previously employed by poets, English or other, but invented (the possible stages of the invention being given elsewhere) the magnificent Spenserian stanza of eight decasyllables and an Alexandrine.   With this he got more room than in either rhyme-royal or the octave —an unsurpassed medium for the individual descriptive effects in which he delighted, and yet one which could combine itself (for the purpose of larger description or of narrative) into most attractive sequence.   He did not, however, confine himself to this in his later poems, but showed himself a master, not merely of the octave in both its forms and of the couplet, but also of two extensive verse combinations more elaborate than the Spenserian itself, but less original, and both really suggested, as the Spenserian was *not*, by Italian.   The first was the sonnet, which, after the successors of Wyatt and Surrey had been apparently afraid to venture on it, had been taken up by Sidney and Watson probably about the same time that he was himself at work upon his *Calendar*, and in which he did very beautiful things.   The other was the still more extensive and complicated arrangement, suggested no doubt by the Italian *canzone*, which he employed in the *Epithalamion* and *Prothalamion*—stanzas of unequal line-length and intertwisted rhyme-order which sometimes extend to a score of lines or thereabouts.

Spenser did not, after the *Shepherd's Calendar*, attempt the lighter kind of lyric, nor anything in trisyllabic measures; while he seems distinctly to eschew trisyllabic substitution in others, though it appears sometimes.   But this was, in fact, a condition of his completing, and informing with full poetic spirit, the prosodic reform of the second and third quarters of the century.   He left English poetry once more provided—and indeed had furnished it long before his

The Faerie Queene.

too early death—with a perfect form of verse, and with a nearly perfect form of poetic diction. This diction, which was almost as much his own work as his stanza, was at the time, and has been since, much misunderstood. Ben Jonson called it "no language"—an insidious proposition which, under the truth that it is no language that was at the time, had been before, or has since been the living speech of any person or group, conveys the falsehood that it is therefore unfit for poetry. It is probable that Chaucer's was, though slightly mixed, much nearer the actual language of his own time, and for that very reason it grew obsolete, and, until it was studied from the antiquarian point of view, carried the verse with it. Spenser's blend of actuality, archaism, dialect, borrowings from French and Italian, and the like, provided a literary medium which, though parts of it too have become antiquated, has as a whole provided patterns for all subsequent poets. The most disputable of his devices, though it has a certain quaint charm of its own, is what is called his "eye-rhyme"—a system of altering the spelling of some words so that they may not only sound alike on the voice but look alike on the page.

CHAPTER III

THE high and (it is believed) thoroughly well-deserved
praise bestowed upon Spenser at the close of the last
chapter must not lead the student to suppose that Spenser
worked alone, that he was the sole restorer and perfecter
of English prosody at this time, or even that his work
included all that was necessary or desirable. That work,
as has been pointed out, tended towards the complete
restoration of regular and at the same time thoroughly
musical and spirited verse, but it kept—except in the
early experiments of the *Shepherd's Calendar*—to the
regular side, avoiding much trisyllabic substitution as well
as "triple time" generally, and eschewing, likewise, strictly
lyrical movements save of the stateliest kind, very much
"broken and cuttit "[1] verse, and the like.

As regards pure triple or anapæstic measures, no great
advance was made until nearly the close of this present
period, though a few isolated attempts can be quoted.
But the principle of trisyllabic substitution was secured,
once for all, by the development of blank verse, and the
variation of lyric was fully maintained by the practice
of a hundred poets, from the contributors, sometimes
quite obscure, to the *Miscellanies* which came later than
Tottel, through Sidney and others of the first great
Elizabethan division, through Drayton and many more

---

[1] A phrase of King James (VI. of Scotland and I. of England); *v. inf.*
Bks. III. and IV.

of the second, down to the famous group of "Caroline,"
"Cavalier," or "metaphysical" poets who were contemporary with Milton.

And first of blank verse.

Blank verse.   The earliest examples of this great metre in Surrey
were, naturally enough, very exact in syllabic length and
somewhat monotonous in arrangement and effect. Deprived of the warning bell of rhyme, and having nothing
but the structure of the verse itself to rely upon, the poet
was almost inevitably tempted to make very sure of that
structure by moulding it singly, and ensuring a distinct
stop at the close. This rather aggravates than relieves
itself in the satiric blank verse of Gascoigne (*The Steel
Glass*) and the dramatic blank verse of Sackville and
Norton (*Gorboduc*); while when the immediate predecessors
of Shakespeare, called the University Wits (Marlowe, Peele,
Greene, and the rest), took up the vehicle for general
theatrical practice, they never completely got clear of
the same fashion—which Shakespeare himself adopted
Before   in his earliest attempts. Admiration, just in itself, for
Shake-   Marlowe has made some try to discover in him, and
speare.   perhaps also in Peele (where there is really a little more
of it), the trisyllabic substitution, the variation of pause,
and the overrunning of sense and rhythm from line to line,
which are necessary to break up this "single-mouldedness."
But, except as to a very few passages where actual passion
melts the ice, they deceive themselves. In the couplet
(*v. inf.*) Marlowe did arrive at enjambment; in blank verse,
hardly ever. The beauty of such verse as his in the
more majestic, as Peele's in the sweeter kind, can hardly be
exaggerated, but neither has yet got complete command of
all means of achieving beauty.

The three chief means which they, on the whole, missed,
and over which Shakespeare (profiting by their advance as
far as they made it) gradually gained the mastery, have
been indicated as the overrunning of the line, the variation
of the pause, and, above all, the employment of trisyllabic
feet. We can see Shakespeare step by step attaining these,

as well as the more doubtful and dangerous redundant syllable, which in his last stage he rather abused, and which Beaumont and Fletcher and later dramatists were to abuse still more. All these means, but especially the three first (for redundance is compatible with single-mouldedness), break up the single-moulded line, and substitute for it (except in cases where it is specially wanted) the verseclauses and verse-paragraphs, which it is the glory of Shakespeare to have perfected. In his certainly earliest plays—*The Comedy of Errors, Titus Andronicus, The Two Gentlemen of Verona, Love's Labour's Lost* to some extent— single-mouldedness still appears strongly. But there are exceptions even in them ; and these exceptions gradually pervade, mellow, and diversify the prosodic composition, till it attains the perfect accomplishment of *As You Like It* and *Hamlet.* Yet a fifth peculiarity and innovation—the lengthening and shortening of lines—though it may have originally been a mere easement or liberty, and is often much abused by other dramatists, becomes in Shakespeare's hands a fresh instrument of concerted music—the frequent regular Alexandrines relieving the decasyllable by direct contrast, and fragments being generally (*v. sup.*) so arranged as to give genuine fractions of the normal scansion itself.

In him,

Practically all the secrets and all the accomplishments shown—perhaps all the accomplishments possible—at this period are to be found in Shakespeare. The differences of the other dramatists are rather rhetorical than strictly prosodic ; and the efforts sometimes made to construct special prosodies for them are mostly lost labour. Beaumont and Fletcher (who seem, from uncertain but pretty strong evidence, to have actually collaborated with Shakespeare in the *Two Noble Kinsmen*) develop his latest mood—that where, as in *Cymbeline, The Winter's Tale,* and *The Tempest,* there is much redundance.[1] They carried it much further than he did, and undoubtedly too far ; though the great poetical

and after him in drama.

---

[1] That, reversing the order, Shakespeare borrowed this from them, is a recent notion, extremely difficult to reconcile with external evidence, and going in the very teeth of internal.

power which both possessed saved them. On the other hand, Ben Jonson, all whose tastes were classical (*i.e.* in favour of restriction and order), adopted a rather hard and limited, .though rhetorically fine, fashion of blank verse. On the others it would be unprofitable to enlarge much here. Massinger is perhaps interesting as working with the most obviously *literary* eye on his predecessors—a tendency which is continued in Shirley. But in the latter there is some, if not much, of a special degeneration which by Shirley's own later days had nearly destroyed dramatic blank verse itself, and which was only arrested by the substitution for it of the "heroic" couplet, as used in the plays called by the same name.

Its degeneration.
   This degeneration, which is most evident in Davenant and Suckling, but which appears to some, though not to a great extent, in Shirley, and in most others of the playwriters up to the closing of the theatres, should be carefully compared with the initial stage of the measure in English. Then, as we saw, the absence of the guiding and preserving influence of rhyme made writers especially and excessively careful of exact syllabisation, of punctilious though monotonous rhythm, and of meticulous separation of one line from another. So also we have seen that, in the second or great period, the restrictions were loosened—that Shakespeare, preserving perfect metrical harmony, substituted an ordered licence for them all. But even he perhaps a little latterly, and his followers Beaumont and Fletcher much more, exceeded in the redundant syllable. The third generation, though including, as in the two cases specially mentioned above, men of no small poetic talent, made the common, the apparently inevitable, but the disastrous mistake of considering beauty not merely as directly connected with apparent irregularity, but as to be secured by irregularity itself. Much of their blank verse is extremely blank, but not verse at all ; nor yet prose, but an awkward hybrid. Not a little is prose pure and simple. It is scarcely surprising that, after the Restoration, the metre should have been regarded as "too mean even for a copy

of verses," and discarded, for more than a few years, in drama itself. Except the broken-down rhyme-royal of the fifteenth century (to which it bears a striking resemblance without the excuse there available) there is no more really disgraceful department of English poetry.

At the very time, however, when this disorganisation of dramatic blank verse was at its worst, and when it had as yet only been used on the rarest occasions for any other purpose, its great restorer began, though he did not for a long time continue, the process of restoration. Milton's *Comus* (1634) exhibits him as a student, and consequently an imitator, of all the three preceding schools, excepting the contemporary degradation, which was impossible to such a born master of harmony. He has now caught, and often directly reproduces, the single-moulded line of Marlowe ; and, on the other hand, he is almost equally inclined to the excessively redundanced endings of Beaumont and Fletcher, even to the extent of frequently making the last foot an anapæst.[1] Yet he not seldom closely approaches Shakespeare himself in the varied modulation, without excessive laxity, of his lines, and in the weaving of them, through overlapping, presence, absence and shifting of pause, and the like, into a verse paragraph. He inserts Alexandrines, but does not use verse-fragments much. And he begins a process—of which he was to be the greatest master—of adding to the colour, and enhancing the form, of lines by striking and important words, especially proper names. But fine as the blank verse of *Comus* is, it is, when we compare it with the lyrical close of the piece itself, evidently in the experimental stage. And it does not show the complete and assured command which is visible in the octosyllables and mixed lyrics.

When, later, he once more employed blank verse (and

Milton's reform of it.

Comus.

---

[1] Not, of course, that this is not sometimes most successful, as in Tennyson's

 And flashing round and round and whirled | *in an arch,*

but that it is dangerous, and if often used would be intolerable.

this time blank verse only) in *Paradise Lost*,[1] there was
nothing of experiment left in it.   The system, in whatever
way it may be interpreted, is quite obviously one which
the poet has completely mastered, and which he is using
without the slightest doubt or difficulty.   It has given the
pattern for all narrative, in fact for all non-dramatic, blank
verse since ; it established, though not quite at once, the
measure as one of the great staples for this general use ;
and though there have been times at which it was not
generally popular, and persons by whom it was heartily
disliked, there has been a sort of general consensus, sometimes grudging, but oftener enthusiastic, that it is one of
the greatest achievements of English poetry.

It is therefore inevitable that the partisans of the
various systems of that poetry on its formal side, of which
accounts were given in the beginning of this *Manual*,
should all try to vindicate it for their own views.   Attempts
are still made (though chiefly by foreigners who naturally
cannot bring the necessary ear) to reduce *Paradise Lost* to
a strict decasyllabic arrangement, no extra syllables being
allowed at all.   This, of course, is merely hideous, and
involves numerous crass absurdities, such as the reduction
of, " so oft " to " soft." [2]

---

[1] Published in 1667, and so more than thirty years after *Comus*.   But
perhaps begun at least fifteen years earlier.

[2] To give a thoroughly satisfactory discussion of Milton's prosody
would need space quite out of proportion here.   The writer has done
what he could, in this direction, in the long chapter devoted to the subject
in his larger *History*.   But some examples, illustrations, and parallel
scannings under different systems may be added to the text of this
Manual.   And first in regard to printing :

(*a*)   In the printed *Paradise Lost* the line

Above *th' A*onian mount, while it pursues

appears with the apostrophe ; but below—

Delight thee more, and Sil*o*a's brook that flowed—

has no attempt to indicate elision by printing.

(*b*)   And chiefly thou, O Spirit, that dost prefer—

if this is to be made strictly dissyllabic, we must pronounce " spir't,'
though not so printed ; but, a little lower—

The accentualists, as such, are not driven to equal straits unless they choose; indeed, though accentual prosody can never give an adequate account of Milton's verse, there is no reason why it should not give a partially correct one. If any one says that Milton employs a verse of five accents—these usually occurring at the even places of a normal line, but not infrequently varied in position, sometimes separated by more than one unaccented syllable, but usually by one only—he will give, in his own language and

Analysis of its versification, with application of different systems.

> Innu|mera|ble force | of spir|its armed

absolutely requires the full value.

(*c*)   Sing, Hea*v'n*ly Muse, that, on the secret top

favours the idea that Milton, as most Elizabethans certainly did, thought " Heaven " a monosyllable.   But compare line 297—

> On Hea|ven's a|zure ; and | the tor|rid clime.

(*d*) Note, too, words like " ominous," " popular," " delicate," printed without attempt to apostrophate, though the middle syllable makes a trisyllabic foot.

Again, consider the comparative euphony of the following lines :

(*e*)   Of glo|ry obscured | as when | the Sun | new risen,

or

> Of glor|- yobscured, | etc.

(*f*)   The form | attempt|ing.   Where|fore do I | assume,

or

> The form | attempt|ing.   Where|fore d'I | assume,

or

> The form | attempt| Wherefore | do I | assume,
> (*ing*).

with the " -ing " sunk or swallowed somehow " extrametrically."

(*g*)   The ani|mal spirits | that from | pure blood | arise,

or

> Th'ani|mal spir'ts | that from | pure blood | arise.

(*h*)   Because | thou hast har|kened to | the voice | of thy wife,

or

> Because | thou'st har|kened to | th' voice of | thy wife.

with his own limitations, a correct, though scanty and
jejune, account of the thing. He will, however, in most
cases be found going on, and entering upon very disputable
matter. He will notice "licences," and will, in some cases,
be inclined to deplore, or even denounce, the variation of
accent just noted. He will also, in most cases, be found
declining to accept the unaccented syllables as they stand
—indeed he has no machinery ready for doing so without
making them a disorderly crowd,—and will endeavour to
dispose of them by some process of "elision," inventing extremely ingenious, but mostly arbitrary and sometimes self-
confessedly inadequate, specifications of the employment of
this. If he is of the class of accentualists who prefer the
term "stress" and its applications, he will probably go much
further still, and allow, or insist upon, the widest variation
in the number of stresses, lines of five being indeed the
average, but four, three, and, in some extreme cases, even
two, being allowed.[1] Further intricate subdivisions will be
found between believers in these theories who, while ruling
out syllables from *scansion* by an elaborate system of
metrical fictions, maintain that they are not to be dropped
in *pronunciation*, and others who, as most people did
unhesitatingly in the eighteenth century, as many did in
the earlier nineteenth, and as a few boldly and consistently
do still, drop the pronunciation altogether, spelling and
pronouncing, as well as scanning, "am'rous," "om'nous,"
"pop'lar," "del'cate," and the like.

The foot system, on the other hand, as it always does,
accepts Milton's verse exactly as it stands, takes no kind of
liberty with it, and merely strives to discover its characteristics. This system finds (with the exception of a very
few daring experiments, no one of which can be called
wrong in principle, though there may be different opinions
about the success of some of them in practice) nothing
different from the general laws of English verse, as observed
at all its best periods, and as visible, if only in the breach

[1] With possible extension to *eight*, and (for aught I can see on the
system) to *ten*.

of them, at all, best and worst.   Milton's normal line is a
five-foot iambic :

$$\smile - \smile - \smile - \smile - \smile -$$

But for these iambics he will substitute trochees or anapæsts, sometimes perhaps tribrachs, very freely ; and his
use of the trochee for this purpose is more lavish and more
audacious than that of any other English poet, so much
so that he will allow two to follow each other at the opening of the line, and frequently adopts a choriambic ending
by placing one at the fourth foot.   On the other hand, he
seldom has the final anapæst which we found in *Comus,*
or perhaps the Alexandrine, though sometimes there are
fractional lines.   By dint of these variations—of which the
trisyllabic (generally anapæstic) foot is the most frequent,
the most successful, and, despite objections, the most
certain—he attains great variety in his line, which he
increases and utilises, for one great purpose, by the same
devices of pause, diction, etc., formerly noticed in *Comus,*
but in a more accomplished manner and to a higher
degree.

The purpose is this, that by these, by equally elaborate and
extraordinarily successful variation of the pause, by devices
of diction, and by the use of brilliantly coloured and heavily
weighted proper names and of others, he may construct
a verse-paragraph similar to that which Shakespeare had
already accomplished, but without the special characteristics
of spoken verse.   He altered his methods a little—though
perhaps not so much as has been sometimes thought—in
Paradise Regained, and still more in *Samson Agonistes,* where,
however, the renewed dramatic intention has to be considered.   And, on the whole, especially when taken in combination with his master Shakespeare, he established not
merely the freedom and order of blank verse itself, but the
whole principle of equivalent substitution in English prosody.

But it was not in blank verse only that Shakespeare Stanza, etc.,
and Milton played, in prosody, almost more than the part in Shake-
which they played in poetry generally.   In their other work speare,
it is quite as true of them that, from it, all the principles of

English versification could be derived by intelligent study. Shakespeare's early long poems, *Venus and Adonis* and the *Rape of Lucrece*—the one in the six-line stanza, the other in rhyme-royal—rank as the greatest stanza-verse of the last decade of the sixteenth century except Spenser's ; while his *Sonnets* are, not merely for their poetic spirit, the greatest in the English form, exhibiting remarkable individuality in the arrangement of the three quatrains, and an unmatched power of bringing the last couplet to bear suddenly, with the utmost prosodic as well as poetic effect. The largely shortened octosyllabic couplets, scattered about his plays and among the smaller (some of them technically " doubtful ") poems, show equal mastery of that form, and have indeed inspired Fletcher, Wither, Milton, and all practitioners of it since. But the songs in the plays are, next to his blank verse, his greatest prosodic triumph. He has got in them all the contemporary variety and much more than the usual contemporary freedom, so that such pieces as those in *The Tempest*,[1] in *Much Ado About Nothing*, and in *As*

[1] Come un|to these | yellow | sands,

And then | take hands :

Courtsied | when you | have and | kiss'd

The wild | waves whist,

Foot it | featly | here and | there ;

And, sweet | sprites, the | burthen | bear.

Hark, | hark !|

Bow-wow. |

The watch-|dogs bark :

Bow-wow.

(Alternate trochaic and iambic rhythm capable of being made all iambic by starting with monosyllabic feet : "Come" | "Court-" | " Foot " | etc.   Monosyllabic equivalence in " Hark, hark ! " to " The watch-|dogs bark.")

You Like It [1] might, had they been attended to and understood, have saved the early critics of Tennyson and some
other nineteenth-century poets from blunders about the
"irregularity," "discord," "un-English character," etc., of
their versification.

Except in this last respect (for he does not much indulge in Milton,
in triple-timed measures), Milton's examples are as striking,
while they are more numerous. In grave stanza of purely
iambic cadence but varied line-length, the ode on the
Nativity is unsurpassed in our poetry. The octosyllabic
couplets (with catalexis) of the *Arcades*, *L'Allegro*, and *Il
Penseroso*, and the already-mentioned latter part of *Comus*,
stand at the head of their class. *Lycidas*, which is written
in lines mainly decasyllabic, though sometimes of different
length, arranged (except in the last stanza) on no identical
principle, is a practically unique combination of rhyme and
blank verse—the ends being sometimes left unrhymed,
but generally rhymed, though on an apparently irregular
system which never violates harmony, but makes—first
each paragraph and then the whole poem—a piece of
concerted music, a definite prosodic symphony or sonata.
And lastly, the choruses of *Samson Agonistes*, when he

[1] Un|der the green|wood tree
    Who loves | to lie | with me,
    And tune | his mer|ry note
    Unto | the sweet | bird's throat,
Come hi|ther, come hi|ther, come hi|ther :
    Here | shall he see
    No en|emy
But win|ter and | rough weather.

("Under | the green-" and "Here shall | he see" would scan equally
well in themselves, but line 5, "Come hither," gives the anapæstic hint
and key.)

had returned to rhyme, apply this system on more extensive principles[1] still, occasionally attempting quite new measures,[2] and getting the utmost possible result out of large variation of line-length in the same or in mixed cadences.　Some of the experiments are less successful than others, and, on the whole, *Samson* displays a *harder* style of verse than the earlier poems; but it is equally important as exhibiting the true principles of English prosody.　Indeed, when Milton had published it, he may be said to have closed the formative period of our versification, not in the sense that he had not left infinite things to be done, but that he

[1] *Oct.*, *Iamb.*, ⎧This, this | is he ; | softly | awhile ;
　　and Troch. ⎩Let us | not break | in up|on him.

Dec.	O change	beyond	report,	thought, or	belief !
Alex.	See how	he lies	at ran|dom, care|lessly	diffused,
Hexasyl.	With lan	guished head	unpropt,
Hexasyl. hyperc.	As one	with hope	aban	doned,
Hexasyl. hyperc.	And by	himself	given o	ver,
Oct.	In sla	vish hab	it, ill-fit	ted weeds	
Tetrasyl.	O'er-worn	and soiled.
Alex.	Or do	my eyes	misre|present ?	Can this	be hē ?
Oct. cat.	That he	roic,	that re	nowned,
Dec.	Irre	sisti	ble Sam	son whom,	unarmed,
Alex.	No strength	of man	or fier|cest wild	beast could	withstand ;
Alex.	Who tore	the li|on as	the li|on tears	the kid ;
Dec.	Ran on	embat	tled ar	mies clad	in iron,
Hexasyl.	And, wea	ponless	himself,	
Alex.	Made arms	ridi|culous,	useless	the for|gery
Dec.	Of bra	zen shield	and spear,	the ham	mered cuirass,
Dec.	Chalyb	ean-tem	pered steel	and frock	of mail
Hexasyl.	Ada|mante|an proof :

Hardly anything here needs remark, except the use made of the old catalectic octosyllable beloved from *Comus* days, with its trochaic cadence, and that of half-Alexandrines or hexasyllables.　There is only one monometer, towards the centre or *waist* of the scheme ("O'er-worn and soiled").

[2] Oh, how | comely it | is, and | how re|viving,

To the | spirits of | just men | long op|pressed,

When God | into the | hands of | their op|pressor

Puts in|vincible | might.

(Catullian hendecasyllable ?)

had, after Chaucer, Spenser, and Shakespeare, almost completely indicated the principles of doing them.

But these principles had been illustrated by others   and others.
during the lifetime of the two,[1] after fashions which even
the most summary account of English prosody cannot
leave unnoticed ; and these fashions, with some general
phenomena of this double lifetime, not always specially
noticeable in Shakespeare and Milton themselves, must be
indicated.   The performances of these two "primates"—
the one in the English, the other in the Italian form of
the sonnet—make it unnecessary to say more of that
form, though it was very largely practised in the last
decade of the sixteenth century, and beyond all doubt
helped much to discipline verse generally.   And the same
is true of the octosyllabic couplet, which, however, was
very beautifully practised by the Jacobean poets Browne,
Wither, and others.   But more must be said of the stanza,
of the decasyllabic couplet, the fortunes of which in this
time were most momentous (and which, as it happens,
was only occasionally practised by Shakespeare,[2] scarcely
at all by Milton[3]), and of the various forms, so far as their
multiplicity does not forbid, of lyric.

The novelty, splendour, and apparent difficulty of the
Spenserian seem to have imposed on contemporaries to
such an extent as to prevent them from copying it in
typical form at all ; while many years passed before it was
attempted in slightly altered forms.[4]   The favourite stanza
in the later years of Elizabeth was the octave, chiefly in
the Italian form, which was very largely written by Drayton,
by Daniel, and many others, including Edward Fairfax
in his very influential translation of Tasso.   Rhyme-royal
fell especially out of favour, though Milton used it in his

---

[1] Milton was eight years old when Shakespeare died, and their combined lives, 1564-1674, more than cover the whole "major" Elizabethan
period, 1557-1660, except part of its incipient stage, 1557-1580.

[2] As a variation to blank verse.

[3] Some quite boyish things, a beautiful passage of the *Arcades*, and
a few couplets in *Comus* are the exceptions.

[4] By the two Fletchers, Giles reducing it to an octave *ababbccc* and
Phineas to a septet *ababccc*.

early days, and Sir Francis Kynaston wrote a long poem in it as late as 1648. The decasyllabic quatrain, alternately rhymed, was used by Davies and others. Yet not merely Ben Jonson (*v. inf.*) but Drayton himself expressed weariness of the stanza generally, and this undoubtedly grew, though it continued to be used. The new favourite was the decasyllabic couplet.

The "heroic" couplet.

It has been said that this couplet, despite its splendid success, and the abundance of varied model for it in Chaucer, was not much used (and never used well save perhaps in *The Friars of Berwick*) by his successors. It acquired, however, without any clearly traceable cause, a considerable hold on the early drama ; and, when it was ejected from this, it revenged itself by turning the stanza out to a large extent in non-dramatic verse. Drayton, in the passage referred to, speaks of the attraction of "the *gemell*," *i.e.* "the *twinned* line," and practised it not a little. Jonson, we are told, thought couplets (made in a fashion the specification of which is unfortunately not clear) "the bravest sort of verses." He did not, however, write them very largely ; but Drayton did. And while Marlowe set a magnificent example in *Hero and Leander*, and others employed the measure independently, the same sort of influence in its favour, which was noticed formerly as exercised in Chaucer's case by the final couplets of rhyme-royal, was beyond all question now exercised afresh by those of the fashionable *ottava*. In fact, the already-mentioned *Tasso* of Edward Fairfax (1600) is one of the recognised originals of a particular form—the stopped or self-ended couplet. This the octave, like the English sonnet, which doubtless had influence too, especially encourages. Drayton and others wrote as Chaucer, we saw, had written, almost indifferently in both kinds, at least so that neither has marked and dominant character. But Marlowe, in striking contrast to his blank-verse practice, decidedly preferred, and practised exquisitely, the opposite or "enjambed" variety.

By degrees, however, there grew up in the seventeenth

century what has been perhaps not incorrectly described Enjambed
as a "battle of the couplets"—certain poets definitely
employing one form, others the other; while in at least
one case [1] the preference is distinctly and combatively
avowed. As a sect, clearly marked, the enjambers or
disciples of Marlowe are the older.   Their most distinguished representatives are, in the earlier part or first
quarter of the century, William Browne, George Wither—
who in the piece called *Alresford Pool* produced one
of the most beautiful separate examples of the kind,—a
rather mysterious person named John Chalkhill, to whom
Izaak Walton was godfather and usher; in the second
and at the beginning of the third, the dramatist Shakerley
Marmion and William Chamberlayne. The latter's poem
of *Pharonnida* [2] is the longest example of the style, and
in flashes and short passages the most poetical of all;
but it also exhibits the defects of that style most flagrantly.
These defects come from the fact that the poet—allowed
to neglect his rhyme as a warning bell of termination
of something, and to use it as a mere accompaniment—
allows his clauses and sentences to run into a sometimes
quite bewildering prolixity, and very frequently neglects
even that modified restriction of the line itself to some
distinct form and outline which both good blank verse
and this form of couplet equally require.   The result,
assisted by the ugly fancy of the time for apostrophated
elisions, sometimes comes near to the contemporary
degradation of blank verse itself which has been mentioned.

There can be no reasonable doubt that these excesses and stopped.
and defects stimulated attention to the stopped form of the
couplet; and as little that this attention was, though not
unmixedly, decidedly beneficial to English verse.   It was
becoming, and had soon become, desirable, not merely
that such things as this excessive enjambment in couplet

---

[1] That of Sir John Beaumont (*v. sup.* p. 78 *et inf.* Book III.).

[2] This, like Marmion's *Cupid and Psyche*, Chalkhill's *Thealma and
Clearchus*, and other pieces exemplifying the form, is a verse-*romance*, a
kind for which that form has special, though dangerous, adaptation.

and as the degeneration of blank verse should be corrected, but that the valuable and indeed inestimable assertion of the right to trisyllabic substitution which blank verse had once more brought out, and which was prompting the use once more of purely or mainly trisyllabic *measures*, should be met, and for a time at any rate restrained, by the counter-assertion of the necessity of rhythmical smoothness and regularity. The language—though there is no reason to believe that the general pronunciation of Shakespeare's time was so different from ours as some have thought—was still going through changes of accent and the like; and, as yet, general notions on prosody were rare, for the most part very ignorant of the actual history of English poetry, and as a rule badly expressed. In these circumstances it is not surprising that the form—even the music—of the stopped and as nearly as possible normal decasyllabic couplet should appeal to many. The accepted growth of it is marked traditionally by the names of Fairfax, Sandys, and, above all, Waller, from whom Dryden (not to be noticed in detail till the next chapter) derived his pattern. But the clearest notion both of the principles and of the attraction of the form is to be obtained from the lines of Sir John Beaumont, quoted and discussed elsewhere.

For the present, however, the stopped couplet—even as such, and in comparison with its rival—was struggling not so much for mastery as for recognition, and Ben Jonson's idea of its being (if he really thought so) "the bravest of all" was nowhere near general acceptance. In particular, the production of lyric between Spenser's time and the Restoration—if not even considerably later—was immense in quantity, almost unique in variety, and never surpassed in poetical merit, though until late in the period it mostly, except in Shakespeare and a few others, confined itself to dissyllabic feet.[1] The poetical miscellanies

---

[1] The continuous anapæst appears, after Tusser, in Elizabethan poetry chiefly in popular ballad ; and it is only about 1645 that literary poets, like Waller and Cleveland, take it up.

of the later Elizabethan time, and the lyrical work of Lyric. Sidney, Drayton, Jonson, Campion, and many others, brought out the song capacity of English as it had never been brought out before ; and in the later portion of the period the poets specially known as " Caroline "—that is to say, of the period of Charles the First, with a smaller but remarkable contingent from the earlier days of his son —Herrick, Carew, Crashaw, Vaughan, Stanley, King, and almost dozens of others down to Rochester, Sedley, and Afra Behn—tried almost infinite varieties of line-length and line-adjustment with delightful results. And it is specially to be noticed that this lyric never broke down as couplet and blank verse were doing—that it always retained the tradition of metrical harmony which Wyatt and Surrey had reintroduced into English literary poetry, and which Spenser had perfected.

CHAPTER IV

HALT AND RETROSPECT—CONTINUATION ON HEROIC VERSE AND ITS COMPANIONS FROM DRYDEN TO CRABBE

Recapitula-
tion. It is desirable, if not absolutely necessary, at this point (*circa* 1660, which, though not in strict number of years or centuries, is in fact the central stage of English prosody) to halt and recapitulate what had been done since the formation of Middle English by the influence of Latin and French upon Old. The conditions of the blend having necessitated a new prosody, that prosody was, as was natural, slowly elaborated; but the lines which it was to take, in consequence of the imposition of strict form upon a vigorous and strongly characterised but rather shapeless material, appeared almost at once. Metre replaced the unmetrical rhythm of Anglo-Saxon; but this metre had to take forms greatly more elastic than the strict syllabic arrangement of French, and differently constituted from the also mainly syllabic arrangement of Lower Latin. And so, in the verse of the thirteenth and earlier fourteenth century, a foot-system, with allowance of equivalent substitution, makes its appearance—roughly, but more and more clearly. Nor is this at all affected by the alliterative revival of the last-mentioned period, which partly makes terms with metre and rhyme, partly pursues its own way—to reach its highest point with Langland, and to die away soon after the close of the fifteenth century. At the very same time with Langland himself, the pure metrical system is brought to its highest perfection by Chaucer. But this perfection depends on

a state of the language which is "precarious and not at
all permanent," and in the fifteenth century English metre,
as far as the Southern and main division of the language
is concerned, falls, to a great extent, into anarchy.

From this anarchy it is rescued, no doubt, as a general
determining influence by the settling once more of pronunciation, but directly and particularly by the efforts of
Wyatt, Surrey, and their minor successors from 1525 to
1575. Then Spenser comes, and performs almost more
than the work of Chaucer, inasmuch as his material is
more trustworthy and has fewer seeds of decay in it.
He, like his predecessors, recoiling from the frightful
disorder of the preceding century, inclines, save in his
earliest work, to a rather strict form of verse, mostly
dissyllabic. But the mere exigencies of the stage, the
nature of blank verse itself when once established, and
the genius of Shakespeare, restore there the liberty of
trisyllabic substitution, and the influence of music helps
to bring in trisyllabic measures — "triple time" — as
such. In Shakespeare first the whole freedom, as well
as nearly the whole order, of English prosody discovers
itself. But this freedom is pushed by others to licence,
and blank verse becomes practically as ruinous a heap as
the rhyme-royal of the fifteenth century, with one form
of decasyllabic couplet keeping it company, if not quite
in actual cacophony, at any rate in disorderly slackness.
Then Milton restores blank verse to almost all the freedom
and more than the order of Shakespeare, infusing also
into all the other metres that he touches this same
combination; so that in these two practically everything
is reached. But poetic fervour dies down; blank verse
becomes for a time unpopular; the age calls for the
more prosaic subject - kinds of verse—satire, didactics,
etc.; prevailing standards of prosody are strictly regulated
to an accomplished but decidedly limited "smoothness."
The results of this, with a few exceptions reserved, we are
to see in the present chapter.

It was fortunate that the poet under whom this "Reign

Dryden's
couplet

of Order" was introduced, was one who had in himself a certain irrepressible vigour and *verve*, which would not tolerate mere monotony.   John Dryden wrote most of his most famous poems in the couplet, and in a stopped form of it; but he did not confine himself thereto, using also the heroic quatrain (which he made an exceedingly fine measure); "Pindarics" (of which the same may be said); occasional, though few, octosyllabics; and lyrical measures of the most varied kind, both dissyllabic and trisyllabic, which sometimes do not fall far short of all but the very best work of the preceding generation.   His couplet itself, moreover, was not quite rigidly stopped; and even if it had been, was so largely varied by the licences of triplet, Alexandrine, and sometimes these two combined, that the purely or mainly mechanical effect with which his successor Pope is charged, and which is undoubtedly to be observed in that successor's imitators, does not impress itself.   Even had these devices (which may be said themselves to have something mechanical about them) not been present, the extraordinary nerve and full-bloodedness of Dryden's verse would have been almost if not quite sufficient to remove the reproach.   The antithetic yet never snip-snap explosion of his distichs; the way in which they fling themselves against the object; the momentum given to them by striking words strikingly placed, ingenious manipulation of pause, unexpected and exciting turns of phrase—are unprecedented. His prosody may be called a somewhat rhetorical prosody, but it is the very highest of its own kind.   It exercised strong and good influence over the whole classical period with which we are dealing in this chapter; a little after the middle of the eighteenth century it effected a diversion from the too monotonous limitation of Pope; and in the very hey-day of the Romantic movement it taught new devices, and revealed new sources of prosodic beauty, to Keats.

Great, however, as are the merits of this couplet verse of Dryden's, and incomparably well as it is adapted for argument, satire, exposition, and other things somewhat extra-poetical in themselves, there is something artificial in its limitations. And it is a matter of experience, that when you make artificial rules for a game, this artificiality always tends to make itself more artificial. Moreover, it is not only fair, but important, to allow that Dryden's licences of triplet and Alexandrine (in the latter case sometimes extended even to a fourteener) require ability and judgment, equal to his own, to prevent mismanagement of them. In clumsy hands something almost as amorphous as the broken-down blank verse and the unduly enjambed couplet of the preceding generation might easily come of them. It is therefore not surprising that, the attention of the average poet being more and more concentrated on this couplet, attempts should be made to reduce the liberties, and perfect the correctness, as much as possible. They are visible even in such writers as Garth, between Dryden and Pope ; they are still more visible in Pope himself, and Pope's. when, some decade after Dryden's death, he began to publish verse. He does not, especially at first, entirely discontinue triplet and Alexandrine, but he uses them more and more sparingly, and indeed sneers at the latter. He draws the pause more invariably to the centre, and sets up a more distinct division between the halves of his line. While separating his couplets more closely, he lightens the vowel-effects of his rhymes, so that there shall be no temptation to linger at couplet-ends. And though he is traditionally said to have had a special fancy for a couplet of his which contains an almost indestructible trisyllabic foot,[1] such feet, as a rule, are quite smoothed out of his verse.

The unmatched regularity, harmony (as far as it went), and accomplishment of Pope's couplet, and his great superiority to all other poets in these respects during the second, third, and fourth decades of the eighteenth century, assisted the general taste, which has been mentioned, in

[1] Lo ! where Mæotis sleeps, and hardly flows

The freez|ing Tana|is through a waste of snows.
The Dunciad, iii. 87, 88.

Their pre-
dominance.

raising his form of couplet to the highest place in popular estimation, as well as—sometimes expressly, sometimes by a sort of silent taking for granted—in formal discussions of poetry. Savage to some extent, Churchill still more, and after him Cowper, reverted, as has been said, to a standard nearer Dryden's. But Johnson, Goldsmith, and others, with the whole mob of inferior writers, followed Pope ; as did also Crabbe, who maintained the practice of the form till the very time of the appearance of Tennyson. The defects, or at least the limitations, of it were indeed sometimes seen, and were commented on, in striking though not fully informed fashion, by poets like Shenstone in the first half of the century, and Cowper again in the second. But it constituted, none the less, the orthodox mode of the whole time, and longer ; and when, nearly at the end of the first quarter of the nineteenth century, Keats's critics found fault with his ignorance or mismanagement of the structure of the English heroic line and couplet, what they meant was, whether they knew it or not, that he managed that line and that couplet differently from Pope.

Eighteenth-
century
octosyllable
and
anapæst.

Although, however, the stopped couplet thus gradually established in the latter part of the seventeenth century, and exercised during the whole of the eighteenth, a sort of tyranny, not every poet nor every metre bowed his or its head to this. Even in the first half of the eighteenth, poets like Collins and Gray practically shook it off, the first only using it in his early and immature work, the second hardly at all. They will therefore be reserved for the next chapter. Others, though using it, also practised metres different from it, and some of these were of a character peculiarly suited to counteract any bad influence that it might have. Among these the most important and the earliest—for both of them passed a considerable portion of their lives in the seventeenth century itself—were Prior and Swift, both of whom, but especially Prior, were proficients in the "Hudibrastic" octosyllable and in the new continuous anapæstic. The octosyllable, with its easy ambling pace, its fluent overlapping, and its often prolonged and fanciful rhymes, corrected the somewhat stiff snip-snap of the larger couplet ; while the anapæst peremptorily brought back trisyllabic rhythm, with all its marvellous refreshments and advantages, and, if only for convenience, suggested substitution of feet.[1] The great literary authority and popularity of these two poets, and the intrinsic charm of Prior, established, for metres that they used, a safe position throughout the period of decasyllabic domination. Even Bysshe put "lines of eight and seven syllables" almost on a level with those of "ten or eleven"; and though he sneered at anapæsts, and introduced them by a singular roundaboutness of expression,[2] did not absolutely bar them in fact.

Blank verse—than which, in its perfection, there is no *Blank verse* more powerful guard and corrective as regards the possible errors of the stopped couplet—was not put in operation, except by Milton at the very beginning of the period, so early as these. In fact, as has been said, it was the degradation of blank verse, almost as much as anything else which encouraged the growth of this form of rhyme. Nor was the all-powerful influence of Milton himself at once felt, except by a very few persons ;[3] while, when it began to be felt, it was not fully understood. Attempts, however, were by degrees made in it ;[4] and, some sixty years after the appearance of *Paradise Lost*, the beginning of Thomson's *Seasons* brought to bear a new, popular, and powerful agency. Although Thomson may have been under the elision and "apostrophation" delusions of his time, he did not attempt to avoid what his younger contemporary, Shenstone, called "virtual" trisyllabic feet. One of his best lines, for instance—

---

[1] In the actual case, of course, dissyllabic feet for trisyllabic ; but this could not but suggest the converse process in dissyllabic verse. And the octosyllable was not used for light verse only ; Dyer in *Grongar Hill* (1726) revived the Miltonic form of *L'Allegro*, etc., with an effect all the more certainly excellent, that it was demurred to by the mistaken critics of the time. [2] *V. inf.* pp. 242-5.

[3] Among whom Lord Roscommon deserves honourable mention.

[4] As by Watts the hymn-writer, John Philips, and Gay.

$$\smile \ \smile \ -$$

The yellow wall-|flower, stain|ed with iron-brown,

contains such a foot naturally, though you may slur and "apostrophate" it into "flow'r"; and there are endless others, ready to suggest themselves to a nice ear, whenever you come across such words as "pastoral" and "impetuous" in—

$$\smile \ \smile \ -$$

Shines o'er | the rest | the pas|toral queen, | and rays

$$\smile \ \smile \ -$$

Impet|uous rush|es o'er | the sound|ing void.

But an even more valuable effect of blank-verse practice was the inevitable reappearance of the verse-paragraph, with its necessary constituents the verse-sentences and verse-clauses, which need not—and, if a good effect is to be produced, *must* not—be made of successive batches of complete lines, still less of batches of equal size. In forging the verse-paragraph, variation of pause, overrunning of sense as regards line-ends, strong breaks in the actual lines (a thing almost abused by Thomson himself, and quite so by his followers, but in itself a caustic to one of the evils of couplet verse), are necessary implements and materials. Accordingly the staunchest devotees of the couplet, such as Johnson, always dislike blank verse ; and when, later, a poet like Cowper takes it up, his action is similarly connected with dislike to the "mechanic warbling" of the Popian style. In his hands, especially in the late and splendid example of "Yardley Oak," almost the full Miltonic variety is recovered. But always, and throughout its practice during the eighteenth century, it acts as a foil, a relief and a refuge to and from the limitations and restrictions of the couplet itself.

and lyric.   Lastly, a similar enfranchising influence was exercised by lyric ; but to a comparatively limited extent. The genius of the latest seventeenth century and of almost the whole eighteenth, except in a few poets (mostly to be kept as exceptions, with Gray and Collins, who were of them, to the next chapter), was by no means lyrical. The healthiest influence of it was supplied by anapæstic forms, especially in light verse. " Pindarics " were at first much used, but were too often of a most prosaic character. " Romance-six " was affected to an almost surprising degree, but for the most part in a rather *Sir Thopas*-like form, exact and sing-song. This was also the fault of most of the common measure or ballad - quatrain, such as the well - known examples of Percy and Goldsmith ; though the *Reliques* of the former gave better models (somewhat tampered with by the editor) forty years before 1800 ; and the mis-cellaneous collections of Durfey and Philips had to some extent done so nearly as much earlier still. The Evangelical revival, by infusing more passion and reality into hymns, had a good effect ; and when we come to Cowper, this influenced his profane as well as his sacred poetry. Nor should we omit to mention—as a really powerful counter-agent to the couplet, with its monotonous regularity, unqualified rhyme, and so on—the irregularly rhythmed prose of Macpherson's *Ossian*, which appeared about the same time as the *Reliques*, and attracted much attention.

By all these things, and by the special influence of the poets to be mentioned in the early part of the next chapter, useful testimony was continuously given, to the effect that, after all, the decasyllabic couplet, especially in the prevailing form, was not the only metre, nor even the only important metre, in English. But its predominance continued, and its characteristics, as has been said, to some extent infected or inoculated its rivals. " Inoculated " rather than " infected," for, once more let it be repeated, this predominance undoubtedly beat into the English tongue, ear, and mind a sense of the importance of real and regular rhythm—a sense which, for another hundred years and more, has prevented, in the freest expatiation of released prosody, any kind of return to the disorder of the whole fifteenth century, and in some respects, at any rate, of the mid-seventeenth.

Merit of eighteenth-century " regu-larity."

CHAPTER V

THE ROMANTIC REVIVAL—ITS PRECURSORS AND FIRST
GREAT STAGE

Gray and Collins.
WE must now take up, somewhat more minutely, the phenomena mentioned in the last chapter as showing revolt against, and recovery from, the partly beneficial but excessive tyranny of the stopped decasyllabic couplet. These may be considered, still briefly but more particularly, under two heads : the first concerning chiefly the influence of individual poets—Collins, Gray, Chatterton, Burns, Blake; the second, agencies various in kind and source. Neither Collins nor Gray can be said to have directly attacked the task—though Gray at least was, as we see from his *Metrum*, not ignorant of the facts—of re-leavening and re-illustrating prosody by an infusion of trisyllabic substitution. With rarest exceptions, they still cling to the iamb as a base-foot. But they rearrange its line-groups in a fashion as alien as possible from that of the couplet. Collins even discards rhyme altogether in the quatrains of *Evening*, and in his famous " Passions " varies his construction as much as possible within the general limits. Gray follows, but improves upon, Dryden in the rhymed decasyllabic quatrain; adapts, with an effect somewhat stiff, but often very beautiful, the Greek system of strophe, antistrophe, and epode in the *Progress of Poetry* and *The Bard*; employs Romance-six with singular felicity in both serious and serio-comic verse; and, though retaining a strongly artificial poetic diction, informs this with new touches and spirit from sources as a rule quite closed to his contemporaries and predecessors—Norse and

Welsh as well as Greek. Both these poets, in short, disregard, to a large extent, equality of line-length, and employ mixed rhymes. Now equality of line-length and strictly *consecutive* rhymes were almost as dear to the chief lovers of the couplet as its unvarying syllabic arrangement and its regular accent.

Gray, it has been said, knew substitution, but did not use it ; the ill-fated genius of Chatterton not only knew it, but used it. It is present, and very effective, in Burns ; but it was not the chief means of good of which Burns availed himself in regard to prosody. His dialect, with its relief from the conventional "lingo" of eighteenth-century poetry, did much ; but the forms which he used, and especially the famous "Burns metre," did more. It would be almost impossible to devise a greater contrast to the couplet ; or—since (which is at least worth noting) the six lines of this stanza contain exactly as many syllables (forty) as two ordinary couplets—to arrange these same numbers in ways more rhythmically different. But the first eighteenth-century poet thoroughly to understand and exemplify the powers of equivalence is Burns's slightly older contemporary, William Blake, whose *Poetical Sketches* appeared as early as 1780, while his *Songs of Innocence and Experience*, and his remaining poems, display a knowledge of the secrets of this equivalence, and a command over them, which had not been shown since Shakespeare. Chatterton, Burns, and Blake.

Blake, however, expressed rather than exercised influence, for his poems remained long almost unknown ; and it may be doubtful whether even the others brought about many conscious prosodic changes. The gradual recovery of knowledge of older English literature, and especially of the ballads, had in all probability much more direct power. Durfey's *Pills to Purge Melancholy*, Philips's *Collection of Old Ballads*, and Percy's *Reliques*—with constantly increasing editions of the Elizabethan dramatists and other writers, even such as Skelton and Occleve— could not but awaken men's minds to the fact that (as Gascoigne had put it in a matter closely connected if not Other influences of change.

absolutely identical) "we had used in times past other kinds of metres" than the stopped couplet.   And towards the end of the century revolt of various kinds appeared— copious though usually very tame ballad; multiplied blank verse of the usual kind; and (in imitation partly of some older English models and of Collins, partly of the German) rhymeless verse of different sorts, the chief early practitioner of which was Frank Sayers of Norwich, a physician and man of letters who was more influential on others than important in himself.   Bowles (after Warton, whose *History of Poetry* worked in the same direction) reintroduced the sonnet.   William Taylor, another member of the Norwich group, revived (again after the German) English hexameters; and though Hayley, Darwin, and others continued the eighteenth-century couplet unchanged, the spirit of the youth of the period was clearly tending in a different direction.

Words-worth, Southey, and Scott.

Of the four great champions of reaction who were born about 1770, Wordsworth, though he illustrates the change generally, and never, in his principal work, uses the stopped couplet, is not very noticeable prosodically.[1]   The three others are, in different ways, of the first importance. Southey, as early as 1796, not merely practised, but, which is much more, practised deliberately, and definitely defended in a letter to an objecting friend, the use of three syllables for two.   Moreover (not confining himself to the ballad metre, which he had employed and which he was specially justifying), he alleged the practice of Milton, frankly stigmatising as "asses" the editors who had endeavoured to disguise this practice as "elision."   Scott —assisted perhaps to some extent by hearing a recitation or reading of Coleridge's unpublished *Christabel*, but undoubtedly also following[2] the example of the innumerable

---

[1] His greatest prosodic achievement is also his greatest achievement in poetry, the "Immortality" Ode.   But, though he varies line-length admirably, the prevailing rhythm is merely iambic; and when, in stanza 4, he tries to vary *it*, the effect is very unfortunate.

[2] Scott was a debtor for something as well to "Monk" Lewis.   See "List of Poets," Book IV.

ballad- and romance-writers with whom he was almost better acquainted than any other man in Britain—produced first ballad-pieces, and then, in and after *The Lay of the Last Minstrel*, continuous narrative poems of great length, for the most part couched in equivalenced octosyllables, but often much varied in rhyme-arrangement and diversified by shorter and longer lines. And there is no doubt that the enormous popularity of these poems of his did more than anything else to familiarise the public ear with metres and cadences as different as possible from the couplet.

But the influence of Coleridge, independent of that *Coleridge.* indirectly applied through Scott, was the most important of all. It was indeed not (as it should have been) exhibited, at once and in bulk, by the simultaneous publication of *The Ancient Mariner* and *Christabel*, the latter of which, though, at least in great part, written at the same time as the former, was separated from it in publication by nearly twenty years. *The Ancient Mariner* itself is in ballad metre, but ballad metre treated in the freest possible fashion, not only with equivalence used at pleasure in individual lines, but with the four lines of the strict quatrain extended to five, or any number up to nine— thereby increasing and varying the stanza-effect in the widest possible manner, though never expanding it into positive paragraphs. More important still, because more apparently novel, though it had been in fact preluded both by Chatterton and Blake, and had been recognised by Gray in the work of Spenser, was the use, in *Christabel*, of continuous octosyllabic couplets, only sometimes, and rarely, broken into stanza, but constantly equivalenced and frequently varied by shorter lines. Of these, Coleridge himself gave in his preface a curiously inadequate account, regarding them—or at least giving them out—as constructed on the principle of counting only the accents. They, however, in fact follow the strictest foot-division, and have been the pattern of all similar verses, with equivalent substitution, since.

Moore.　　Moore, who comes in point of date between this group and the second great trio of Byron, Shelley, and Keats, is very important prosodically.　Since the earlier seventeenth century at latest, music, though it had had much and rather deleterious influence on theories of English prosody, had had little on its practice, a few light things excepted. But Moore was an accomplished musician both in theory and practice, in composition and in execution ; he belonged to a race distinguished for song-gift ; and the great majority of his almost innumerable lyrics were directly composed for old airs or adapted to new.　The consequence was, almost inevitably, that they present a variety of cadence and rhythm which had hardly ever before been seen. Occasionally this variety oversteps the bounds of pure prosody, allowing, as in the well-known "Eveleen's Bower," [1] a syllable which, corresponding to an *appoggiatura* in music, requires, in strict scansion, to be slurred or else to be considered extra-metrical, as in the "Song to a Portuguese Air," [2] and others, further licences.　He was himself aware of this, and it did little harm ; while the tunefulness of his trisyllabic measures, and the great range of "broken and cuttit" line-arrangements which his work presented, were both of the first importance in promoting variety and freedom of metrical arrangement.

His expertness in the two arts, however, and his

[1] And wept | behind [the] clouds | o'er the maid|en's shame.

That stain | upon [the] snow | of fair Ev|eleen's fame.

[2] Where three lines like the following occur :

Should those | fond hopes | e'er for|sake thee,

Which now | so sweet|ly thy heart | employ,

On our thresh|old a wel|come still found,

and are quite irreconcilable.

constant combination of them, as well as perhaps his Byron. inferiority (though this is only relative) in strictly poetical power, somewhat reduce Moore's importance as compared with that of Byron, Shelley, and Keats. The first-named was the least of the three in prosody, as in poetry ; but his prosodic merits have, as a rule, been far under-valued, even by his adorers as a poet. He affected, and perhaps really to some extent felt, much greater admiration for the eighteenth-century poets, and for those who mainly or partly followed them in his own time, than for the innovators of the Romantic school ; and he himself wrote the stock couplet with correctness and vigour. But he chose for his principal serious poem, *Childe Harold*, the Spenserian, which "regular" classical critics had always disliked ; and, though he never achieved its proper character, did finely in it sometimes, and undoubtedly restored its popularity. Again, he chose for his greatest serio-comic pieces, *Beppo* and *Don Juan*, the *ottava* ; while his minor tales were in Scott-*Christabel* octosyllables. In lyric, too, he showed varied power, and once turned [1] what had been a burlesque before in its exact, and a very sing-song metre in its restricted, form into a thing of remarkable prosodic beauty, to be made more beautiful still by Praed and Mr. Swinburne. His most consummate prosodic achievement is undoubtedly the above-mentioned octave of *Don Juan*, which can hardly be surpassed, either in suitability to its subject, or in the way in which the particular characteristics of the metre itself are brought out.

But the greatest poets are naturally, and almost inevitably, the greatest prosodists ; and this was well seen in the case of the two whom we have yet to mention, Shelley Shelley :
his longer
poems. and Keats, who also present a valuable and interesting contrast in this as in other ways. It is probable that in all cases Shelley began with direct though not studious imitation. His early and almost worthless poems were based on "Monk" Lewis and others of that type ; his first striking thing, the opening of *Queen Mab*, is a sort of

[1] In the "Haidee" song. *V. sup.* Scanned Conspectus, § XLIV.

variation on that of Southey's *Thalaba* ; and his first great poem, *Alastor*, had Wordsworth evidently before it ; while *Laon and Cythna* (*The Revolt of Islam*) would probably not have been in Spenserians if *Childe Harold* had not adopted them, nor perhaps *The Witch of Atlas* in octaves but for *Beppo.* Yet, as soon as he has attained poetic gift, he goes off from his models entirely, and, without much apparent care for preconceived forms, achieves the most marvellous beauty in whatever he touches. In *Prometheus Unbound* especially, the blank-verse dialogue, and the abundant lyrical choruses and interludes, not only exhibit wholly astonishing variety and individual excellence, but adapt themselves to each other, as nowhere else in drama. The Spenserians of *Adonais*, taking some liberties, attain, at their best, absolute perfection ; of the octosyllabic couplets, shortened or not in several minor poems, almost as much may be said ; and the octaves of *The Witch of Atlas* (with the very best of Keats's *Isabella*) are the greatest examples of that metre in English for serious use. He even tries the often failed-in *terza rima*, and does beautiful things in it, though perhaps not such beautiful examples of it.

His lyrics.   But it is in his lyrics that Shelley's prosodic, like his poetic, power shows highest. Those in *Prometheus Unbound* have been spoken of ; but the numerous and glorious short and separate pieces defy enumeration or specification here. The two popular favourites, "The Cloud" and "The Skylark," would each serve as a text for an exemplary lecture on English prosody, and a dozen others, with dozens more added to them, would do the same. None is ever really "irregular" : to say, as has been said of "The Cloud," that it defies ordinary scansion, is simply to say that the speaker does not understand either the poem or ordinary scansion, or both (see above, Book I. p. 100). But almost all exhibit, in endless variety of relief and colour, the great laws of equivalence and substitution, and the enormous advantage of varied and even complicated metre, rhyme, line-length, and stanza-arrangement.

Shelley never seems to have studied metre much, and, as has been said, his first pattern is the merest starting-point for him.   But he touches none that he does not adorn ; none that he does not make matter of delight ; and none, likewise, in which he does not supply a text for infinite technical instruction as well.

The case of Keats is curiously different.   He too—as Keats. indeed practically everybody does—begins with imitation, but it is imitation of a different kind.   Chapman, Spenser, the sonneteers, the Jacobean poets probably, Leigh Hunt certainly, supply him not merely with hints and " send-offs," but with carefully studied models.   He hits, in conse-quence, first in his *Juvenilia* and then in *Endymion*, upon a very much enjambed form of decasyllabic couplet—a form opposed to all the traditions of Pope, and deemed horrible by the orthodox critics of the day.   But he sees for himself the defect of this, and applies himself earnestly to the study of Dryden and Milton as tonics and astringents. The results are the fine, less fluent, still slightly overrun, but tripleted and Alexandrined heroics of *Lamia*, and the splendid blank verse of *Hyperion*.   But he has not confined himself to these, or to their lessons ; and he has never confined himself to the mere lessons of any poet or of any period.   He produces in turn the touching octaves of *Isabella* ; the magnificent Spenserians of *The Eve of St. Agnes* ; the Sonnets, most of them among the finest ex-amples of the form in English ; the varied stanza-measures of the Odes ; the unique ballad adaptation [1] of *La Belle*

---

[1] With "long measure," but with the last line cut down to a mono-meter :

O ! what | can ail | thee, knight-|at-arms,
Alone | and pale|ly loi|tering ?
The sedge | has with|ered from | the lake,
And no | birds sing.

This last line being sometimes exquisitely equivalenced in the first foot :

∪ ∪   —   ∪   —
And her eyes | were wild.

.   .   .   .

∪ ∪   —
On the cold | hill side.

Dame sans Merci ; and lastly, two forms of octosyllabic couplet—the mainly catalectic or seven-syllabled form of some earlier poems, and the complete one of *The Eve of St. Mark*, which overleaps all other examples back to Gower, picks out the finest qualities of Gower's own form, and rearranges them in an example unfinished in itself, but serving as a guide, in the production of a great body of finished and admirable work, to the late Mr. William Morris.   In no poet is the lesson—which it was the business of this generation to exemplify, and should be of this chapter to expound—of ordered variety, in foot, in line, in stanza, more triumphantly shown.

CHAPTER VI

THE LAST STAGE—TENNYSON TO SWINBURNE

THE lesson of the last chapter, if properly learnt, will From Keats to Tennyson. have shown the substitution of a more really "correct," because wider and freer, view of English prosody than that which had produced the narrow and blinkered pseudo-correctness of the eighteenth century, and the way in which this extension was, whether consciously or unconsciously, utilised by the great poets of 1798-1830. Consciously, however, this lesson was not learnt by all of these poets themselves; yet it spread, and rapidly became the general, if not yet the acknowledged, principle of English poetry. It is observable in most and in all the best of what have been called the "Intermediates"— the poets who were born between 1790 and 1810, such as Beddoes and Darley,[1] Macaulay and Praed. But in

---

[1] Especially in these two, as here:

Half Alex.	Winds | of the West, | arise !
Alex.	Hesper|ian bal|miest airs, | O waft | back those | sweet sighs
Dec. couplet.	{ To her | that breathes | them from | her own | pure skies, { Dew-drop|ping, mixt | with Dawn's | engold|ened dyes
Half Alex.	O'er my | unhap|py eyes !
Fourteener.	From prim|rose bed | and wil|low bank | where your | moss cra|dle lies,
Alex.	O ! from | your rush|y bowers | to waft | back her | sweet sighs—
Half Alex.	Winds | of the West, | arise !

(DARLEY.)

If thou | wilt ease | thine heart
Of love | and all | its smart,
Then sleep, | dear, sleep ;

Tennyson at once and in Browning—the one born just before, the other just after, the end of the first decade of the nineteenth century—it manifests itself in the most unmistakable degree ; so much so, indeed, as to have actually puzzled, if not shocked, Coleridge himself, the greatest restorer of its mainspring.   Tennyson's first volumes are open to many just criticisms.   But if the student will turn to the scanned examples of the " Hollyhock Song" and the "Dying Swan" given previously, he will see that the young poet, so far from having "begun to write without knowing very well what metre is," had begun with an almost absolutely perfect knowledge of it, whatever his shortcomings in other matters might be.[1]

Tennyson himself.   The variety of metres in which this accomplishment was shown was extraordinary, and was no doubt felt by contemporaries to be bewildering.   Even from the poets of the first Romantic school they had been principally (though of course not entirely) accustomed to lines of the same length, couched in more or less uniform metre throughout.   The pieces which composed the two volumes of 1830 and 1832, even before they were revised and augmented in 1842, contained a greater variety of metres than had been seen in the same bulk of work of any single English poet from Chaucer to Keats.   There was blank verse, if not at first quite of the absolute perfection which it reached ten years later, of a new and remarkable pattern, adjusting the Miltonic paragraph to a much more fluent movement, and quite discarding the Thomsonian

> And not | a sor|row
> Hang a|ny tear | on your | eyelash|es ;
>   Lie still | and deep,
> Sad soul, | until | the sea-|wave wash|es
>   ◡ ◡ — ◡ —
>   The rim | o' the sun | to-mor|row
>   In east|ern sky.   (BEDDOES.)

The redundant syllables are specially marked off here, to bring out their contrast with the acatalectic lines.

.[1] Macaulay's prosody is mostly plain sailing ; but in *The Last Buccaneer* he has (perhaps following Moore) attempted a rather unusual rhythm.   See *Hist. Pros.* iii. 135-137.   For Praed *v. sup.* p. 114.

stiffness.   There were Spenserians (in the opening of the
" Lotos-Eaters ") of the very best kind.   There was a little
very fine decasyllabic couplet.   But the great majority of the
poems were lyrics, couched in a dazzling variety of metres.
It was not only that the poet expanded the apparent but
not real " irregularity " of Shakespeare into examples such
as the two noted above.   It was not merely that, as in the
" Lotos-Eaters " itself and " The Vision of Sin,"[1] he arranged different metres in the same piece on the principles
of an elaborate musical symphony.   The way in which he
handled metres previously known must have startled—indeed we know that it did startle—the precisians still more.

A good instance of this is the threefold rehandling of
the old decasyllabic quatrain, familiar to everybody from
Dryden's *Annus Mirabilis* and Gray's *Elegy*.   This quatrain
itself, as a consequence of its gravity, is rather apt to be
monotonous.   Simple shortening of the even verses gives
rather better outline, but not much less—in fact even
greater—monotony.   In three different poems Tennyson
handles it in three different ways.   " The Poet "[2] is
couched in 10, 6, 10, 4, giving a succinct and rather
sententious metre, which suits admirably for the sharply
cut cumulative phrases of that fine piece.   But, by this
shortening, ten syllables, the equivalent of a whole line,
were lost ; and this gave too little room for description,
and especially for the series of pictures, in scene- or figure-
painting, which form so large a part of the other two poems
and communicate to them such extraordinary charm.   So,
in the " Palace of Art," Tennyson " eked " the stanza,
extending the second line to eights and the fifth to sixes.[3]

Special example of his manipulation of the quatrain.

---

[1] This did not appear till 1842.

[2] The poet in a golden clime was born,
      With golden stars above ;
Dower'd with the hate of hate, the scorn of scorn,
      The love of love.

[3] I built my soul a lordly pleasure-house,
      Wherein at ease for aye to dwell.
I said, " O Soul, make merry and carouse,
      Dear soul, for all is well."

This, besides actually giving a little more room, admits more varied "fingering," together with an effect of outline, which is wonderfully attractive—a taper, but with a swell in it. In the "Dream of Fair Women"—more narrative and with larger aims—he wanted more space still, and a form that would link itself better. He gets this by keeping *three* decasyllables with a final six.[1] This is an exceedingly cunning as well as beautiful device, for, on the one hand, the large majority of decasyllables, batched in threes, assists the narrative effect, which is always hard to achieve with stanzas of very irregular outline ; and, on the other, the short final line serves at once as finial to the individual stanza, and hinge to join it to the next.

Many examples could be given, and may be found in the larger *History*, but these will suffice, with the addition that Tennyson continued his experimentation to the very last, as in the remarkable metre of "Kapiolani," and that his handling of blank verse, like Shakespeare, became almost perilous in its freedom, by the temptation that it offered to others to traverse the bounds, though he himself never actually did so.

Browning.   Browning, who was to illustrate the prosodic lesson of the century with, if possible, an even greater variety, did not exactly begin in that direction ; though his prosodic practice was almost equally independent after the very first. That "very first"—*Pauline*—showed a distinct effort to imitate the blank verse of Shelley ; and this was continued, though with more idiosyncrasy, in the dramatically arranged, but not really dramatic, *Paracelsus*, which had, however, one or two beautiful lyrics of a kind also to some extent Shelleyan. The blank verse in these two is not much equivalenced, nor even very much enjambed, but it runs with a peculiar *breathlessness* from verse to verse, even if each be fairly complete in itself. And this breathlessness continues—being, indeed, the main

---

[1] I read, before my eyelids dropt their shade,
   The Legend of Good Women, long ago
Sung by the morning star of song, who made
   His music heard below.

source of the much-talked-of " obscurity " of the piece—
in *Sordello*.   Here the couplet used is utterly opposed to
that of the eighteenth century ; but, once more, it is by
no means the enjambed variety of the seventeenth.   It is
almost a kind to itself, progressing in immense involved
paragraphs (often largely parenthetic) after a fashion which
almost drowns the rhyme, even if there be definite stops
at the end of the verses.

Fortunately, after this, in *Bells and Pomegranates*, he
devoted a large part of his attention to lyric, in which he
produced examples exquisite in quality and inexhaustible
in variety.[1]   His octosyllables in *Christmas Eve* and

---

[1] A few examples may be given :—

(1) Oh ‖ heart ! oh ! | blood that | freezes, | blood that | burns !
         Earth's re|turns
     For whole | centu|ries of | folly, | noise, and | sin !
         Shut them | in
     With their | triumphs | and their | glories, | and the | rest ;
         Love is | best.
                                    (*Love among the Ruins.*)

(Regular trochees alternately trimeter and monometer, but both catalectic.   *One* monosyllabic substitution.)

    (2) What hand and brain went ever paired ?
        What heart alike conceived and dared ?
        What act proved all its thought had been ?
        What will but felt the fleshly screen ?
          We ride | and I see | her bosom heave.
        There's ma|ny a crown | for who can reach,
        Ten lines, a statesman's life in each !
        The flag stuck on a heap of bones,
        A soldier's doing ! what atones ?
        They scratch his name | on the Ab|bey stones.
          My ri|ding is bet|ter, by their leave.
                                    (*The Last Ride Together.*)

(Iambic dimeter stanza ; three or four trisyllabic substitutions.)

    (3) Oh, | what a dawn | of day !
        How the March | sun feels | like May !
            All is blue | again
            After last | night's rain,
        And the South | dries the haw|thorn spray.
            On|ly, my Love's | away !
        I'd as lief | that the blue | were grey.

(Iambic-anapæstic with monosyllabic feet admitted into partnership.)

Easter Day are daringly equivalenced, and rhymed still more daringly, but very effective ; and much later, in *Fifine at the Fair*, he almost succeeded in making the continuous Alexandrine a real success.   But the bulk of his immense work in later days was written in blank verse, as strongly equivalenced as his octosyllables.   Browning was never an incorrect prosodist ; even his rhymes, though frequently extravagant, are almost always defensible ; and it is a vulgar error to think him even rough in verse, though he was so in diction.   But he, once more, pushed the lesson of variety to its extreme in one way.

Mrs. Browning.   His wife, both before and after she became his wife, gave a third important example of this attention to lyric, and this determination to give it the most multitudinous and original forms.   She had one unfortunate, and indeed disgusting, prosodic defect — a toleration of, if not a positive preference for, really atrocious rhymes.   But her ear for metre was quite differently tuned, and often exquisite ; though (as was *not* the case with her husband) her bad rhymes, and, as was the case with him, though in a different way, her extravagant diction, sometimes created a false idea of metrical carelessness.

Matthew Arnold.   But, in a way, the most remarkable witness to the general tendency of the period was to be found in Mr. Matthew Arnold, who disapproved of Tennyson, and must (though personal friendship seems to have prevented him from saying so) have disapproved of the Brownings still more. For all Mr. Arnold's "classical" tastes, in different senses of that word, he became "romantic" in his variety of lyric forms, in his handling of them, in his dealing with the

---

(4) Is all | our fire | of ship|wreck wood,
　　Oak : and | pine?
　Oh, for | the ills | half-un|derstood,
　　The dim | dead woe |
　　Long : a|go
　Befallen | this bit|ter coast | of France !
　Well, poor | sailors | took their | chance :
　　I : take | mine.

(Iambic-trochaic ; or, if monosyllabic initial feet be granted in some lines, all iambic, and perhaps better so.)

couplet, and in the adoption of elaborate stanza forms for his longer poems. Only his blank verse is of somewhat classical pattern, and of this he did not write very much.

In the poets who specially represent the last half of the nineteenth century (with, in one case and the chief of all, an actual extension over nearly the whole of the first decade of the twentieth)—and who consisted mainly of the school often, though not very accurately, called Pre-Raphaelite— these tendencies are exhibited to a still greater extent, and in some cases, beyond all doubt, consciously followed and elaborated. In Dante and Christina Rossetti, brother and sister — more remarkable for genius perhaps than any brother and sister in history, literary or other,—but especially in the brother, the Italian and English elements blended. Dante showed, though in great variety, more of the Italian tendency to slow and stately music ; Christina, more of the English to light and rapid movement as well. But both thoroughly mastered the secrets of equivalence, as well as those of largely broken and variegated line-length and stanza-arrangement. The sonnets of both are the finest, on what is called the Italian model, in our language, and Christina's command, both of simple song metres and of regular short verse—almost Skeltonic in apparent character, but far apart from doggerel—is specially noticeable. She is indeed one of the most daring of experimenters in metrical licence, but, even more than Browning's, her verse, with all its audacity, never transgresses the laws of prosodic music.[1]

[1] (*a*) Morning | and eve|ning
   Maids heard | the gob|lins cry :
   " Come buy | our or|chard fruits,
   Come buy, | come buy :
   Apples and | quinces,
   Lemons and | oranges,
   Plump unpecked | cherries,
   Melons and | raspberries."

(Where, as almost always, the dactylic lines can be made anapæstic with anacrusis, " Mel|ons and rasp|berries," etc.)

(*a*) Iamb and trochee followed by dactyl and trochee.

(margin note: Later poets —The Rossettis.)

Earlier to appear than Rossetti, except in little-read periodicals, but a younger man, was William Morris, whose

(*b*) She clipped | a pre|cious gold|en lock,
She dropped | a tear | more rare | than pearl,
Then sucked | their fruit | globes fair | or red.
Sweeter | than hon|ey from | the rock,
Stronger | than man-|rejoic|ing wine,
Clearer | than wa|ter flowed | that juice.

(*c*) But ev|er in | the noon|light
She pined | and pined | away ;
Sought them | by night | and day,
Found them | no more, | but dwin|dled and | grew grey ;
Then fell | with the | first snow,
While to | this day | no grass | will grow
Where she | lies low :
I plant|ed dai|sies there | a year | ago
That nev|er blow.

(*d*) Laughed every | goblin
When they | spied her | peeping :
Came towards her | hobbling,
Flying, | running, | leaping, |
Puffing and | blowing.

(2) Where sun|less riv|ers weep   Led by | a sin|gle star,
Their waves | into | the deep,   She came | from ver|y far,
She sleeps | a charm|èd sleep :   To seek, | where sha|dows are,
Awake | her not.   Her plea|sant lot.

(3) Come to | me in | the si|lence of | the night ;
Come in | the speak|ing si|lence of | a dream ;
Come with | soft round|ed cheeks | and eyes | as bright
As sun|light on | a stream ;
Come back | in tears,
O mem|ory, | hope, love, | of fin|ished years.

(4) One by one | slowly,   Clear stainless | spirits,
Ah | how sad | and slow !   White, as | white as | snow ;
Wailing and | praying   Pale spirits, | wailing
The spir|its rise | and go :   For an | over|throw.

(5) ''Oh ! whence | do you come,|| my de|ar friend, | to me ?
With your gold|en hair || all fallen | below | your knee,

(*b*) Pure iambic dimeter with a trochee or two.
(*c*) Iambic, with length varied from two to five feet.
(*d*) Dactyl and trochee, or mere trochee.
(2) Iambic.   (3) Iambic, with some trochaic beginnings.
(4) Dactylic-trochaic and iambic alternately.
(5) Really '' irregular.''   Norm dimeter anapæstic—
◡ ◡ − ◡ ◡ − ◡ ◡ −
but largely varied in rhythm and length. Best scanned as above, with strong pause, making *five* feet.

place in the history of English prosody is a very important one. In his first book, *The Defence of Guenevere*, he tried, with remarkable success, a very large number of lyrical metres, sometimes exhibiting great originality of substitution. He passed from this to a still more remarkable revival of the enjambed decasyllabic couplet in *The Life and Death of Jason* and part of *The Earthly Paradise*, following not so much Keats as the best of the early seventeenth-century examples. With this, in *The Earthly Paradise* itself, he combined octosyllabic couplet of almost more exceptional quality still—very little equivalenced, but varied by pause and fingering in a manner which only Gower in his very finest passage, and Keats in the fragment of the *Eve of St. Mark*, had achieved. He also wrote excellent rhyme-royal. In *Love is Enough*, besides many more beautiful lyrical devices, he endeavoured a sort of alliterative semi-metrical rhythm of fifteenth-century kind, which has not pleased every one; but in *Sigurd the Volsung*, while still hovering about the same period, he pitched upon one of the numerous arrangements of the fourteener and perfected it into a thoroughly great metre.[1]

Although not an artist in quite so many kinds of verse as Morris, and confining himself as a rule to strict metre, Algernon Charles Swinburne was, however, by far the greatest metrist of this group and time, and one of the greatest in the history of English poetry. In his copious critical work he did not bestow much explicit attention on matters prosodic; but when he did, made important remarks, and once gave one of the most important to be found definitely expressed by any English poet. This was

Mr. Swinburne.

And your face | as white || as snow|drops on | the lea,
And your voice | as hol||low as | the hol|low sea ? "

(This last extract is a most audacious, but quite justifiable, fingering of the ordinary five-foot iambic line, with substitutions and adaptations which give it now anapæstic, now trochaic undertone. The first exhibits, in a batch of five from *Goblin Market*, the same audacity and the same success in varying line-*length* as well as constitution ; (2), (3), and (4), with more of what is commonly called " regularity," show the same various address.)

[1] For examples of Morris's prosody see Scanned Conspectus.

to the effect, that English would always lend itself readily and successfully to any combinations of iamb, trochee, or anapæst, never to those of dactyl and spondee. He himself produced magnificent verse which looks like dactylic hexameter or elegiac, but is really (and was meant by him for) anapæstic work with anacrusis and catalexis. He wrote beautiful choriambics and more beautiful Sapphics. But these, at least the last two, were merely experiments and *tours de force*. He also experimented in the artificial French forms (*v. inf.*). But his principal work was straightforward composition in the direct lines of the English poetical inheritance, utilising to the utmost all the liberties of equivalence and substitution on the principles of Tennyson, but never abusing them, and informing particular metres with a spirit that made them entirely his own. His blank verse, though sometimes exceedingly fine, was also sometimes a little too voluble ; and of his couplets much the same may be said in both ways. But in lyric—giving that word the widest possible extension—he is unsurpassed as to variety and individuality of practice, while, in two striking cases, he made improvements of the most remarkable kind on previous improvements made by others.[1]

---

[1] Examples of lyric :

(1) You have cho|sen and clung | to the chance | they sent | you,
    Life sweet | as per|fume, and pure | as prayer ;
But will | it not one | day in heav|en repent | you?
    Will they sol|ace you whol|ly, the days | that were ?
Will you lift | up your eyes | between sad|ness and bliss ?
Meet mine | and see | where the great | love is,
And trem|ble and turn | and be changed ? | Content | you,
    The gate | is strait ; | I shall not | be there.

(Anapæstic dimeter with iambic substitution and redundance.   A most perfect combination.)

    (2) If love | were what | the rose | is
        And I | were like | the leaf,
    Our lives | would grow | togeth|er
    In sad | or sing|ing wea|ther,
    Blown fields | or flower|ful clo|ses,
        Green plea|sure or | grey grief :
    If love | were what | the rose | is
        And I | were like | the leaf.

(Pure iambics.   Dimeter catalectic and brachycatalectic by turns.)

The first of these was the fresh adaptation (after Fitz-Gerald, but with an important difference) of the decasyl-labic quatrain in *Laus Veneris*. The translator of *Omar Khayyám* had, with great effect, made the first, second, and fourth lines rhyme together, leaving the third entirely blank. Mr. Swinburne made the third line of each of his pairs of quatrains rhyme as well, a completion of the music which has a very fine effect. And a still greater achievement was the shortening of the last line of the "Praed Metre," which makes one of the most beautiful arrangements to be found in English. But it is perhaps only in these two that even guidance of any definite kind can be assigned. For the most part the prosodic effect is produced by original extension of the general laws, and by entirely individual fingering of particular metres. Nothing in the whole range of English poetry is more remarkable than the handling, in this way, of the ordinary Long Measure with alternate redundance in "At a Month's End ";[1] and the examples of other varied metres, also given below, will complete the exposition, as far as it can be done in anything but a monograph of great extent.

Many poets, in the later years of the nineteenth cen- Others. tury, have been remarkable for prosodic accomplishment; but, except in the outside department of experiment in quantitative and classical metres, they have rarely touched principle. Arthur E. O'Shaughnessy [2] and James Thomson

---

(3) When the | game be|gan be|tween them | for a | jest,
    He played | king and | she played | queen to | match the | best.
    Laughter | soft as | tears, and | tears that | turned to | laughter,
    These were | things she | sought for | years and | sorrowed | after.

(Trochaic trimeter catalectic ; quite pure throughout.)

[1] As a | star feels | the sun | and fal|ters,
    Touched to | death by | divin|er eyes—
    As on | the old gods' | untend|ed altars
    The old fire | of with|ered wor|ship dies.

("Long measure"; but completely transfigured by the redundance and double rhyme in the odd places, and the ·trochaic and anapæstic substitution.)

[2] We | are the mu|sic-mak|ers,
    And we | are the dream|ers of dreams,

the Second showed extraordinary proficiency, the first in
the more rapid, the second in the statelier variation of
metre. Canon Dixon, who was sometimes extremely happy
in lyric,[1] wrote, in *Mano*, the one long English poem in

Wan|dering by lone | sea-break|ers,
  And sit|ting by de|solate streams :
World-los|ers and world-|forsakers,
  On whom | the pale | moon gleams ;
For we | are the mov|ers and shak|ers
  Of the world | for ev|er, it seems.

(Anapæsts used with singular skill.)

The stars are dimly seen among the shadows of the bay,
And lights that win are seen in strife with lights that die away.

The wave is very still—the rudder loosens in our hand ;
The zephyr will not fill our sail, and waft us to the land ;
O precious is the pause between the winds that come and go,
And sweet the silence of the shores between the ebb and flow.

. . . .

Say, shall we sing of day or night, fair land or mighty ocean,
Of any rapturous delight or any dear emotion,
Of any joy that is on earth, or hope that is above,
The holy country of our birth, or any song of love ?

. . . . . .

Our heart in all our life is like the hand of one who steers
A bark upon an ocean rife with dangers and with fears :
The joys, the hopes, like waves or wings, bear up this life of ours—
Short as a song of all these things that make up all its hours.

(The old fourteener—but made almost new by the great variation of
pause, by occasional redundance, and by the grouping of the lines.)

[1] If ev|er thou | didst creep
From out | the world | of sleep,
When the sun | slips | and the moon | dips,
If ev|er thou | wast born ;
Or upon | the starv|ing lips
Of the gray | uncol|oured morn.

(Especial effect produced by the anapæsts and monosyllabic feet of
line 3.)

Thou go|est more | and more
To the sil|ent things : | thy hair | is hoar,
Emp|tier thy wear|y face : | like to | the shore
Far-ru|ined, and | the deso|late bil|low white
That recedes | and leaves | it waif-wrin|kled, gap-|rocked, weak.
The shore | and the bil|low white
Groan|—they cry | and rest | not : they | would speak
And call | the eter|nal Night

terza rima, but without removing the objections which
seem to hold, in our language, against the arrangement
that is so magnificent in the *Divina Commedia*.   In the
late 'seventies a fancy came in, and remained for some
time, of reviving the artificial French (and to some extent
English) metres of the fifteenth and earlier centuries—
ballades, rondeaux, triolets, etc.   Mr. George Meredith,
when he employed verse and not prose, used a considerable
number of odd measures unusually rhythmed, as well as
others perfectly adjusted to the demands of the ear.   Mr.
Henley and others carried on the rhymeless revival from
Mr. Arnold, and yet others, such as the late Mr. John
Davidson, while using rhyme reviled it.   A few attempts
have recently been made at "*stress*-metres"—rebellious to
any uniform system of scansion, even with full liberty of
substitution, and, in fact, irregularly rhythmed prose.   But
nothing really good and unquestionably poetic has been
produced which will not obey the principles set forth in
this treatise, and everything really good has furnished fresh
illustrations of them.[1]

> To cease | them for ev|er, bid|ding new | things is|sue
> From her | cold tis|sue :
> Night | that is ev|er young, | nor knows | decay,
> Though old|er by | eter|nity | than they.

(Very fine "modern Pindaric," with extremely well-managed substitution.)

[1] For some supposed exceptions *v. sup.* last section of Scanned Conspectus, pp. 128-130.   One of the most interesting things in the study of
prosody is the tracing of the history of lyric forms.   Examples have been
given above, and more will be found below ; but *completeness* is here again
impossible.   Again, also, the "principles," properly followed out, will
carry the student safely through all such investigations, as, for instance,
that into the connection of Mr. Swinburne's "Anima Anceps" with
Curran's "Deserter," and the entire pedigree of both.   Perhaps it may
be well to add that, where a choriambic effect occurs ($-\smile\smile-$), choice
is often, if not always, open between scansion as trochee and iamb or as
monosyllabic foot and anapæst.   This has been already indicated expressly in some examples.   See, especially, pp. 183, 184, 212.

CHAPTER VII

RECAPITULATION OR SUMMARY VIEW OF STAGES OF ENGLISH PROSODY

I. OLD ENGLISH PERIOD

PROSODY rhythmical, not metrical; determined exclusively by alliteration and accent. Combinations of accented and unaccented syllables perhaps classifiable, but seldom, if ever, reducible to any combination corresponding to the flow of later Middle and Modern English verse, though the *principle* (of syllabic irregularity in corresponding lines) *survives as the most important basis of that verse itself.* Rhyme, except in the piece specially entitled "Rhyming Poem" and other very late examples, practically non-existent; the instances collected from other places being very few and quite possibly accidental.

II. BEFORE OR VERY SOON AFTER 1200

Earliest Middle English Period.

No pure and unmixed alliterative-accentual verse of the old kind, but a choice between pure syllabic metre of iambic type (*Ormulum*), less regular but clearly metrical (*i.e.* "*foot*-measured") verse, iambic or trochaic (*Paternoster, Moral Ode*, etc.), and singular mixtures of the alliterative kind (badly done), and the metrical kind (sometimes done rather better) (*Layamon, Proverbs of Alfred*).

III. Middle and Later Thirteenth Century

Second Early Middle English Period.

The metrifying process going on, with stronger emphasising of the metrical character and almost complete discarding of the alliterative (*King Horn*, late in the century, has sometimes been claimed as an exception, but without good reason). Definite forms emerge: the two great kinds of octosyllabic couplet—more strictly *syllabic* (*Owl and Nightingale*), or less so (*Genesis and Exodus*); the fifteener-fourteener or seven-foot iambic (*Robert of Gloucester*); the *rime couée* or "Romance-six" (*Proverbs of Hendyng*). Of pure alliterative verse there is no trace whatever.

IV. Earlier Fourteenth Century

Central Period of Middle English.

The metrical development attains complete predominance in the *Romances* (chiefly octosyllabic couplet or "Romance-six"), and in lyrics such as those of the Harleian MS. 2253. In both there is considerable *equivalence*, or substitution of trisyllabic (and perhaps also monosyllabic) for dissyllabic feet. The fourteener begins to break itself down into the ballad measure of eight and six, with or without full alternate rhyme. Decasyllabic couplet appears (as it had done even earlier) sporadically. But at an uncertain time—probably about the second third of the century—alliteration again makes its appearance, sometimes alone (*William of Palerne*), sometimes in company with some rhyme-arrangement (*Sir Gawain and the Green Knight*); and the two methods continue side by side (though with the alliteration always in the minority and seldom quite pure) for the best part of two hundred years, till well within the sixteenth century itself.

V. Later Fourteenth Century

Crowning Period of Middle English.

The tendencies already indicated, and shown after 1350 by Laurence Minot, the writers in the Vernon MS., and others, culminate in three remarkable poets—Langland, Gower, and Chaucer. The first, who is probably the oldest (though the most probable theory of his work puts it in stages from the sixth or seventh to the last decade of the century), eschews rhyme altogether, and (as far as he can, but not entirely) declines metrical form —preferring a modernised Old English line, strongly middle-paused, and regularly, but not lavishly, alliterated. Gower, with a little rhyme-royal, employs elsewhere, throughout his voluminous English work, octosyllabic couplet, nearer to the French or strictly syllabic norm than that of any other Middle English writer, though with some tell-tale approaches to variety. Chaucer, between the two, represents the true development of English prosody proper. He practises, from the (disputed) *Romaunt of the Rose*, to the (certain) *House of Fame*, the octosyllabic couplet; varies it remarkably and consciously; and gets from it effects excellent in their way, but never, apparently, quite satisfactory to himself. He adopts or imitates from the French, besides minor forms, the great rhyme-royal or *Troilus* stanza. He has, in his prose, curious "shadows before" of blank verse. But his greatest metrical achievement is the taking up—whether wholly from French or with some consciousness of earlier sporadic attempts in English is disputed, but certainly in the perhaps unconscious line of those attempts—the decasyllabic or heroic couplet, which is first the sole vehicle of his *Legend of Good Women*, and secondly the main vehicle of *The Canterbury Tales*.

VI. Fifteenth and Early Sixteenth Centuries

The Decadence of Middle English Prosody.

The prosodic accomplishment of Chaucer, while representing all that Middle English was capable of attaining, represented more than it was capable of maintaining.   His followers in Middle Scots, employing not the actual vernacular, but a " made " literary language, carried out his lessons for some time with great success.   But those in Southern English appear to have—except in more or less pure folk-poems—succumbed partly to influences of change in pronunciation (which are very imperfectly understood, though the disuse of the final valued *e* is the certain and central fact), partly to a loss of understanding (which is still more obscure in its nature and causes) of the metres themselves.   From Lydgate to Hawes, rhyme-royal most of all, decasyllabic couplet (not so often tried) hardly less, and octosyllabic to a somewhat minor degree, exhibit the most painful irregularity, clumsiness, and prosaic effect, there being sometimes no regular rhythm, and nothing at all but the rhyme to give a poetical character to the composition.   The "doggerel" of Skelton is a pretty obvious attempt to escape from this.   Only ballad, carol, and the like seem to escape the curse.

VII. Mid-Sixteenth Century

The Recovery of Rhythm.

In the second quarter of the sixteenth century attention seems to have been drawn to the " staggering state " of prosody; by the end of that quarter, or a very little later, we know from positive evidence that it was theoretically felt. But much earlier Sir Thomas Wyatt, and, in his tracks, Henry Howard, Lord Surrey, expressed the fact practically by their imitations of Italian forms.   Both tried the sonnet ; Wyatt attempted, with little success, *terza rima* ; and Surrey, with more, tried blank verse. The regular quantification or accentuation necessary for the reproduction of these forms evidently gave them (and Wyatt more particularly and naturally, as the pioneer) a great deal of trouble ; but they managed it—if not universally or perfectly—somehow ; and they kept the practice up in lyric measures less strictly imitated. They also popularised—if they did not introduce —a new combination-variation of the old long lines into the so-called "poulter's measure" or couplet of twelve-fourteen syllables, easily breaking down into six, six, eight, six. Their example was followed by many poets between 1550 and 1580, iambic regularity establishing itself rather at the expense of poetic variety, but with an immense gain to the ear. A very important, though not in itself very poetical, development was also made in the regular anapæstics of Tusser ; and the drama, taking up at last Surrey's blank verse, in the meantime experimented with all sorts of forms, regular and doggerel.

VIII. Late Sixteenth Century

The Perfecting of Metre and of Poetical Diction.

This invaluable if not always very stimulating period of drill and discipline (in which Wyatt and Surrey themselves, with Sackville later, are the chief and almost the only poets who transcend experiment) passes, a little before 1580, into one of complete poetic and proportionately complete prosodic accomplishment, with Spenser and his companions and followers for non-dramatic poetry, with Peele and Marlowe preluding Shakespeare in dramatic blank verse. The greatest pioneer, one who not only explores but attains, is Spenser ; and he, after presenting in the *Shepherd's Calendar* the most remarkable record of experiment in the history of English poetic form, proceeds to the perfect structure and exquisite diction of the *Faerie Queene.* He, however, hardly touches blank verse, and, after the *Calendar*, eschews the lighter lyric. But both these are

taken up by others; and while lyric attains all but the
highest possible stage of that diversity in harmony which is
especially required by it, the possibilities of blank verse are
more than suggested in Shakespeare's predecessors, and are,
in the dramatic range, exhausted by Shakespeare himself.
Outside the drama, however, and blank verse, the abiding
fear of doggerel keeps back the due development of
regularised substitution : verse is mostly iambic. But here
also Shakespeare pierces the heart of the mystery, and the
songs in his plays are as prosodically complete as his blank
verse itself. There is much practice in sonnet, and, towards
the end of the century, "riding rhyme" or heroic couplet,
which had fallen into some disuse, is revived, chiefly for
satiric or semi-satiric purposes (as by Spenser in *Mother
Hubberd's Tale*, by Hall, Donne, and Marston in their
definite satires, etc., and for "history" by Drayton.

IX. EARLY SEVENTEENTH CENTURY

*The further Development of Lyric, Stanza, and Blank Verse.
Insurgence and Division of the Couplet.*

Between the latest years of the sixteenth and the
earliest of the seventeenth century there is naturally
little difference, but the total transformation is rather
rapid. Blank verse no sooner attains its absolute perfection in Shakespeare than it begins to show signs of
overripeness, in the great tendency to redundance which
even he shares in his latest plays, and which distinguishes
Beaumont and Fletcher. Stanza does not, after the
similar consummateness of Spenser, show a similar formal
decline; but there arises a distaste for it. Only lyric
perseveres in practically full flourishing ; and even exhibits
a certain further quintessence of beauty, though some loss
of strength. Meanwhile, the decasyllabic couplet revives
in a complicated fashion. It does not yet make much
recovery of drama, but is very largely practised by
Drayton, is declared (at least on Drummond's authority)

to be "the bravest sort of verse" by Jonson, and made, towards the end of James the First's reign, the subject of a formal critical-poetical encomium by Sir John Beaumont. But it is a house divided against itself, and it is not till the "stopped" form (in which the rhymes sharply punctuate the sense) conquers the "enjambed" (which in *this* sub-period is the favourite) that it attains complete popular favour.

X. MID-SEVENTEENTH CENTURY

Milton.

The period, or sub-period, which may be called "mid-seventeenth century," on one side continues the developments described in the last section, and on another begins those which will be described in the next. But it contains almost the whole work of Milton, who belongs in one sense to both, in another to neither. If he had written no blank verse, he would still be of the first rank as a practical prosodist, in virtue of his stanza-forms, such as that in the "Hymn on the Nativity"; of his remarkably varied octosyllabic couplet in *L'Allegro, Il Penseroso, Arcades,* and *Comus*; of the almost unique strophes, with irregular rhyme, in *Lycidas*; of the *Sonnets,* adjusted not to the Elizabethan-English, but to the commoner Italian forms; and of the peculiar choric arrangements of *Samson Agonistes.* But it is undoubtedly as the introducer of blank verse for general poetic practice, and as the modulator of that verse in the directions previously described, that he stands as one of the very greatest masters of English prosody. For, on the one hand, he rescues "blanks" from the chaos into which, by the laches of the dramatists, they were falling; and, on the other, he establishes for ever (though it may sometimes be mistaken by individuals and periods) the principle of foot-equivalence and substitution in the individual line, with that of combination of several lines into a verse-paragraph.

XI. THE LATER SEVENTEENTH CENTURY

Dryden.

For the moment, however, the work of Milton produces no effect, and though Dryden, his younger contemporary, uses, with great effect, a large variety of metres, his main importance, in the general history of prosody, consists in the establishment of the stopped heroic couplet as at once the most popular and the most dignified of English metres. But he does not at once make it into the strictly decasyllabic, strictly middle-paused kind which dominates the following century. On the initiation (partly at least) of Cowley, he varies it with the Alexandrine, which he sometimes includes in a triplet, while the same extension to three similarly rhymed lines, in decasyllable only, is still more frequent. He does not exactly introduce, but popularises and for a time maintains, the same couplet in drama, but uses it most successfully in satiric and didactic verse, of extraordinary weight and vigour, while entirely destitute of monotony. He himself and his minor but more lyrical contemporaries, Rochester, Sedley, Afra Behn, etc., continue the older Caroline tradition of song in varied measures, but it dies out. On the other hand, his practice (suggested, doubtless, by Davenant's *Gondibert*) of the decasyllabic quatrain, and the majestic if not fully Pindaric strophes of his *Odes*, supply models which serve to vary the unbroken prevalence of the couplet, and are followed by Gray and others, during the succeeding century, with exceptionally fine results.

XII. THE EIGHTEENTH CENTURY

The summary of the history of eighteenth-century prosody has been foreshadowed in the above lines. Addison, Garth, and others follow Dryden; and Pope further "corrects" him in a couplet which becomes polished to the extreme, but, when handled without almost supreme genius, is distinctly monotonous.   And this couplet, with almost complete and definite acceptance by theorists and little overt protest on the part of practitioners, assumes the position of premier metre in English for long poems, continuing to hold it throughout the hundred years. Lyric, too, confines itself to relatively few forms, chiefly iambic—the " common " and " long " measure, the Romance-six, the decasyllabic quatrain, the regular or irregular Pindaric ode.   There are, however, certain privileged exceptions to the uniformity.   Two poets not in their first youth at the beginning of the century—Prior and Swift—secure a position for the light octosyllable and for anapæstic measures; Gray and Collins raise the ode ; Thomson—preceded by one or two minor poets, and followed by a considerable number, some of whom are not so minor—takes up "the manner of Milton," that is to say, blank verse.   Even in the first half of the century Shenstone timidly pleads for trisyllabic substitution, while in the second half Chatterton and Blake boldly practise it ; and that study of old (and especially ballad) English verse, of which Percy's *Reliques* is the central example, slowly but surely leads the way to a restoration of its principles.

XIII. The Early Nineteenth Century and the Romantic Revival

In no department of poetic practice does the great Romantic revival, after forerunnings in Chatterton and Blake, show itself, in the latest years of the eighteenth century, and the earliest of the nineteenth, more perceptibly than in that of prosody.   Only one of its masters —Wordsworth—slights this revival in theory, while he is not of the first mark in practice.   But Coleridge, in *The Ancient Mariner* and *Christabel*, restores and perfects equivalence on a doubtful principle, but with consummate practical effect.   Southey, less effective practically, is both sounder and more original in theory; Scott takes up

Coleridge's example in all his verse-romances, and completely vindicates the freedom of lyric; Byron, affecting admiration of the couplet, achieves his own best work in Coleridge-Scott octosyllables, in Spenserians, in octaves, and in lyric; Shelley pushes the various and unfettered lyrical movement to its almost inconceivable farthest; and Keats revives (after Leigh Hunt) the enjambed couplet in decasyllable, recovers an octosyllabic form unknown since Gower and only partially utilised by him, writes exquisite Spenserians and beautiful octaves, comes perhaps nearest Milton in blank verse and nearest Dryden in the other kind of couplet, and achieves forms of ode, classical and Romantic, of astonishing flexibility and charm. By and in these, and in many minors from Moore downwards, the freedom of prosody, and the great instrument of that freedom, the equivalenced foot, are championed and practised with almost all the variety possible.

XIV. The Later Nineteenth Century

The process of varying and extending the forms of prosody, by the special instrument above noticed and others, and under the direction of a general effort to give those forms a wider visual and audible appeal to the mind's senses, continues in the two later groups or stages—of which the chief representatives are, in the first case, Tennyson and Browning; in the second, Mr. Swinburne, the Rossettis, and William Morris—with constant recovery or fresh invention of prosodic effect.

It is on the continuity of this history that the student should keep his eye. Looked at partially, it may seem to lack this continuity; looked at as a whole, it will be seen to exhibit exactly the alternate or successive predominance of different tendencies and developments in which all healthy life-history consists. No partial and inconsecutive explanations as to widely differing pronunciation of vowels at different times, none of "quantity" having the prefer-

ence at one time and "accent" at another, or of certain
feet inclining to these things respectively, are necessary, or
should be entertained.   The birth, progress, and perfecting
of the foot under the guidance of equivalent substitution,
now vividly present, now apparently in abeyance, but
always potentially existing—this is "the mystery of this
wonderful history," the open secret of English prosodic life.

BOOK III

HISTORICAL SURVEY OF VIEWS ON PROSODY

CHAPTER I

BEFORE 1700

IN hardly any language are studious investigations into the form of verse likely to be early, and in a language with such a history as English they could not possibly be so. We have indeed, from the early fourteenth century, some remarks of Robert of Brunne on kinds of verse—"cowee" (Romance-six), "baston,"[1] "enterlace" (pretty obvious), etc., but with no explanation or discussion ; and Chaucer himself (who, in this respect as in others, is slavishly followed by Lydgate[2]) makes apologies for roughness and inexperience.[3] In Gower (*Conf. Am.* iv. 2414) there is a reference, but after Chaucer and not yet quite satisfactorily explained, to the difference between "rhyme" and "cadence," while in the Scottish chronicler Wyntoun there is another reference[4] to "cadence." Again, in Chaucer we have the Parson's famous disclaimer of indulgence in "rum ram ruf," because the speaker is "a Southern man." But not one of these things makes the slightest pretence to be even a prosodic discussion, let alone a prosodic treatise ; and it is

Dearth of early prosodic studies.

---

[1] Perhaps general for a stanza. Certainly used in one case for a six-lined one of four longer lines and two shorter.

[2] In his *Troy Book* he says that, "as tho" [at that time] he "set aside truth of metre," "had no guide in that art," and "took no heed of short and long."

[3] *House of Fame*, Book III., where he disclaims intention to "shew art poetical," speaks of his "rhyme" as "light and *lewed*" [unlearned], admits that "some verses" may "fail in a syllable," and precedes (possibly patterning) Gower in distinguishing "rhyme" and "cadence."

[4] He says that the substitution of "Procurator" for "Emperor" "had mair grievèd the *cadence* Than had relievèd the sentence [meaning]."

233

not till towards the end of the third quarter of the sixteenth century—when a whole generation had already followed Wyatt in endeavouring to effect, in practice, the reform of the prosodic breakdown from Lydgate to Hawes, if not even to Barclay—that the first English prosodic treatise appears in the shape of Gascoigne's *Notes of Instruction* (1572-75). They had been a little anticipated in time by remarks of Ascham's, and perhaps of others, on a new fashion of classical "versing," on which more presently ; but this, though essentially prosodic in character, had not yet formed the subject of a regular treatise, and its exponents implicitly or expressly declined all meddling with "beggarly rhyme," *i.e.* with the form of English poetry proper.

Gascoigne.

Gascoigne's little book [1] is very short, very practical, very sensible, and—except in one unlucky remark, which (or rather the misunderstanding of it) has done harm to the present day—in the main, perfectly sound. He dwells on the importance of accent and of the observation of it ; and he was quite right, for even Wyatt had been very loose in this respect, and the desire to get out of the doggerel of the fifteenth century [2] had led novices in precision to strain the accent, in order that they might keep the quantity. But he insists also—and with more than a century of awful examples to justify him if he had cared to use them—on "keeping metre"—on not wandering from lines of one length or character to those of another as the rhyme-royalists of the preceding century constantly do. He gives rules for the pause, leaving rhyme-royal itself free in that respect. He mentions especially, besides rhyme-royal, "riding rhyme" (Chaucerian couplet), "poulter's measure " (the alternate Alexandrine and fourteener), and octosyllables. He deprecates poetic commonplaces ("cherry lips" and the like), and gives some positive

---

[1] For editions, etc., of this and other books named and discussed in this survey, see Bibliography.

[2] The passage referred to above (p. 166) as illustrating this, in the *Mirror for Magistrates* (ed. Haslewood, ii. 394, and see *Hist. Pros.* ii. 188), is anterior to Gascoigne.

rules for pronunciation ("Heav'n" is to be always mono-syllabic).

The excepted unlucky point is his remark that "com-monly nowadays in English rhymes we use no other than a foot of two syllables, whereof the first is depressed and made short, and the second elevated or made long." He says that "we have used in times past other kinds of metres," giving as example the anapæstic line— His remark on feet.

> No wight | in this world | that wealth | can attain ; [1]

laments the restriction to iambs, and shows a remarkable appreciation of Chaucer's "liberty that the Latinists do use," *i.e.* equivalent substitution, though he may not have quite correctly understood this.

The desire for order and regularity in all this is very noticeable, and perfectly intelligible to any one who has appreciated (see last Book) the hopeless breakdown, due to the neglect of these qualities, in English prosody between 1400 and 1530. Gascoigne's statement about the iamb is, moreover, true of the majority of his own contemporaries, though it overlooks such a writer as Tusser. But it would be a grievous mistake (and unfortunately it has often been committed) to accept this not quite accurate declaration of ephemeral fact, accompanied as it is, more especially, by another expression of regret for that fact—as a rule and principle governing Elizabethan and English poetry.

Gascoigne's little treatise was followed at no great intervals, but after his own death, by more elaborate dealings with the subject—some of them exclusively or mainly devoted to the new craze for classical metres, others treating the subject at large and merely referring to the "versing" attempts. The order of these compositions, with a very brief sketch of their contents, may now be given.

---

[1] Observe that this *might* be scanned

> No wight | in this | world that | wealth can | attain.

But then it would not be "another kind of metre." The remark is not without bearing on the suggested possibility of Spenser's "February" being mistaken heroic.

Spenser and Harvey.

In the winter of 1579-80, the date of the appearance of the *Shepherd's Calendar*, Spenser and his pragmatical friend Gabriel Harvey exchanged certain letters (which we have) dealing with the " versing " attempt that Spenser himself makes. An experiment in quantified trimeter refers to "rules" on the subject made by a Cambridge man named Drant, but does not (unfortunately) give them, and asks for Harvey's own. Harvey blows rather hot and cold on the matter, approving the system, but criticising the details.

Stanyhurst.

Next, in 1582, came the *Preface* to Richard Stanyhurst's translation of the *Aeneid*, a book famous for the strange language in which it is written, but, as far as its Preface is concerned, a very sober and scientific attempt to do an impossible thing. Stanyhurst endeavours to arrange a set of rules for determining the quantity of every syllable in English, *not* necessarily according to its Latin or other derivation, but on principles germane to the language itself. He does not and cannot succeed ; but his attempt is interesting, and rather less contrary to facts than some recent attempts of the same kind.

Webbe.

He was followed, in 1586, by William Webbe, whose *Discourse of English Poetry* is notable for the enthusiasm displayed by the author towards Spenser (the *Shepherd's Calendar* had appeared some years previously) ; for his curiously combined enthusiasm as regards the classical metres which Spenser had tried and dropped ; for the first *published* sketch of the history of English poetry (erroneous, but interesting) ; and for a certain number of desultory remarks on prosodic subjects, mostly brought round to the classical fancy, though showing the interest which these questions were exciting. But between Stanyhurst and Webbe one book of the kind had appeared, and another had been perhaps composed, though not printed, in the

King James VI.

same year—1584. The first was King James the Sixth of Scotland's *Rewlis and Cautelis* for the making of verse in his native dialect. Obligation has been traced in it to Gascoigne and to the great French poet Ronsard. It is very clear and precise, but of no wide interest, being simply an analysis of recent actual Scots verse with some peculiarities of terminology. It is our first methodical book of prosody, and some of its titles, such as " cuttit and broken " verse for the metres of very irregular line-length which were growing so fashionable, and which were to excite the displeasure of the eighteenth century, are distinctly useful. Not so perhaps another—" tumbling verse "—which is of uncertain application to alliterative-anapæstic or to mere doggerel rhythm—which has complicated the question of "cadence" (*v. sup.*), (of this it has been, perhaps correctly, thought to have been intended as an English translation), and which was adopted rather arbitrarily by Guest (*v. inf.*).

The other book, written in or before 1584, though not published till 1589, was the most elaborate treatment of English prosody yet attempted, and continued to be so until Mitford's treatise (*v. inf.*) nearly two hundred years later. The *Art of English Poesy*, as it not too arrogantly called itself, has no certain author, but has been by turns attributed to two brothers, George and Richard Puttenham. It is, in the original, a treatise of some 257 well-filled pages. About half of these is indeed occupied by an immense list of the fancifully devised " Figures of Speech " which the Greek rhetoricians had excogitated, and which apply (in so far as they have any real application at all) not more to poetry than to prose. But the First Book contains an elaborate discussion or defence of poetry generally, ending with a sketch of English poets, probably, if not certainly, written earlier than Webbe's. And the Second is a very full and formal handling of the formal part of poetry, the discussion being carried so far as to include those artificial figures in squares, lozenges, altars, wings, etc., which more than one age fancied, but which, in English, hardly survived the satire of Addison. Puttenham, however, takes great pains to point out the exact form of different regular stanzas ; arranges line-lengths ; dwells on rhyme, pause, accent, and other matters of importance ; considers the classical "versing" (though he does not like it) ; and, in short, treats the whole

Putten-ham (?)

subject, as far as his lights and opportunities permit, in a really business-like manner. It was somewhat unfortunate that he came a little too soon, neither the *Faerie Queene* nor probably any of the greatest plays of the "University Wits" having appeared at the time he wrote—nothing, in short, of the best time and kind but the *Shepherd's Calendar*.

The later years of the sixteenth century were less fruitful in regular prosodic discussion, though the old wrangle about "versing"[1] continued at intervals between Harvey and Nash, and some scattered observations on prosody exist, by Drayton and others. But in the earliest years of the seventeenth the first-named dispute, after hanging about for more than half a century since Ascham's day, was laid to rest, for the time and (except in scattered touches) for

Campion and Daniel. nearly two centuries afterwards, by the poet Thomas Campion's tractate on certain new forms of verse (not hexameters) devised by himself, and the reply of another poet, Samuel Daniel, in his *Defence of Rhyme*. Campion, an exquisite master of natural rhymed verse, did not wholly fail with his artificial creations of " English elegiacs," " English anacreontics," etc.— metres based mainly on iambs and trochees, though with some trisyllabic feet grudgingly allowed. He not merely does not support the dactylic hexameter, but pronounces against it ; and his main objection seems to lie against rhyme. He also, like Stanyhurst, attempts a scheme of English quantity, though he admits the abundance of " common " syllables with us. Daniel in his answer confined himself to generalities, but with the most triumphant effect—basing his defence of rhyme on " Custom and Nature "; alleging the omnipotence of delight which is unquestionably given by and received from rhyme ; and asking why, when in polity, religion, etc., we notoriously and profoundly differ from the Greeks and Latins, we are to imitate them in verse ? He points out, again with absolute truth, that Campion's own versification is mostly or wholly nothing but old forms stripped of rhyme,

---

[1] At this time the technical phrase for classical-quantitative versification without rhyme.

and urges the hopelessness of adjusting, even on the reformer's own system, English quantity to classical. With this the thing became, and was long wisely allowed to be, *res judicata.*

In a sense this little book, or rather pamphlet, may be said to conclude the first batch or period of prosodic study in English. For the whole of the seventeenth century after it, though one of the most important practically in the entire history, sees very little theoretical discussion. Ben Jonson had, we are told, written a treatise against both Campion and Daniel, especially the last, praising couplets "to be the bravest sort of verses, especially when they are broken like hexameters," and against "cross-rhymes and stanzas." But we have not his own authority for this, which is only reported by Drummond, and the exact interpretation to be put upon "broken like hexameters" is absolutely uncertain. The surfeit of stanza [1] is, however, an obvious fact, and is borne witness to by Drayton, in the remarks above referred to, and by others— things culminating in the verse precepts of Sir John Beaumont (*v. sup.*) recommending the stopped distich in a form which is almost eighteenth century. Had Jonson finished his *English Grammar* and given the prosodic section which he promised, we should know more. As it is, there is nothing of importance before the Restoration except the *English Parnassus* of Joshua Poole, published posthumously, with a remarkable Preface signed "J. D.," which in point of time might be—but which there is not the slightest reason except date and initials to suppose to be—Dryden's. This Introduction is partly historical and not ignorant, while the author shows good sense and taste by objecting to "wrenched" rhymes ("náture" and "endùre"), to the habit of "apostrophation" or cutting out syllables supposed to be extra-metrical, and substituting apostrophes,[2] which

[margin notes:] Ben Jonson, Drayton, Beaumont.

Joshua Poole and "J. D."

---

[1] Which, let it be remembered, had dominated English poetry, in rhyme-royal, for nearly two centuries from Chaucer to Sackville, and then in the Spenserian, the octave, and others, for three-quarters of a century more. These surfeits always recur, though the octosyllabic couplet has suffered least from them.   [2] "Wat'ry," "prosp'rous," and even "vi'let."

was infesting the printing of the day, and was, to the great corroboration of prosodic heresies, not got rid of for a century and a half. He dislikes, too, the heavily over-lapped verses then prevalent.

Milton.   Milton, inferior to no English poet in his practical importance as a master of prosody, and perhaps superior to all except Shakespeare, has nothing about it in the pre-ceptist way, except his rather petulant outbreak against rhyme [1] in the advertisement to *Paradise Lost* (an outbreak largely neutralised by his own practice, not only earlier, but later), and the reference to "committing short and **Dryden.** long" in Sonnet XIII.[2]   And Dryden almost repeats the tantalising conditions of Jonson's attitude to the subject. He tells us that he actually had in preparation a treatise on it; but nothing more has ever been heard of this, and, large as is the amount of his work in literary criticism, his references to this part of it are few and are mostly vague.   He does indeed tell us that no vowel can be cut off before another when we cannot sink the pronunciation of it, and if this observation be extended to elision generally it is important.   But, on the whole, the most significant passages on prosody of the later seventeenth century are the work of a more obscure writer, Samuel **Woodford.** Woodford, in his Prefaces to Paraphrases of the *Psalms* (1667) and the *Canticles* (1678).   Here criticising, as no one else did, Milton from the prosodic point of view soon after date, he recognises and defends trisyllabic feet, but is dis-inclined to blank verse, regarding (and actually arranging)

---

[1] As "the invention of a barbarous age to set off wretched matter and lame metre," "a barbarous and modern bondage," contrasting with "apt numbers, fit quantity of syllables, and the sense variously drawn out from one verse to another."

[2] This phrase, which has been treated as enigmatic, is quite clear in the context, addressed to Lawes the musician as one

> Whose tuneful and well-measured song
> First taught our English music how to span
> Words with just note and accent, not to scan
> With Midas' ears, committing short and long.

That is to say, Lawes was not guilty, as most composers notoriously are, of laying musical stress on a syllable that could not prosodically bear it.

it as rhythmed prose.   The references of Lord Roscommon
and one or two others in verse, as well as of critics of
shadowy notoriety like Rymer and Dennis in prose, are
mostly trivial.

In this first division of English prosodists there is Comparative
observable a want of thoroughness—at first sight perhaps barrenness
strange, but easily explicable—which makes most of their of the whole.
work little more than a curiosity.   The only book which
attempts to grapple somewhat methodically with the whole
subject—that attributed to Puttenham—labours under two
fatal disadvantages.   The first is that the writer has a
most imperfect knowledge, or rather an almost unmixed
ignorance, of what has come before him ; and the second
is that he naturally cannot know what will come after
him, while what actually did come immediately after him
happens to be one of the greatest bodies, in bulk and merit
and variety, of English poetry.   The two most gifted persons
who think of treating it, Jonson and Dryden, do not actually
do so ; and it may be more than doubted whether, had
they done so, ignorance of the past would not still have
stood in their way.   It is true that Dryden's *obiter dictum*,
that you must not elide what you must pronounce, is a
sort of ark of salvation which carries all the elements of a
sound prosody in it.   But it is not certain that the writer
quite saw its full bearing, and that bearing was certainly not
seen by others.   On the other hand, Gascoigne's innocent
but unlucky remark about the single two-syllabled foot
expresses an opinion which, though wholly erroneous,
undoubtedly did prevail very widely throughout the whole
period.   The evidence of its falsity was indeed constantly
accumulating in blank verse during the first half of the
seventeenth century, in definite trisyllabic metres during
the second.   But this evidence was ignored or disobligingly
received; and when, at the very beginning of the eighteenth,
Bysshe once more attempted formulation of prosodic
orthodoxy, he arranged a code which, as long as it was
observed, half maimed the sinews and half throttled the
song of English poetry.

CHAPTER II

FROM BYSSHE TO GUEST

Bysshe's *Art of Poetry.* IN 1702, just after the beginning of the new century, there appeared a book which, though it received little directly critical notice, and was spoken of with disapproval by some who did notice it, was repeatedly reprinted, and which expressed, beyond all reasonable doubt, ideas prevalent largely for a century or more before it, and almost universally for a century or more after it. This was the *Art of Poetry* of Edward Bysshe. The bulk of it is composed of dictionaries of rhyme, etc. But a brief Introduction puts with equal conciseness and clearness the following views on English prosody.

"The structure of our verses, whether blank or in rhyme, consists in a certain number of syllables; not in feet composed of long and short syllables." He works this out carefully—explaining that verses of double rhyme will always want one more syllable than verses of single; decasyllables becoming hendecasyllables, verses of eight syllables turning to nine, verses of seven to eight. "This must also be observed in blank verse." Then of the several sorts of verses. Our poetry, he thinks, admits, for the most part, of but three verses—those of ten, eight, or seven syllables. Those of four, six, nine, eleven, twelve, and fourteen are generally employed in masques and operas and in the stanzas of lyric and Pindaric odes. We have few entire poems composed in them; though twelve and fourteen may be inserted in other measures and even "carry a peculiar grace with them." In deca-

syllabic verse two things are to be considered—the seat
of the accent and the pause. The pause ought to be
at the fourth, fifth, or sixth syllable. The strongest
accent must be on the second, fourth, and sixth. But he
says nothing about accent in the last four places; indeed he
is less explicit about the second half of the line throughout.
And he says less about accent generally than about pause,
though he is sure that "wrong placing" of it is as great
a fault in English as a false quantity was in the classical
languages. To make a good decasyllable you must be
careful that the accent is neither on the third nor on the
fifth—a curious crab-like way of approaching the subject,
but bringing out in strong relief the main principle of all
this legislation, "Thou shalt not." The verse of *seven*
syllables, however, is most beautiful when the strongest
accent *is* on the third.

More curious still is his way of approaching trisyllabic
metres. As such, he will not so much as speak of them.
"Verses of nine and eleven syllables," it seems, "are of
two sorts." "Those accented on the last save one" are
merely the redundant eights and tens already spoken of.
"The other [class] is those that are accented on the last
syllable, which are employed only in compositions for
music, and in the lowest sort of burlesque poetry, the
disagreeableness of their measure having wholly excluded
them from grave and serious subjects." These are neither
more nor less than anapæstic three- and four-foot verses;
though for some extraordinary reason Bysshe does not
even mention the full twelve-syllable form under any head
whatever. I suppose the "lowness and disagreeableness"
of the thing was too much for him, and as he had dis-
allowed feet he had, at any rate, some logical excuse in
making nothing of them. He admits triplets in heroic,
and repeats his admission of Alexandrines and fourteeners.
"The verses of four or six syllables have nothing worth
observing," though he condescends to give some from
Dryden.

Under the head of "Rules conducing to the beauty

of our versification," and with the exordium, "Our poetry being very much polished and refined since the days of Chaucer, Spenser, and other ancient poets," we find that you must avoid hiatus; *always* cut off the *e* of "the" before a vowel; never allow such collocations as "thy *i*ambics" or "into *a* book"; never value such syllables as "amazèd" and "lovèd," but always contract them; avoid alliteration; never split adjective from substantive, or preposition from verb, at the end of a line. "Beauteous" is but two syllables, "victorious" but three. You must not make "riot" one syllable as Milton does.[1] You *may* contract "vi'let" and "di'mond," and if you do, should write them so. "Temp'rance," "diff'rent," etc., are all right; and you may use "fab'lous" and "mar'ner." But Bysshe acknowledges that "this is not so frequent." And he rejects or doubts some of the more violent and most hideous apostrophations, such as, "b'" for "by," but has no doubt about "t' amaze," "I'm," "they've," and most others. Rhyme is not very fully dealt with, but for the most part correctly enough—so far as Bysshe's principles go. Stanzas of "intermixed rhyme" (like rhyme-royal, the octave, and the Spenserian) "are now wholly laid aside," for long poems at least. Shakespeare invented blank verse to escape "the tiresome constraint of rhyme." Acrostics and anagrams "deserve not to be mentioned."

Its importance. If any one has read this account carefully he will perceive at once what Bysshe's ideals and standards are. They put the strict decasyllabic couplet, with no substitution, no overrunning of lines, a fixed middle pause, and as nearly as possible an unvaried iambic cadence, into the principal place—if not quite the sole place of honour—in English poetry. They frown upon stanzas, upon varied metres of any kind, and even upon unvaried anapæstic or "triple" measures. Strict syllabic scansion, with a consideration of accent, is the only process allowed; and even Dryden, just dead, and still regarded as the greatest

[1] Of course Milton does *not*.

of English poets, is directly though gently reproached for too great variety and laxity, as well as indirectly blamed for using "low" and "disagreeable" forms. The author seems to have been a very obscure person, of whom little or nothing is known; but any one who really knows English poetry will see that he practically expresses the mind that dominated it during almost the whole of the eighteenth century.

Either from Bysshe's starting the question; or from the same general influence which made him start it; or from the supposed tendency, not to be too hastily accepted, of a lull in creative poetry to be followed by an access of criticism—there is, from this time onward, no lack of prosodic work. John Brightland, in an *English Grammar* (1711), opposed Bysshe on the subject of accent; and he was also spoken of disparagingly by Charles Gildon, who produced two books, *The Complete Art of Poetry* (1718) and the *Laws of Poetry* (1721). Gildon was a pert and rather superficial writer who deservedly came under the lash of Pope; and, though neither quite ignorant nor quite stupid, he initiated a course of error which has never yet been stopped, by confusing prosody with music and arranging it by musical signs. Between Bysshe and his two critics Dr. Watts had, in the preface to his *Horae Lyricae*, given some prosodic remarks indicating discontent with the monotony of the couplet, an appreciation (not unmixed with criticism) of Milton, and other good things. But, before long, the question whether Accent or Quantity governs English verse — often complicated with the attempt to interpret this latter by musical notation— absorbed an altogether disproportionate amount of attention. The works of Pemberton (1738), Mainwaring, Foster, Harris, Lord Kames, Webb, and Say (1744) must be consulted by exhaustive students of the subject, and will be found duly commented upon in the larger *History* by the present writer. But they hardly need detailed notice here, any more than the later lucubrations of Lord Monboddo, Tucker, Nares, Fogg, and others.

Minor prosodists of the mid-eighteenth century.

Their general tendency—which was indeed, as has been said, the general tendency of the century, correctly harbingered by Bysshe—was to concentrate attention on the heroic line, and indeed to regard it as strictly iambic, trisyllabic feet being wholly rejected, and even trochaic substitution either rejected likewise, as by Pemberton, or regarded as a more or less questionable licence. But the subject was also handled by persons of more literary importance, and in some cases, though not in all, of more insight and more knowledge.

Dr. Johnson.   The most remarkable exponent of the general prosodic ideas of the century is undoubtedly Dr. Samuel Johnson, who, though he wrote no special prosodic treatise, dealt with the subject in his *Dictionary*, in the *Rambler* (especially in connection with Milton), and in his *Lives of the Poets*. Except that Johnson does admit feet—or at least their names—his doctrine in the *Dictionary* hardly differs from Bysshe's as to the syllabic norm of lines, the strict regularity of accent constituting "harmony," and the duty of compounding superfluous syllables by elision, synalœpha, etc. He applies these doctrines in the *Lives*, and still more in his papers on Milton, Spenser, etc., in the *Rambler*. The spondees in Milton's lines—

Both stood,

Both turned,

and the trochees in his

Uncropped falls to the ground,

and in Cowley's

And the soft wings of peace cover him round,

are condemned as "inharmonious." He objects to Milton's "elisions"—that is to say, the devices necessary on his own system to avoid trisyllabic feet—and so to these feet themselves. He thinks the Spenserian stanza, *Lycidas*, and the end of *Comus* bad, because the lines and rhymes are not regularly arranged. In short, he is an unhesitating — and almost the greatest — believer in the sheer, alternately accented, middle - paused, syllabically

limited decasyllable; though, with perhaps inevitable in-
consistency, he does admit that, without variation of
accent, the series of sounds would be not only very
difficult but "tiresome and disgusting," while maintaining
at the same time stoutly that this variation "always injures
the harmony of the line considered by itself."

The inconveniences of this rigid system were not, how-   Shenstone.
ever, entirely unnoticed.   At an uncertain time, but probably between 1740 and his death, the poet William
Shenstone urged, in a posthumously published Essay, the
beauty of what he called "virtual dactyls"—that is to say,
words like "watery" and "tottering,"—distinctly arguing that
"it seems absurd to print them otherwise than at full length"
—the "otherwise" being the established practice, based
upon definite theory, of the century.   Johnson's friend the
elocutionist Sheridan, in his *Art of Reading* (1775), calls it   Sheridan.
absurd (as it certainly is) to regard "echoing" as metrically "ech'ing."   And, later, the poet Cowper, though
using ambiguous and irresolute terminology on the subject,
admits the "divine harmony" of Milton's "elisions"—by
which, he explains in the most self-contradictory way,
"the line is *lengthened*."   While much earlier, at the very
middle of the century, John Mason, a little-known dissent-   John Mason.
ing minister, who was, like Sheridan, a teacher of elocution, quoting and scanning the lines—

> And many an amorous, many a humorous lay,
> Which many a bard had chanted many a day,

observes that this, "though it increases the number of
syllables, sweetens the flow of the verse," "gives a sweetness
that is not ordinarily found in the common iambic verse."
It would be impossible to state more correctly or more
definitely the case for the equivalent substitutional trisyllabic foot in English.   But, as we shall see, it was to be
nearly two generations before considerable poets boldly
adopted (even then not always distinctly championing) the
idea, and an entire century, if not more, before the principle
was thoroughly accepted and understood.

Two deliberate prosodists, in two books published within a twelvemonth of each other, are memorable as (if not exactly starting) formulating, in a more elaborate way than had ever been done before, the one a mischievous and false, the other the only true method of dealing with prosody.   Joshua Steele, in his *Prosodia Rationalis* (1775),

Mitford. is not always wrong; and William Mitford is not by any means invariably right—in fact, he partly shares Steele's error.   But his *Harmony of English Verse* (1774) is even then to a great extent, and in its second edition, thirty years later, much more, occupied with a careful historical inquiry as to the actual successive forms of his subject from the earliest period.   At first he had not even Tyrwhitt's invaluable *Chaucer*—which appeared in the year after Steele's book—to guide him : later he availed himself of the great accessions to the study of Middle and Elizabethan English which the intervening generation had seen.   And so, though he believed too much in accent, and relied too much on the dangerous assistance of music, he frequently came right.   He has no doubt (as it is astonishing that an historical student should have any doubt) about trisyllabic feet ; he likes what he calls "aberration of accent," *i.e.* trochaic substitution ; and he shows the possession of a fineness and cultivation of ear not as yet noticeable in any English prosodist, by observing the presence of anapæstic rhythm in the revived alliterative verse of Langland.   Except the inadequate and perfunctory, as well as of necessity merely inchoate, sketches of Webbe and Puttenham, this was the first attempt really to take English poetry into consideration when studying English prosody ; and it had its reward.

Joshua
Steele.   On the otner hand, Steele, who has been followed by many other prosodists of the same school, entirely neglected the historical contents of his subject, approaching it absolutely *a priori*, deciding that it is essentially a matter of music, and basing his scansions on purely musical principles.   This led him to begin with an anacrusis

in every case, and so to invert the whole rhythm of the
line. He has been praised for his views on "time" in
the abstract, and may deserve the praise ; while he was
certainly right in regarding pause as an important metrical
constituent. But whatever merit there may be in his
principles from an abstract point of view, his concrete
practice is simply atrocious, and proves him to have had
absolutely no ear for English verse whatever. He makes
six feet or "cadences with proper rests," at least, and
sometimes more, in every heroic line, so that he would
scan one famous line thus—

O | happiness, | our | being's | end and | aim,

and he arranges the opening lines of *Paradise Lost* for
scansion thus—

Of | man's | first diso|bedience | and the | fruit of | that for- |
bidden | tree | whose | mortal | taste brought | death | into the |
world | and | all our | woe, | Sing, | Heavenly | Muse.

It must be perfectly evident to any one who will read
these examples, even to himself, but still more aloud, not
merely that they entirely destroy the actual cadence and
rhythm of the actual verses, but that they provide a
new doggerel which is absolutely inharmonious, unrhythmical, and contrary to every principle and quality
of English poetry. It would doubtless be possible to
accommodate them with a tune ; in fact, any one who
has ever looked at a "set" song will see how they correspond to it. But then any one who has ever looked at
a set song must, in a majority of cases, have been con-
vinced at once that musical arrangement has nothing
to do with prosodic.

It was inevitable that the "Romantic" movement— Historical
one of the principal causes and features of which was a and Romantic prosody.
demand for variety, while another was its disposition to
return to older modes—should be largely concerned with
prosody ; but, with some notable exceptions, this concern-
ment did not take the form of actual prosodic deliverances
or discussions. Gray, one of the chief precursors of the Gray.

movement, had projected a regular history of English
poetry, and has left invaluable notes under the general
head of *Metrum*—notes in which he goes back, deliberately
and directly, to Middle English, discovers therein the
origin and nature of the metre of Spenser's *February*, etc.,
and has very good remarks about others.   But it was not
till the stir of the revolutionary period that much more
was done, and even then more was done than said.   The

Taylor and Sayers. German explorations of William Taylor of Norwich induced
English writers to follow the German attempt at accentual
hexameters; and another of the Norwich group, Frank
Sayers, not merely wrote, but expounded and defended in
prose, rhymeless metres of a choric character; both being
—in part, if not mainly—revolts from the mechanical

Southey. His importance. heroic couplet.   Before the end of the century, long
before Coleridge published the explanatory note on
Christabel metre, and not improbably before he had even
thought of that note, Southey had not only used trisyllabic
equivalence in his *Ballads*, but had formally and independently defended it as such in a letter to his friend

Wordsworth. Wynn.[1]   Wordsworth says very little about metrical detail

---

[1] The passage is of importance and must be given :—

"And now . . . I proceed to the indictment of my ears.   If the
charge had come from Dapple it would not have surprised me.   One
may fancy him possessed of more than ordinary susceptibility of ear;
but for the irritability of yours, I cannot so satisfactorily account.   I
could heap authority on authority for using two very short syllables in
blank verse instead of one—*they take up only the time of one.*[1]   'Spirit'
in particular is repeatedly placed as a monosyllable in Milton; and some
of his ass-editors have attempted to print it as one, not feeling that the
rapid pronunciation of the two syllables does not lengthen the verse more
than the dilated sound of one.   The other line you quote is still less
objectionable, because the old ballad style requires ruggedness, *if this
line were rugged*; and secondly, because the line itself rattles over the
tongue as smoothly as a curricle upon down-turf :

$$- \; \cup \; \cup \quad - \; \cup \; \cup \; - \; \cup \; \cup$$

I have made candles of infant's fat.

This kind of cadence is repeatedly used in the *Old Woman* and in the
' Parody.'"[2]

The quantification, it should be observed, is original.

---

[1] Italics added.

[2] *Letters of Robert Southey*, ed. Warter (London, 1856), i. 69.

in his famous Preface to the second edition of the *Lyrical Ballads* and its successors—appearing to think, and indeed in one place asserting, that "harmony of numbers" comes of itself to a person who has other poetical qualifications.

His two just-mentioned friends, however, lodged, at a slightly later period, two of the most important preceptist documents of English prosody, though they were documents differing very widely in the extent and character of their importance. These were Coleridge's note on the *Coleridge.* metre of *Christabel*, and Southey's Preface to the *Vision of Judgment*. The latter is too long to give, and is written from a mistaken point of view; but it, and the much-ridiculed poem which it accompanied, undoubtedly restarted the practice of attempting to write English hexameters, which has been continued, with some intervals and some episodes, but at times most busily, ever since. The former must be given at length, and some comment made on it :—

"The metre of the *Christabel* is not, properly speaking, *Christabel,* irregular, though it may seem so from its being founded *its theory* on a new principle, namely, that of counting, in each line, *and its* *practice.* the accents, not the syllables. Though the latter may vary from seven to twelve, yet in each line the accents will be found to be only four. Nevertheless this occasional variation in number of syllables is not introduced wantonly, or for the mere ends of convenience, but in correspondence with some transition in the nature of the imagery or passion."

What *Christabel* metre really was has been expounded earlier, and its author's account of it is not a little surprising. When he called its principle "new" he must have forgotten—not exactly the Middle English writers, whom he very likely did not know, nor perhaps Gray, though the latter's remarks on Spenser's *February* were actually published before *Christabel*, but—Spenser himself and Chatterton (both of whom he certainly knew, if not Blake also), as well as the very ballad-writers whom he had himself imitated in the *Ancient Mariner*. His mention of "accents" and not "feet" argues an erroneous and inadequate theory which leaves much of the beauty of his own work unexplained ; while it can be shown from the text itself that the variation of syllables, though metrically beautiful, often does not correspond at all with any special point of sense, passion, imagery, or anything else. But his practice more than cured any wound which his theory may have inflicted.

Prosodists from 1800 to 1850. In comparison with Southey's and Coleridge's remarks, and still more with the practice of the latter in *Christabel* and the *Ancient Mariner*, the preceptist prosody of the extreme end of the eighteenth century, and the first third of the nineteenth becomes, except for exhaustive students of the subject, a mere curiosity, and not a very interesting one. Prosodic remarks, mostly erroneous or inadequate, found their way into popular handbooks, such as Walker's *Dictionary* (almost wholly wrong) and Lindley Murray's *Grammar* (partially right). The musical theories of Steele were taken up by others, such as Odell, Roe, and, above all, the republican lecturer Thelwall, who, escaping the consequences of his earlier extravagances, became a teacher of elocution. The new Reviews gave opportunity for occasional critical remarks on the subject—the most notable of which was the *Quarterly* review, by Croker, of Keats's *Endymion,*—usually embodying the cramped and ignorant doctrinairism of the preceding century. Southey's hexameters started a large amount of writing on that subject. In 1816 John Carey, compiler of the best-known Latin *Gradus* and author of many "cribs" and school editions, repeated most of the errors of Bysshe, but did grudgingly allow trisyllabic feet ; and in 1827 William Crowe, a minor poet and Public Orator at Oxford, wrote a treatise of *English Versification*—good in method, but bad in principle —condemning the adjustment of very short to longer lines, etc. Nothing of this period comes in importance near to that second edition of Mitford (1804, with most of the historical matter added) which has been noticed. But in 1838—after the appearance of Tennyson and

Browning, but when no public attention had been paid to them—appeared the most elaborate, ambitious, and, partly at least, valuable work that had yet been written on the subject—the *History of English Rhythms*, by Edwin Guest, then Fellow, afterwards Master, of Gonville and Caius College, Cambridge.   Guest took nearly two years between the publication of the first and second volumes of his book, and admittedly changed his opinions on some points, but his main theories are unmistakable.   He goes entirely by accent, denying metrical quantity in English altogether, and imposing curious arbitrary rules (such as that two adjoining syllables cannot be accented without a pause) on accent itself.   But he possessed an immense and truly admirable knowledge of English verse—Old, Middle, and Modern—up to his time ; and he lavished this, in a manner useful, indeed invaluable, to the present day, on the support of general theories which, unfortunately, are quite unsound.

For Guest seems to have conducted his work under the influences of three different obsessions, no one of which he ever worked out thoroughly in all its bearings, which do not necessarily imply each other, and two of which are even rather contradictory.

The first[1] was the belief that our verse is wholly dependent upon accent, and that "the principles of accentual rhythm," whatever they are, govern it exclusively.

The second[2] was that the laws of English versification generally are somehow not only dependent on those of *Old* English versification, but identical with them, and always to be adjusted to them.

The third[3] was that, somewhere about the early

---

[1] The evidence of this obsession is concentrated in Book I. chap. iv. pp. 74-101 ; but diffused over the entire treatise.

[2] This seems to have presented itself to him throughout as a matter of course, not requiring demonstration and hardly likely to be contested ; it is perhaps most categorically affirmed at Book II. chap. iii. p. 184.

[3] This also is pervading.   It "gathers itself up" most in the context just cited, and at pp. 301 and 400-402, the two last among the most surprising instances of complete misunderstanding of history by a real historical scholar.

Guest.

thirteenth century, and increasingly till the end of the fourteenth, there took place a succession of alien invasions which never resulted in a coalescence or blending, but merely in the presence of two hostile elements; and that while the perfect English versifier will cling to the older and only genuine one, he must, if he does not so cling, give it up altogether, and have nothing to do with anything but "the rhythm of the foreigner."

Now what has been already and will be later given in this book seems to show that these propositions are in fact false.

In the first place, though accent plays a large part in English prosody, that prosody is as far as possible from being purely or exclusively accentual.

In the second, the oldest English poetry and its younger varieties are so utterly different that the same laws cannot, except *per accidens*, apply to them.

In the third, instead of two jarring elements, we find before us, from the thirteenth century, at least, onwards, a more and more distinct and harmonious blend of language, resulting, of necessity, in a more and more distinct and harmonious blend of prosody.

But there is also a *fourth* principle, which he adds to, rather than deduces from, the other three:—

That the collocation of accented and unaccented syllables forms *sections*,[1] which in turn form, and into which can be reduced, all English verse.

On these principles he went through the whole body of English verse from Caedmon to Coleridge, arranging it with infinite trouble on the "sectional" system, and classifying the verses as those of "four accents," those of "five," and so on, with suitable distinctions for stanzas, etc. Unfortunately—to mention only the crowning and fatal fault which makes mention of all others in such a book as this unnecessary—he finds himself in perpetual

---

[1] Perhaps it should be said that a "section" is a bundle of "accented" and "unaccented" syllables extending in possible bulk from *three* syllables with *two* accents (Guest's minimum) to *eleven* syllables with *three* accents. Of a pair of these, similar or dissimilar, a verse consists.

conflict with the practice of the greatest English poets in
their most beautiful passages. Shakespeare and Milton go
"contrary to every principle of accentual rhythm," and
use devices which "they have no right" to use. Coleridge
and Burns employ sections which "have very little to
recommend them." Spenser's verse is "wanting in good
taste," and Byron's versification "has never been properly
censured." It may seem incredible that a writer of learning
and acuteness should not have seen the absurdity of his
position when he tells beautiful poetry—sometimes admitted
by himself as such—that it has no business to be beautiful
because it does not suit his rules. But the fact disposes
of him, and of the rules themselves, without its being
necessary—though it would be easy—to prove their want
of intrinsic justification.

CHAPTER III

LATER NINETEENTH-CENTURY PROSODISTS

Discussions on the *Evangeline* hexameter. THE amount of prosodic writing during the last seventy years has been very large. In the earliest and latest parts of the period it was principally devoted to the subject of English hexameters—in the first, in regard to the accentual attempts of Longfellow, to which *Evangeline* gave immense popularity ; in the last, to the counter-attempts at "quantitative" versification, in which the feet are constructed, not with reference to accent or to the way in which the words are ordinarily pronounced, but to independent and even opposed temporal value derived from the special sound attached to the vowel ("ĭdol," long ; "fïddle," short, etc.), or, on semi-classical principles, to what is called "position." To analyse the individual views of critics on these two bodies of questions would be here impossible, and reference must be made to the larger *History*, to Mr. Omond's treatises, or to the original works, the most important of which will be found duly entered in the Bibliography. But we may summarise results under three heads.

I. The "accentual" or *Evangeline* hexameter has, as has been said, been at times far from unpopular ; but it has always dissatisfied nicer ears by a certain *inappropriateness* which has been differently appraised, but which is evidently pointed at by the apology of its first extensive practitioner, Southey, that he could not get spondees enough, and had to be content with trochees. This inappropriateness has since been characterised by an un-

surpassed expert in theory and practice—Mr. Swinburne
—in the blunt assertion that to English "all dactylic and
spondaic forms of verse are unnatural and abhorrent."

II. On the other hand, the so-called quantitative verse
is repulsive to the same ears (unless, like Tennyson's
experiment, it is accommodated to ordinary pronunciation)
by the very fact that it sets that pronunciation expressly
at defiance, and makes sheer jargon of the language.

III. Considering these facts, some (among whom the
present writer is included) regard an apparent English
hexameter, such as that of Kingsley's *Andromeda*, and, still
more, that of certain verses of Mr. Swinburne himself, as
an admirable and glorious metre, but as not dactylic at
all—scanning it as a five-foot anapæstic with anacrusis
(odd syllable at the beginning) and hypercatalexis (ditto
at the end).[1]

Of more general prosodic inquiry some selection-
summary must be given. Guest's original work does not
seem to have produced much effect, save on specially
scholarly writers interested in the subject, like Archbishop
Trench ; though the reprint of it, forty years later, had,
as we shall see, a great deal of influence. Except on the
hexameter matter, there was little done between 1840 and
close upon 1870. It was, however, unfortunate that, at
the very opening of this time, Latham's *English Language*
embodied some very inadequate remarks on prosody,
including the symbol *xa* for an iamb, which has too much
permeated English text-books since. The works of Arch- Mid-century
deacon Evans and E. S. Dallas, both published in 1852, prosodists.
are important only to very thorough-going students. The
latter was acute, but fanciful and inclined to jargon. The
former, regarding stress as the only basis of modern
versification, indulged in a curious undervaluation of
English poetry generally : we must "forget all about
classical poetry to be satisfied with blank verse " ; English
lyric has been " under an evil genius, and always a blank " ;
and Shakespeare and Milton "gained exceedingly " by

---

[1] For examples of all these see Scanned Conspectus.

translation into Greek and Latin.   Any intelligent reader
can judge of such a tree by such fruits.

Of really earlier date than these (for their author died
in 1846) were Sidney Walker's remarks on *Shakespeare's
Versification*, posthumously published in 1854, which contain
some useful metrical observations.[1] Dallas's book produced
at least two important reviews, each of which extended
itself into a more important prosodic tractate.   The first
of these was by the late Professor Masson, who afterwards rearranged his prosodic ideas in a minute and very
scholarly study of Milton's versification, appearing in his
larger edition of the poet.   Professor Masson perhaps
admitted some unnecessary feet, such as the amphibrach,
but his views are on the whole extremely sound.   The
other essay was by Coventry Patmore—a poet, a man of
distinct originality in many ways, and a really learned
student of preceding prosodists—in fact, by far the most
learned up to his time.   This essay is full of suggestive
and ingenious notions, but exceedingly crotchety, and, for
persons not thoroughly grounded in the subject, unsafe.
It has the merit of recognising the division of verse into
what it calls, by a rather ponderous term, "isochronous
intervals" (that is to say, feet equivalent in time), and of
recognising, likewise, the important metrical as well as
rhetorical part played by pause.   But it exaggerates this
part in an impossible fashion, making a full pause-foot at the
end of every heroic line ; and its attention to "accent" is
also excessive and, in fact, inconsistent.

On the whole, however, it was not, as has been said,
till the very eve of 1870, when the Præ-Raphaelite school
had made its appearance, that any considerable amount
of prosodic writing came.   Then, and in the very same
year, 1869, there was a remarkable outburst, including *A
Complete Practical Guide to the Whole Subject of English
Versification* (by E. Wadham), which represents a modified

---

[1] Especially one which the student should apply for himself, that
Shakespeare's incomplete lines are mostly regular fractions of complete
ones, scanning correctly on the same system (*v. sup.* p. 130).

Bysshian system—believing in elision ; thinking trisyllabic feet bad, though they may exist, especially at the cæsura ; discountenancing both blank and anapæstic verse ; and applying to the whole subject a new terminology which has not been generally accepted.   Then came also a *Manual of English Prosody* by R. F. Brewer (reissued many years afterwards as *Orthometry*), which contains a very large amount of information on the details of the matter, but little appreciation of its more important aspects.   Much briefer, but, despite some errors, sounder on the whole, and giving no bad introduction to the subject, was the *Rules of Rhyme* of Tom Hood, son of the poet.   Greater influence than that of any of these has been exercised by the prosodic part of Dr. Abbott's *Shakespearian Grammar*, published in this year, and of his *English Lessons for English People*, issued (and partly written by J. R. Seeley) two years later. Unfortunately, not a few of the principles of these books are either demonstrably unsound or very doubtful, the worst of all being the insistence on "extra-metrical" syllables, or, in other words, the confession that English prosody cannot account for English poetry.   1869 also saw the beginning of a very important work, Mr. A. J. Ellis's *Early English Pronunciation*, which has had a great effect on some views of prosody, and contains a very elaborate scheme of syllabic values for quality and degree of force, weight, etc.

In 1874 Mr. John Addington Symonds, a critic, prose-writer, and even poet of no mean rank, published an essay, which he afterwards expanded into a tractate, on *Blank Verse*, denying that *any* preconceived metrical scheme will explain this, and arguing that each line must be treated separately according to its own sense.   More minute than any book since Guest's, and written with definite purpose to teach poets their business, was Mr. Gilbert Conway's *Treatise of Versification* (1878), which reverts to eighteenth-century theories, not merely of the scansion but of the pronunciation of words like "om*i*nous" and "del*i*cate" ; thinks Milton "capricious" and "inconsistent" ; and

Those about 1870,

proceeds entirely on the principle that the base and back-bone of English prosody is accent. Two years later Mr. Ruskin issued his *Elements of English Prosody*, employing musical notation, but using the names of feet very strangely applied. And a year later Mr. Shadworth Hodgson published a paper on "English Verse," perhaps not uninfluenced by Guest, and advocating (as several writers about his time began to do) "stress" systems of scansion, the stress being allotted according to various considerations of sense and otherwise. Another stress-man —still more influenced, though partly in the way of correction, by Guest—was the late Professor Fleeming Jenkin, who in 1883 wrote in the *Saturday Review* some papers, republished after his death, and advocating "sections," of which there may be as many as four in a normal heroic line, though this may, on the other hand, have as many as seven or even eight "beats" on strong syllables. Much sounder than any of these—indeed, on practical matters almost irreproachable—was Professor J. B. Mayor's *Chapters on English Metre* (1886), on which he founded later a *Handbook* of the subject (1903).

and since.   In the last twenty or thirty years there has been an increasing number of books on prosody, the names of the most important of which will be found in the Bibliography. The most important of all is perhaps Mr. Robert Bridges' *Prosody of Milton*, increased in subsequent editions to something like a manual of Stress Prosody, and containing material also for estimating the recent attempts, by Mr. Bridges himself and by the late Mr. W. J. Stone, to revive the writing of English hexameters on a quantitative, not an accentual, basis. There have also been many attempts (of which perhaps the most remarkable is a treatise on monopressures, taken up and applied by Professor Skeat) which would reduce prosody to a branch of medical physics or physiology, by basing it on the mechanical action of the glottis or larynx. And strong and repeated efforts have also been made to bring the subject entirely under the supervision of music—using musical notation, musical terms such as "bar," and the like. The most widely influential of these was the work of the American poet and critic Sidney Lanier; the most recent, that of Mr. William Thomson of Glasgow. On the other hand, the writings of Mr. Omond, though some doubt may be entertained as to details, have the merits of absolute soundness on the general principles of the subject, and may be studied with ever-increasing advantage.

These principles—general, and in relation to the Summary. methods of treatment more especially dealt with in the last paragraph or two—may be briefly summarised before this sketch of our prosodist history is closed. Systems of stress prosody are unsatisfactory, because the unstressed syllables of the line, and their connection or grouping with the stressed ones, are of quite as much importance to total effect as stresses themselves, and because attention to stress seems to beget the notion that regularity of time and time-interval is of no importance.[1]

Physiological-mechanical systems are altogether insufficient, even if not wrong, because they only refer to the raw material of prosody; because, in their nature, they must be applicable to verse and prose alike, and to all kinds of verse; with the additional disadvantage that, as actually explained by their advocates, they usually make verse-arrangements of the most inharmonious and unpoetical character.[2]

This latter objection applies with even greater force to the musical theorists, whose explanations of verse invariably confuse rhythm or overturn it altogether, while their whole system ignores the fact, that music and prosody are quite different things—that they may perhaps be accommodated

---

[1] Thus Mr. Bridges, though he himself does *not* neglect the unstressed, and even makes combination of the two kinds which are actually feet, would allow sometimes *four* and sometimes only *three* stresses in a heroic line. Later stress (or "stress-*cum*-music") prosodists have even proposed to recognise *two* "bars" only in such a line.

[2] Thus it has been proposed to scan a line of Goldsmith:

The sheltered | cot, | the culti|vated | farm.

in particular cases, but that this accommodation is by no means frequent.

In some cases, chiefly those of foreigners who have undertaken the study of English verse, return has been attempted to the rigid syllabic methods of Bysshe and his followers.   But it is usually admitted by these persons that the method does not suit nineteenth-century poetry, and they are open therefore to the fatal charge of having to suppress part, and a most important part, of the historical life of the subject.

On the other hand, the system of corresponding foot-division, with equivalence and substitution allowed, which has been followed in this book, is open to none of these objections.   It neither neglects nor suppresses any part of the line in any case, but accounts fully for all parts. It applies to poetry only, and, to a large extent at least, explains the difference between good poetry and bad.   It adjusts itself to the entire history of English verse, since the English language took the turn which made it English in the full sense.   It requires no metrical fictions, no suppression of syllables, no allowance of extra-metrical ones, no alteration in pronouncing, no conflict of accent and quantity.   No period or kind of English poetry is pronounced by it to be wrong, though it may allow that certain periods have exercised their rights and privileges more fully than others.   In short, it takes the poetry as it is, and has been for seven hundred years at least ; bars nothing ; carves, cuts, and corrects nothing ; begs no questions ; involves no make-believes ; but accepts the facts, and makes out of them what, and what only, the facts will bear.

BOOK IV

AUXILIARY APPARATUS

CHAPTER I

GLOSSARY

(THE miniature glossary which I prefixed to my larger *History* having been found useful, and indeed some complaints having been made that it was not fuller, I have determined to go to the other extreme here, with a special view to those readers who may be approaching the subject for the first time. Excepting words like "trisyllabic," etc., which can hardly be thought to require explanation, an attempt has been made to include almost every technical, and especially every disputed, term.)

ACCENT.—This term, which is perhaps the principal centre of dispute in matters prosodic, and which, even outside strict prosody, is not a little controversial, may be defined, as uncontroversially as possible, in the words of a highly respectable book of reference,[1] "A superior force of voice, or of articulative effort, upon some particular syllable." It is prosodically used as equivalent (with some slight differences) to "stress," and is regarded by a large— perhaps the most numerous—school as constituting the foundation-stone of English prosody. The inconveniences and insufficiencies of this view will be found constantly indicated throughout this book. On the question, almost more debated, what constitutes, and in different languages and times has constituted, accent itself—whether it is loudness, duration, "pitch," or what not of sound—no pronouncement has been or will be attempted in this volume.

[1] Webster's *Dictionary*.

ACEPHALOUS.—A term applied to a line in which the first syllable, according to its ordinary norm or form, is wanting, as in Chaucer's

⌃ Twen|ty bo|kès clad | in blak | or reed.

ACROSTIC.—An arrangement, not perhaps strictly prosodic, by which the initial syllables of the lines of a poem make words or names of themselves, as in Sir John Davies's *Astræa*, where these initials in every piece make " Elizabetha Regina." The process is now chiefly confined to light verse ; but there is nothing to be said against it, unless the sense is strained or perverted to get the letters.

ALCAIC.—A Greek lyrical measure, used by and named after the famous lyrical poet Alcæus, but most familiar in the slightly altered Latin form of Horace. Like all these forms, it is only a curiosity in English, and, even as such, has shared the endless and hopeless controversies as to accentual and quantitative metre. No one, however, is ever likely to get nearer to the real thing than Tennyson in

> Me rather all that bowery loneliness,
> The brooks of Eden mazily murmuring,
> And bloom profuse, and cedar arches,
> Charm as a wanderer out in Ocean.

The strict Horatian form (the last syllables being, as usual, common) is :

$$- - \cup - - - \cup \cup - \cup \cup$$
$$- - \cup - - - \cup \cup - \cup \cup$$
$$- - \cup - - - \cup - \cup$$
$$- \cup \cup - \cup \cup - \cup - \cup.$$

ALEXANDRINE.—A line of twelve syllables or six iambic feet. This measure (traditionally said to have taken its name from the Old French poem on Alexander) became the favourite metre for the *chansons de geste* or long narrative poems in that language, and then practically the staple of French verse to the present day. But though it is early traced—as a whole or as two halves—in English, it never established itself as a continuous metre with us. Only two pieces of importance, Drayton's *Polyolbion* and Browning's *Fifine at the Fair*, so employ it. On the other hand, it is constantly found scattered about early English verse ; appears—questionably according to some, unquestionably according to the present writer—in Chaucer ; was an ingredient in the "poulter's measure" (*v. inf.*), so popular with the poets of the second and third quarters of the sixteenth century; was used by Sidney continuously in sonnet ; forms, as a concluding line, the distinguishing feature of the great Spenserian stanza ; is very frequent in Shakespeare and the other Elizabethan dramatists; and was adopted by Dryden (though latterly, and then not quite always, rejected by Pope) as a relief and variation to the heroic couplet. It also supplies a frequent ingredient in Pindaric verse and in various lyrical stanzas. For its perfection it almost requires a central cæsura at the sixth syllable.

In Dryden (probably from insufficient information), in Warton (less excusably), and in some more modern writers (without any excuse at all), "long Alexandrine," or sometimes even Alexandrine by itself, is used to designate the fourteener, "seven-beat," or seven-foot iambic line. This ignores the derivation, contravenes the established use of French, the special home of the metre, and introduces an unnecessary and disastrous confusion.

ALLITERATION.—The repetition of the same letter at the beginning or (less frequently) in the body of different words in more or less close juxtaposition to each other. This, which appears slightly, but very slightly, in classical poetry, has always been a great feature of English. During the Anglo-Saxon period universally, and during a later period (after an interval which almost certainly existed, but the length of which is uncertain) partially, it formed, till the sixteenth century, a substantive and structural part of English prosody. Later, it became merely an ornament, and at times, especially in the eighteenth century, has been disapproved. But it forms part of the very vitals of the language, and has never been more triumphantly used than in the late nineteenth century by Mr. Swinburne.

AMPHIBRACH.—A foot of three syllables—short, long, short ($\cup - \cup$)—literally "short on each side." According to some, this foot is not uncommon in English poetry, as, for instance, in Byron's

$$\cup \quad - \quad \cup \qquad \cup \quad -\cup$$
The black bands | came over
$$\cup \quad - \quad \cup \quad \cup \quad -$$
The Alps and | their snow,

as well as individually for a foot of substitution. Others, including the present writer, think that these cases can always, or almost always, be better arranged as anapæsts—

$$\cup \quad - \quad \cup \quad \cup \quad -$$
The black | bands came o|ver
$$\cup \quad - \quad \cup \quad \cup \quad -$$
The Alps | and their snow,

and that the amphibrach is unnecessary, or, at any rate, very very rare in English.

AMPHIMACER ("long on both sides").—Long, short, long ($- \cup -$)—an exactly opposite arrangement to the amphibrach, also, and more commonly, called *Cretic*. It is more than doubtful whether this arrangement, *as an actual foot*, ever occurs in English verse or is suitable to English rhythm; but the name (preferably Cretic) is sometimes useful to designate a combination of syllables belonging to more feet than one, and possessing a certain connection, as expressing either the quantity of a single word or that of a rhetorical division [1] of a line.

---

[1] NOTE ON MUSICAL AND RHETORICAL ARRANGEMENTS OF VERSE

It has been said above (Book I. Chap. V. Rule 41, p. 35) that certain additional arrangements of verse may be made for musical or rhetorical purposes. This no doubt requires explanation and example, the latter especially. It shall now have them.
Tennyson's

The watch|er on | the col|umn to | the end,

and Mr. Swinburne's

The thun|der of | the trum|pets of | the night,

are both regular and unexceptionable "heroics," "five-foot iambics,"

ANACRUSIS.—A syllable or half-foot prefixed to a verse, and serving as a sort of "take-off" or "push-off" for it. This, frequent in Greek, is by no means rare in English, though there are numerous disputes as to its application. It has sometimes been proposed to call it with us "catch"; and, whatever it be called, it comes into great prominence in connection with the question whether the general rhythm of English verse is iambic or trochaic, while it is almost the hinge of the whole matter on the other question whether the English hexameter is really dactylic or anapæstic.

ANAPÆST.—A trisyllabic foot consisting of two shorts

"decasyllabic lines," etc. But in reading them the voice will not improbably be tempted (and need not resist the temptation) to arrange them as

> The watcher | on the column | to the end

and

> The thunder | of the trumpets | of the night

respectively, while in the case of the latter line other dispositions are possible. In blank-verse paragraphs especially, the poet is likely to suggest a great deal of such scansion. No doubt there are in this arrangement four-syllable divisions and three-syllable ones like amphibrachs, etc.; but that does not matter, because the line has already passed the regular prosodic tests. And no doubt the sections, or whatever they are to be called, are not strictly substitutable; but then on this scheme, which is not positively prosodic and applies to the individual line only, they need not be. So, too, there is no harm in dividing Hood's famous piece, for musical purposes, into ditrochees :

> I remember | I remember,
> How my little | lovers came,

or even in making what are practically eight feet out of

> All : peo : ple : that : on : earth : do : dwell,

in order to get an impressive musical effect. Here also the lines have passed the prosodic preliminary or matriculation ; as in the one case trochaic tetrameters catalectic split in half; in the other, as ordinary "long measure."

Now it is this necessary preliminary which the plain- and fancy-stress prosodists neglect ; putting their stress divisions not on the top, but in the place of it. And the probable result would be, if the proceeding were widely followed—as, indeed, it has been already to some small extent,—the creation of a new chaos like that of fifteenth-century South-English verse generally, or of blank verse and heroic couplet in the mid-seventeenth.

and a long ($\cup \cup -$). Almost as soon as English poetry proper makes its appearance, this measure or cadence appears too; for a time chiefly as an equivalent to the iamb. In the revived alliterative metre it to a great extent ousts the trochee, and to one almost as great dominates the doggerel of the fifteenth century. As a continuous metre the early examples of it are well marked, though not very numerous; but in the sixteenth century it seems (no doubt with the help of music) to have caught the popular ear, and from the late seventeenth has been thoroughly established in literature. It is perhaps the chief enlivening and inspiriting force in English poetry, and, while powerful for serious purposes, is almost indispensable for comic.

ANTI-BACCHIC or ANTI-BACCHIUS.—A trisyllabic foot opposite to the Bacchic as a definite foot—a short followed by two long ($\cup - -$). Of very doubtful occurrence anywhere in English verse; though the same remark applies to it as to the amphibrach, the amphimacer, other trisyllabic feet, and all tetrasyllabic, in regard to secondary or rhetorical use.

ANTISPAST ("pulling against"). — A four - syllabled foot—short, long, long, short ($\cup - - \cup$)—opposed to the choriambic. Like all four-syllabled feet, it is not wanted in English poetry, being always resolvable into its constituents, the iamb and trochee. But the combined effect may sometimes be represented by it—with this *caveat*, as in other cases.

ANTISTROPHE.—See STROPHE.

APPOGGIATURA.—A musical term which has no business whatever in prosody, but which has been used by some (*e.g.* Thelwall) to evade the allowance of equivalence, and the substitution of trisyllabic for dissyllabic feet. Its definition in music is "a short auxiliary or grace-note forming no essential part of the harmony." The nearest actual approach to it in English verse would appear to be the extra syllables found (by licence very rare until recently) in such lines as Scott's in the "Eve of St. John," Moore's in

" Eveleen's Bower " and elsewhere, and Macaulay's in
" The Last Buccaneer "—*e.g.* :

And I'll chain | the bloodhound | and the ward*er* | shall not sound.[1]

ARSIS and its opposite, THESIS, are two terms much used
in prosody, though unfortunately with meanings themselves
attached in diametrical opposition to the same word.
The words literally mean " lifting up " and " putting down "
respectively. At first, among the Greeks themselves, the
metaphor seems to have been taken from the raising and
putting down of the *foot* or *hand*; so that " arsis " would
make a light or short, and " thesis " a heavy or long
syllable. By the Latins, and by the great majority of
modern prosodists in reference even to Greek, the metaphor
is transferred to the raising or dropping of the *voice*, so
that " arsis " lengthens and " thesis " shortens. This,
which, whether the older or not, seems to be the better
use, is followed here.

ASSONANCE.—An imperfect form of rhyme which counts
only the vowel sound of the chief rhyming syllable. This
principle was the original one of rhyme in French, and
has always held a considerable place in Spanish. But in
English it has never established itself in competent literary
poetry ; though it is frequent in the lower kind of folk-song,
and though attempts to naturalise it—in forms even further
degraded—were made by Mrs. Browning, and have been
suggested since. As an instrument of vowel-music, very
delicately and judiciously used at other parts of the line
than the end, it has its possibilities, but must always be
an offensive substitute in rhyming verse, and an almost
equally offensive intruder in blank.

ATONIC (" without accent "). — When employed in
prosody, is applied to those languages which, though
they may use accentual symbols, have nothing in the

---

[1] See the larger *History* for fuller discussion of this. Such lines will
often scan trochaically (or in some other way) so as to take in the outside
syllable ; but the question then arises *whether such scansion will suit the
context*.

pronunciation that can be made the base of an actual scansion—the chief example being French.

BACCHIC or BACCHIUS.—A three-syllable foot—long, long, short ($-\ -\ \smile$)—the opposite of anti-Bacchic and subject to the same observations.

BALLAD (rarely Ball*et*).—A word common to most European languages, but used very loosely, and to be carefully distinguished from *Ballade* (see following item). Its original connection is with singing and dancing (Italian *ballare*), and it came, centuries ago, to be used for any short poem of a lyrical character. It has, however, a special application to short pieces of a narrative kind ; and "The Ballads" has, as a phrase of English literary history, frequent reference to the body of such compositions of which the pieces about Robin Hood are early examples. It is most commonly, though not universally, written in the "ballad metre" described below.

BALLADE, on the other hand, is a term arbitrarily restricted to a measure originally and mostly French, but frequently written in English during the late fourteenth and early fifteenth centuries, and revived in the nineteenth. It consists usually of three stanzas and a *coda* or *envoi*, written on the same recurrent rhymes, with a refrain at the end of each. (See example above, p. 126.)

BALLAD METRE or COMMON MEASURE. — The most usual quatrain in English poetry, consisting, in its simplest form, of alternate octosyllables and hexasyllables ; the even lines always rhyming, and the odd ones very commonly. In the best examples, old and new (but less frequently in the late sixteenth, early seventeenth, and almost whole eighteenth century), the lines are largely equivalenced, and it is not unusual for the stanza to be extended to five or more. The most perfect example of ballad metre is Coleridge's *Ancient Mariner*.

BAR and BEAT.—Two musical terms used by stress-prosodists and others who refuse the foot-system. " Bar " is strictly the division between groups of " beats," loosely the groups themselves. "Beat" is the unit of time or measure. On a sound and germane system of prosody neither is needed.

BLANK VERSE, on the analogy of blank cartridge, etc., might be held to designate any kind of verse not tipped, loaded, or filled up with rhyme. As a matter of fact, however, and for sound historical reasons, it is not usually applied to the more modern unrhymed experiments, from Collins's "Evening" onwards, but is confined to continuous decasyllables. This measure (which, *mutatis mutandis*, had already been used by the Italians and Spaniards in the early sixteenth century, and of which curious foreshadowings are found in Chaucer's prose *Tale of Melibee* and elsewhere) was first attempted in English by the Earl of Surrey in his version of the *Æneid*. For a time it was very little imitated, but in the latter half of the century it gradually ousted all other competitors for dramatic use. It was still out of favour for non-dramatic purposes until Milton's great experiments in the later seventeenth; while about the same period it was for a time itself laid aside in drama. But it soon recovered its place there, and has never lost it; while during the eighteenth century it became more and more fashionable for poems proper, and has rather extended than contracted its business since.

BOB AND WHEEL.—An arrangement (see pp. 48, 49) by which a stanza hitherto usually alliterated, but not rhymed, finishes with one much shorter line of usually two syllables, and then a batch, usually four, of lines not quite so short, but still shorter than the staple, and rhymed among themselves.

BURDEN.—The same as REFRAIN (*q.v.*).

BURNS METRE.—An apparently artificial but extremely effective arrangement of six lines, 8, 8, 8, 4, 8, 4, rhymed *aaabab*, which derives its common name from the mastery shown, in and of it, by the Scottish poet. It is, however, far older than his time, having been traced to Provençal originals in the eleventh century, and it is very common in the English miracle plays of the late fourteenth and fifteenth, and not unknown in the metrical romances, as in *Octovian Imperator*. Disused in Southern English by the time of the Renaissance, it seems to have kept its hold in Northern, and Burns received it either immediately from Fergusson or perhaps from Allan Ramsay. (See also below, in list of Form-origins.)

CADENCE.—In general, a term applied to the combined rhythm of a line or batch of lines. In one or two early passages of Wyntoun, Gower, and others, it seems to be employed in some special sense as opposed to, or separated from, rhyme, and has been conjectured to signify alliterative rhythm. But this is very uncertain, rather improbable, and in the Gower case impossible.

CÆSURA ("cutting"). — A term applied, in classical prosody, to the regular provision of a word-ending at a certain place in the line, usually coinciding with a half-foot. The commonest cæsuras in Greek and Latin are penthemimeral ("fifth half"), or in the middle of the third foot, and hepthemimeral ("seventh half"), at the middle of the fourth. At one time, in the earlier writers on English prosody (*e.g.* Dryden), there grew up a strange habit of using the term "cæsura" to express elision or hiatus— to neither of which has it the least proper reference. Correctly used, it is, in English, equivalent to "pause" (*q.v.*), but restricted to the *principal* pause in a line.

CAROL.—A term, like "ballad," of rather loose application, but generally confined to religious lyrics of a definite song-kind. The original O.F. *karole* referred to a rather elaborate *dance* with singing, and from this there has been a certain tendency to associate the carol with much broken and indented measures in prosody.

CATALEXIS ("leaving off").—A term of great importance, inasmuch as there is no other single one which can replace it; but a little vague and elastic in use. Strictly speaking, a *catalectic* line is one which comes short, by a half-foot or syllable, of the full normal measure;

a *brachycatalectic* ("short leaving off"), one which is a whole foot *minus*; and a *hypercatalectic* ("leaving over"), one which has a half foot (or perhaps a whole one in rare cases) too much. The terms "catalexis" and "catalectic" are sometimes used loosely to cover all these varieties of deficiency and redundance in their several developments. *Acatalectic* means a fully and exactly measured line, without either excess or defect.

CATCH.—See ANACRUSIS. The sense of "catch" as referring to a song in parts, with much substitution and repetition, is musical, not prosodic.

CHANT-ROYAL.—A larger and more elaborate *ballade*: five stanzas of eleven verses each and an *envoi* of from five to eight.

CHORIAMB.—A four-syllabled foot consisting of a trochee (or "choree") followed by an iamb (– ◡ ◡ –). Although the remarks made on other four-syllabled feet apply here, as far as the ultimate analysis of English verse is concerned, the great frequency of juxtaposed trochees and iambs in English, and the natural way in which they seem to cohere, make choriambic cadence or rhythm suggest itself more frequently than any other of the compound feet. Mr. Swinburne wrote intentional and continuous choriambics of great beauty.

CODA ("tail").—A musical term used in prosody by analogy, and signifying a final stanza or batch of verses, often couched in a form differing from the rest of the poem, such, for instance, as the final octave of *Lycidas*.

COMMON.—The quantity or quality in a syllable which makes it susceptible of occupying either the position of a "long" one or that of a "short." This gift, well recognised and frequent enough in Greek and Latin prosody—especially in regard to Greek proper names,—is still more widely spread in English. Almost all monosyllables, other than nouns, are common; and in a very large number of others the syllable can be raised or lowered to long or short by considerations of arsis, thesis, stress, emphasis, position, etc.

COMMON MEASURE (for shortness, especially in reference to hymns, "C.M.").—The same as ballad metre, but usually restricted to eights and sixes without substitution. (See also below, Chapter IV.)

CONSONANCE. — In strictness merely "agreement of sound"; but sometimes used to designate *full* rhyme by vowel *and* consonant, as opposed to "assonance," *i.e.* rhyme by vowel only.

COUPLET.—In proper English use this refers to a pair of verses only; and it probably should be, though it is not always, limited to cases where the members of the pair are exactly similar, as in the heroic couplet, the octosyllabic couplet. The original French word is much more elastic, and is applied to the long mono-rhymed *tirades* of Old French poems, to stanzas of more verses than two, and even to whole lyrics, usually of a light description. (See also DISTICH.)

CRETIC.—See AMPHIMACER.

DACTYL.—A trisyllabic foot—long, short, short (– ◡ ◡). This foot, thanks to the great position of the dactylic hexameter in Greek and Latin, disputes, in those prosodies, the place of principal staple with the iambic; and, from the mid-sixteenth century onwards, almost constant endeavours have been made at imitating that metre in English, and consequently at working the dactyl in our language. It was, however, early discovered, even by favourers of classical "versing," that there is something awkward about the English dactyl. And in fact, though we have a very large number of words which are fair dactyls regarded separately, they are no sooner set in a verse than they seem to slip or waggle into other measures, and especially the anapæst. When, by some chance or by some sleight of the poet, they are found, they are usually either continuous, or in connection with, and substituted for, the trochee. To the classical combination of dactyl and spondee English is obstinately rebellious.

DI-IAMB.—A double iamb—short, long, short, long

(∪ – ∪ –). Not wanted in English ; and not even express-ing, as some of the four-syllable feet do, a quasi-real compound effect.

DIMETER.—A combination of two couples of the same foot, iambic, trochaic, or anapæstic. Thus the ordinary octosyllable is an iambic dimeter, and the familiar swinging four-foot anapæst, a dimeter anapæstic. In ancient prosody, "-meter" was never used in this kind of combination, with reference to *single-feet* metres, unless these feet were in places specifically different. Thus "hexameter" means a line of six single feet, of which, though the first four may vary, the fifth must normally be a dactyl and the sixth a spondee ; "pentameter," a line of five feet, dactyls or spondees, but rigidly distributed in two halves of two and a half feet each. Of late years, in modern English prosody-writing, though fortunately not universally, a most objectionable habit has grown up of calling the heroic line a "pentameter," the octosyllabic iambic a "tetrameter." This is grossly unscholarly, and should never be imitated, for the proper meaning of the terms would be *ten* feet in the one case, *eight* in the other.

DISPONDEE.—Double spondee (– – – –). Even more than the di-iamb, and much more than the ditrochee, this combination is not wanted in English.

DISTICH.—A synonym for " couplet," but of wider range, as there is no reason why the verses should be metrically similar. There is, however, in the practical use of the word, an understanding that there shall be a certain completeness and self-containedness of *sense*.

DITROCHEE.—A double trochee—long, short, long, short (– ∪ – ∪).—The remarks on the di-iamb apply here, but not quite so strongly. There are a few exceptional cases

– ∪ – ∪

in Milton, as in the famous "Universal reproach," where the ditrochaic effect, whether beautiful or not, is too notice-able not to deserve specific definition.

DOCHMIAC.—A foot of five syllables, admitting, with the possible permutations of long and short in the five places, a large number of variations. This foot, not strictly necessary even in Greek prosody, is quite unknown in English, and, if used, would simply split itself up into batches of two and three. But it probably has a real existence in the systematisation of English *prose* rhythm.

DOGGEREL.—A word (the derivation of which can be only, though easily, guessed) as old as Chaucer; always used with depreciating intent, but with a certain difference, not to say looseness, of exact connotation. Doggerel is often applied to slipshod or song-song verse; sometimes to verse burlesque or feeble in sense and phrase. But it is better restricted to verse metrically incompetent by false rhythm and quantification, or by insufficient or superfluous provision of syllables and the like.

DUPLE.—A term used by some prosodists in combination with "time" and in contradistinction to "triple," to express a characteristic of verse which is nearest to music, and which perhaps is musical rather than really prosodic. Controversies are sometimes carried on in regard to the question whether trisyllabic feet (such as anapæsts, dactyls, and tribrachs) are, when substituted for dissyllabic, in "duple" or in "triple" time; but this question appears to the present writer irrelevant and extraneous.

ELISION.—The obliteration of a syllable, for metrical reasons, when a vowel at the end of a word comes before one at the beginning of another. This strict classical meaning of the term is extended ordinarily, in the English use of it, to the omission of a syllable within a word, or the fusion of two in any of the various ways indicated by the classical terms *crasis* ("mixture"), *thlipsis* ("crushing"), *syncope* ("cutting short"), *synalœpha* ("smearing together"), *synizesis* ("setting together"), *synecphonesis* ("combined utterance"), and others. Perhaps the most useful phraseology in English indicates "elision" for actual *vanishing* of a vowel (when it is usually represented by an apostrophe), and "slur" for running of two into one. These two processes are of extreme importance, for upon the view taken of them turns the view to be held of Shakespeare's and Milton's blank verse, and of a large number of other measures.

END-STOPPED.—A term largely applied, especially in Shakespearian discussion, to the peculiar self-contained verse which is noticeable in the early stage of blank-verse writing, and which Shakespeare was one of the first to break through. In the text of the present volume this form is called "single-moulded," its characteristics not appearing to be confined to the end.

ENJAMBMENT.—An Englishing, on simple analogy, of the French technical term, *enjambement*, for the overlapping, in sense and utterance, of one verse on another, or of one couplet on another. Enjambment of the couplet appears in Chaucer and other writers early; was overdone and abused in the first half of the seventeenth century; was rejected by the later seventeenth and still more by the eighteenth, but restored to favour by the Romantic movement.

ENVOI.—The *coda* of a *ballade*, etc., with the especial purpose of *addressing* the poem to its subject.

EPANAPHORA (" referring " or " repetition ").—The repetition of the same word or group of words at the beginning of successive lines. This, originally a rhetorical figure, becomes, especially with some of the Elizabethans and with Tennyson, a not unimportant prosodic device; and, in the hands of the latter, assists powerfully in the construction of the verse-paragraph.

EPANORTHOSIS (" setting up again," with a sense also of " correction ").—Also a rhetorical figure, and meaning the repetition of some word, *not* necessarily at the beginning of clause or line. This also can be made of considerable prosodic effect; for repetition, especially if including some slight change, is necessarily associated with emphasis, and this emphasis colours and weights the line variously.

EPITRITE.—A four-syllabled foot consisting of three long syllables and one short (– – – ⌣). The shifting of this latter from place to place makes four different kinds of epitrite. Like its congeners, it is not needed in English

poetry, though spondaic substitution (in the trochaic tetrameter, etc.) may sometimes simulate it ; and the fact that
few English words have clusters of definitely long syllables
makes it rare even in prose.

EPODE.—The third and last member of the typical
choric arrangement in a regular ode. See STROPHE.

EQUIVALENCE means, prosodically, the quality or faculty
which fits one combination of syllables for substitution in
the place of another to perform the part of foot, as the
dactyl and spondee do to each other in the classical
hexameter, and as various feet do to the iamb in the
Greek iambic trimeter and other metres. It is, with its
correlative, Substitution itself, the most important principle
in English prosody ; it emerges almost at once, and, though
at times frowned upon in theory, never loses its hold upon
practice.

EYE-RHYME.—A practice (most largely resorted to by
Spenser, but to some extent by others) of adjusting the
spellings of the final syllables of words so as to make the
rhyme clear to the eye as well as to the ear. It is sometimes forced, and perhaps never ought to be necessary ; but
it is so associated with the beauties of the *Faerie Queene* as
to become almost a beauty in itself, though hardly to be
recommended for imitation.

FEMININE RHYME—FEMININE ENDING.—Terms applied
to the use of words at the end of a line with the final (now
mute) *e.* " Feminine " rhyme is sometimes extended to
double rhyme in general, but this is not strictly correct.

"FINGERING."—A term used in this book for the single
and peculiar turn and colour given to metre by the
individual poet.

FOOT.—The admitted constituent of all classical
prosody, and, according to one system (that adopted
preferentially in this book), of English likewise, though with
variations necessitated by the language. " Foot " (πούς,
pes) is " that upon which the verse runs or marches."   A
Greek foot is made of Greek " long " and " short " syllables ;

an English foot of English. The possible combinations of these have Greek names which are convenient, and the fact that the conditions of "length" and "shortness" are different in the two languages need cause no misunderstanding whatever. But a comparatively small number are actually found in English poetry. All, however, are separately described in this Glossary, and for convenience' sake a tabular view of them is given on the next page.

It should, moreover, perhaps be added that, at most periods of English poetry, monosyllabic feet, such as hardly exist in classical prosody, are undoubtedly present. These can be regarded, if any one pleases, as made up to dissyllabic value by the addition of a pause or interval. Nor is there any valid objection to the admission of a "pause foot" entirely composed of silence. These two kinds of feet, however, are comparatively rare, and require no specific names.

FOURTEENER.—A line of seven iambic feet which emerges as almost the first equivalent of the old long A.S. line in English, as early as the *Moral Ode*, etc. At first it is oftenest a "*fif*teener," from the presence of the final *e*; but this drops off. Very largely used by Robert of Gloucester and others in the late thirteenth century; varied in *Gamelyn*; much mixed up with the doggerel of the fifteenth; frequent in the sixteenth, both alone and as "poulter's" measure; and splendidly used by Chapman in his translation of the *Iliad*. Sometimes employed to vary heroic couplet by Dryden. A favourite metre ever since the beginning of the nineteenth century. Splits into "ballad-measure."

GALLIAMBIC.—A classical metre of which the most famous, and only substantive, example is the magnificent *Atys* of Catullus, but which has been imitated in two fine English poems, Tennyson's great *Boadicea* and Mr. George Meredith's *Phaethon*. Both of these have given a rather trochaic-dactylic swing to the metre, which is probably unavoidable in English. The late Mr. Grant Allen

TABLE OF FEET

Feet of Two Syllables.	Of Three.	Of Four.	Of Five.
Iamb, ˘ — Pyrrhic, ˘ ˘ Spondee, — — Trochee, — ˘ (The trochee ("running foot") was sometimes also called "choree," χορεῖος, or χόρος ("dancing foot"), and this form appears in "*choriambic*.")	Amphibrach, ˘ — ˘ Anapæst, ˘ ˘ — Anti-Bacchic, — — ˘ Bacchic, ˘ — — Cretic, — ˘ — Dactyl, — ˘ ˘ Molossus, — — — Tribrach, ˘ ˘ ˘ (The Cretic was also called amphi*macer*; its arrangement being just the opposite to the amphi-*brach*.)	Antispast, ˘ — — ˘ Choriamb, — ˘ ˘ — Di-iamb, ˘ — ˘ — Dispondee, — — — — Ditrochee, — ˘ — ˘ Epitrite { ˘ — — — (four forms) { — ˘ — — { — — ˘ — { — — — ˘ Ionic *a majore*, — — ˘ ˘ ,, *a minore*, ˘ ˘ — — Pæon { — ˘ ˘ ˘ (four { ˘ — ˘ ˘ forms) { ˘ ˘ — ˘ { ˘ ˘ ˘ — Proceleusmatic, ˘ ˘ ˘ ˘	Dochmiac. (See under head.)

endeavoured to make out, and attempted in his translation
of the *Atys*, an iambic basis with anapæstic and tribrachic
substitution, but unsuccessfully.   Ionic *a minore* (*v. sup.*) is
the ancient suggestion ; and, with an accentual liberty not
unsuitable to its half-barbaric associations, it fits Catullus
pretty well.   But Ionics, as has been said, do not suit
English (*v. inf.* p. 285, *note*).

GEMELL or GEMINEL ("twin").—Terms applied by
Drayton to the heroic couplet.

HEAD-RHYME.—A name sometimes applied—it may be
thought unjustifiably, and beyond all question in a way
likely to mislead—to alliteration.   See RHYME.

HENDECASYLLABLE.—An eleven-syllabled line.   There
is a classical metre specially so called, executed with
particular success by Catullus, and imitated by Tennyson
in the piece describing it :

So fantastical is the dainty metre.

But the term is not infrequently used of the staple
Italian line, of English heroic or decasyllabic lines with
redundance, etc.

HEPTAMETER.—It is rather doubtful whether the word
is wanted in English, for if applied to the fourteener it
would (see METRE and DIMETER) be a complete misnomer;
and not less so, according to correct analogy, if applied to
the seven-foot anapæst, where it would properly designate
fourteen feet or forty-two possible syllables—a length which
not even Mr. Swinburne has attempted.   He himself,
however, by oversight, used it of this line, which is
properly a tetrameter brachycatalectic.

HEROIC.—A word applied, with only indirect propriety,
to the decasyllabic or five-foot couplet, and with hardly any
propriety at all to the single line of the same construction ;
but occasionally convenient in each case.   The origin of
the employment is the use of this line and couplet in the
"heroic" poem and "heroic" play of the seventeenth
century.   It has therefore the same sort of justification as

"Alexandrine." There was also an earlier habit, as in Dante's *De Vulg. Eloq.*, of calling it (in its Italian or hendecasyllabic form) the "noblest" or most dignified line; and this connects itself with the Greek practice of calling the hexameter—the *Epic*-verse—"heroic."

HEXAMETER.—The great staple metre of Greek and Latin epic, in which the line consists of six feet, dactyls or spondees at choice for the first four, but normally always a dactyl in the fifth and always a spondee in the sixth—the latter foot being by special licence sometimes allowed in the fifth also (in which case the line is called spondaic), but never a dactyl in the sixth. To this metre, and to the attempts to imitate it in English, the term should be strictly confined, and never applied to the Alexandrine or iambic trimeter.

HIATUS.—The juxtaposition of vowels either in the same word, or, more especially, at the end of one word and the beginning of the next. At different times, and in different languages, this has been regarded as a beauty and as a defect; but in English it entirely depends upon circumstances whether it is one, or the other, or neither. For a considerable period—roughly from 1650 to 1780, if not 1800—it was supposed—without a shadow of reason —that English poets ought to elide one of such concurrents and indicate it only by apostrophe, so that not merely did "the enormous" become "th' enormous," and "to affect" "t' affect," but "violet" was crushed into "vi'let," and "diamond" into "di'mond." But this has been almost entirely abandoned, though there are still "metrical fictions" on the subject.

IAMBIC.—A foot of two syllables—short, long ($\smile$ –)—the commonest in almost all prosodies,[1] and (though this is sometimes denied) the staple foot of English.

INVERTED STRESS.—A term used by accentual or stress prosodists to designate the substitution of a trochee for an

---

[1] Professor Hardie reminds me of Quintilian's assertion (*Inst. Orat.* IX. iv. 136) that even in Latin, iambs "omnibus pedibus insurgunt."

iamb. Unnecessary, if not erroneous, from the point of view of this book.

IONIC.—A foot of four syllables, consisting of a spondee (– –) and a pyrrhic (◡ ◡). With the spondee first it is called "Ionic *a majore*"; with the pyrrhic first, *a minore*. Neither movement is common in English verse, and, if it were, it would hardly require any joint name. But when the music is uppermost, as in "Vilikins and his Dinah," it suggests itself, with the alternative of the third pæon:

◡ ◡ – ◡̆   ◡ ◡ – ◡̆   ◡ ◡ – ◡̆   – –
Now as Dinah | was a-walking | in the garden | so gay.[1]

---

[1] NOTE ON IONIC *A MINORE* AS APPLICABLE TO THE EPILOGUE
OF BROWNING'S *ASOLANDO*

It has been proposed to scan the beautiful last words of Robert Browning—

> At the midnight, in the silence of the sleep-time,
>   When you set your fancies free—
> Will they pass to where, by death, fools think, imprisoned
> Low he lies who once so loved you, whom you loved so,
>   —Pity me?

as an example of English Ionic *a minore*;[1] not (as it is taken by the present writer) as trochaic—

◡ ◡ – ◡   ◡ ◡ – ◡   ◡ ◡ – ◡̆
At the midnight | in the silence | of the sleep-time;

not

– ◡ – –   – ◡ – ◡   – ◡ – ◡̆
At the | midnight | in the | silence | of the | sleep-time.

Perhaps those who propose this have been a little bribed by conscious or unconscious desire to prevent "accenting" *in* and *of*; but no more need be said on this point. The trochees, or their sufficient equivalents, will run very well without any violent INN or OVV. But when the piece is examined by ear of body and ear of mind (for the mind's ear is as important as the mind's eye) it will be found that Ionic scansion is unsatisfactory. It is perhaps not utterly fatal to the first line (though it gives an unpleasantly "rocking-horsy" movement), and perhaps still less to the second, where the catalexis itself saves this effect to some extent. But the junction and severance of sense which it suggests in the third—

◡ ◡ – –   ◡ ◡ –   – ◡   ◡ – –
Will they pass to | where, by death, fools | think, imprisoned,

---

[1] ◡ ◡ – –   Third pæon (◡ ◡ – ◡) has also been suggested, but the same counter-arguments apply to it.

LEONINE VERSE.—A term not strictly applicable to English, but sometimes found in prosody-books. It means the peculiar mediæval Latin hexameter with middle and end rhymed, as in

> Post cœnam *stabis* : seu passus mille me*abis*.

Browning comes nearest to it in such lines as

> On my specked *hide*, not you the *pride*.

LINE.—The larger integer of verse, as the foot is the smaller, and the stanza or paragraph the largest. It is usually indicated, in printing or writing, by independent beginning and ending on the page—whence the name,—but this is accidental and arranged for convenience of the eye. As a rule, however, it should not be encroached upon lightly, and, even when enjambment is practised, the individual line should have a thinkable self-sufficiency. Nor should two lines be separated when they clamour for union, as in the case of some modern rhymeless experimenters (Mr. Arnold, Mr. Henley, etc.) and in some of the early Elizabethans (Grimoald, Googe, and others).

---

is very ugly. And this same junction or severance becomes impossible in the short lines concluding the stanzas. To suit the Ionic measure these must run—

$$\cup \cup \; -$$

Pity me

$$\cup \cup \; -$$

Being—who?

$$\cup \quad \cup \; -$$

Sleep to wake

$$\cup \quad \cup \; -$$

There as here,

a set of jumpy anapæsts which upsets the whole pathos and dignity of the

composition when compared with "Pity | me"; "Sleep to | wake";

and "There as | here"; while it makes

Being | —who?

into a mere burlesque, and flies in the face of Browning's specially indicated pause.

LONG and SHORT are words which, until comparatively
recently, have been taken as the bases of all prosodic
analysis. They represent two values which, though no
doubt by no means always identical in themselves, are
invariably, unmistakably, and at once, distinguished by
the ear; and the combining of which, in ordinary
mathematical permutation, constitutes the feet, or lowest
integers, of metrical rhythm. This nomenclature—which
presents no initial difficulties, is sufficient for all practical
purposes, and commends itself at once to any unprejudiced
intelligence—seems first to have excited question and
suspicion towards the end of the seventeenth century.
It is disagreeable to both accentual and syllabic prosodists
(see chapters devoted to these), and it appears to disturb
some who would not class themselves with either. It is
indeed quite possible to work either system with "long"
and "short," applied uncontentiously to the natural values
of rhythmed speech in English poetry. But a punctilio
arises as to the definition of the words. "Does length,"
some people ask, "really mean 'duration of time' in pronouncing?" This question, and others, seem to the present
writer unnecessary. We need not decide what *makes* the
difference between "long" and "short"; it is sufficient
that this difference unmistakably *exists*, and is felt at once.
Whether it is due to accent, length of pronunciation,
sharpness, loudness, strength, or anything else, is a question
in no way directly affecting verse. The important things
are, once more, that *it exists*; that verse cannot exist
without it; that it is partly, and in English rather
largely, created by the poet, but that this creation is
conditioned by certain conventions of the language, of
which accent is one, but only one.

LONG MEASURE ("L.M.").—The octosyllabic quatrain,
alternately rhymed.

LYDGATIAN LINE.—An arrangement of extraordinary
hideousness, which occurs rather frequently in Lydgate;
and which has been assigned by the merciful to incom-
petence or carelessness; by other critics, who defend it,

to what must have been deliberate bad taste. It is a line
of nine syllables only, the missing one being not, as in the
Chaucerian *acephala*, at the first, but occurring somewhere
in the middle, and at the cæsura. An uglier metrical
entity probably nowhere exists than such a line as

If an|y word | in thee | ʌ be | missaid.[1]

MASCULINE RHYME.—A rhyme where the rhyming
syllable is single, and ends in a consonant, without any
mute *e* following. Less correctly, a monosyllabic rhyme.

METRE.—In the wide sense, collections of rhythm
which correspond, both within the collection, and, if
there be such, with one or more other collections adjoining. In the narrow, collections dominated by a single
foot-rhythm, as "iambic metre," "anapæstic metre," etc.

MOLOSSUS.—A foot of three long syllables (– – –).
Practically impossible in English *verse*, being too bulky
for a rhythm-integer with us, but admissible as a musical
arrangement.

MONOMETER.—A line consisting of one foot only, or
one pair of feet. See DIMETER.

MONOPRESSURE.—A term invented to express a theory
that the divisions of metre are associated with, and determined by, some physical throat-conditions. Unnecessary
and unworkable.

OCTAVE.—A stanza of eight lines.

OCTOMETER.—A term properly applied to eight-foot
dactylic metre, such as Tennyson's *Kapiolani*; improperly
to Mr. Swinburne's eight-foot anapæsts.

ODE.—A name used in English with great laxity, and
not perhaps to be tied down too much without loss. The
word itself, in Greek, means simply a song. But the choric
odes of the Greek dramatists, and the non-dramatic odes of
Pindar, being couched in a peculiar form—irregular at first
sight, but exactly correspondent when examined,—have

---

[1] It would become tolerable as a four-foot anapæst, and perhaps partly
suggested such a line ; also as an octosyllable with substitution.

created a certain tendency to restrict the term ode, sometimes with the epithet "regular," to things similar in
English (see, in list of poets, Cowley, Congreve, Gray).
On the other hand, the Latins—especially Horace, whose
influence has been even wider—extend the term to pieces
in short, obviously regular stanzas identically repeated,
and the majority of English odes are of this kind.

OTTAVA RIMA.—A special form of octave derived from
the Italians, and composed of eight decasyllabic lines
rhymed *abababcc*. There are other decasyllabic octaves,
such as that used by Chaucer in the *Monk's Tale*, and by
Spenser after him, with or without that adoption of the
Alexandrine which turns it into the Spenserian.

PÆON.—A foot of four syllables—one long and three
short—arranged in varying order. The commonest English
foot in rhythmical prose, but unnecessary in English verse.

PAUSE.—A break in the line as metrically read or
heard, which is almost always coincident with the end
of a word, and which very frequently, but not always or
so often as in the former case, coincides with a stop in
punctuation. It is not necessary that every line should
have a pause ; and the place of the pause, when it exists,
is practically *ad libitum* in most, if not all lines, while there
may be more pauses than one. The attempt to curtail
liberty in these three respects has been the cause of some
of the worst mistakes about English prosody, especially
when it takes the form of prescribing that the pause
should always be as near the middle as possible. Variety
of pause is, in fact, next to variety of feet, the great secret
of success in our verse ; and it is owing to this that
Shakespeare and Milton more especially stand so high.
On the other hand, this variety requires the most careful
adjustment ; and if such adjustment is neglected, the lines
will be uglier than continuously middle-paused ones,
though not so monotonous.

PENTAMETER.—See DIMETER. As properly used, a line
of five feet—dactyls or spondees—divided into two batches

of two and a half each.   As improperly used, a five-foot iambic line in English.

PINDARIC.—Strictly the regular ode (see STROPHE) of Greek poetry ; but extended by, and still more in imitation of, Cowley to any lyrical composition in irregularly rhymed stanzas of different line-lengths.   According to Dryden, the Alexandrine line, frequent in Cowley's odes, was so-called, "but," he most properly adds, "improperly."

POSITION.—In the classical prosodies a short or common vowel before two consonants (but not every two) was said to be long "by position" ; and efforts have been made to determine English quantity in the same way.   No rule of the kind can be laid down ; doubled or grouped consonants after a vowel usually shortening the pronunciation, and sometimes lengthening the value.

POULTER'S MEASURE.—A term used by Gascoigne, and said to be derived from the practice of poulter[er]s in giving twelve to the dozen in one case and thirteen or fourteen in another.   It is applied to the combination of Alexandrine and fourteener which was such a favourite with the earlier Tudor poets, and which broke up into the "Short Measure" of the hymn-books.

PROCELEUSMATIC.—A double pyrrhic, or foot of four short syllables (‿ ‿ ‿ ‿).   Not needed, if not also impossible, in English.

PYRRHIC.—Foot of two short syllables (‿ ‿).   Very doubtfully found in English ; but not impossible.

QUANTITY.—That which fits a syllable for its place as "long" or "short" in a verse.

QUARTET or QUATRAIN.—A group of four lines usually, indeed with the rarest exceptions, united in themselves, and separated from others, by rhyme.

QUINTET.—A similar group of five lines.

REDUNDANCE.—An extra syllable at the end of the line, not strictly part of its last foot.

REFRAIN.—A line recurring identically, or with very slight alteration, at the end of every stanza of a poem. Probably one of the oldest of all poetic features— certainly one of the oldest in English. The same as "burden." Refrains or burdens are not uncommonly meaningless collections of musical-sounding words.

RHYME.—The arrangement of two word-endings— identical in vowel and following consonant or consonants, but not having the same consonant *before* the vowel—at the conclusion of two or more lines, or sometimes within the lines themselves.

RHYME-ROYAL.—The stanza of seven decasyllabic lines, rhymed *ababbcc*, which occurs in Chaucer's *Troilus*, and which traditionally derives its name from its use in *The King's Quair*, though its extreme popularity for a long period is perhaps the real reason.

RHYTHM.—An orderly arrangement, but not necessarily a correspondent succession, of sounds.

RIDING RHYME.—An old name for the decasyllabic couplet, obviously derived from its appearance in Chaucer's Tales of Pilgrims "riding" to Canterbury.

RIME COUÉE or TAILED RHYME. — Translations in French and English of the Latin *versus caudatus*, and not very happy from the English point of view, though justified by origin (see Origin-List). The verse to which they refer is the sixain of two eights, a six, two more eights, and another six. Two tails are not common in English *fauna* ; and one might prefer to call the verse "waisted and tailed." It is, however, in the old Romances (where it is common, and from its commonness in which it is better called the "Romance-six") often found in multiples of three other than six; and it is at the batch of three that the title looks—the couplet of eights constituting the body, and the odd six the tail.

ROMANCE-SIX.—See RIME COUÉE.

RONDEAU—RONDEL.—French (and sometimes English) forms in which lines are repeated at regular intervals.

SAPPHIC.—A classical metre consisting of three longer lines and one shorter (called an Adonic) arranged in the following scheme :—

$$- \cup - - - \cup \cup - \cup - \triangledown$$
$$- \cup - - - \cup \cup - \cup - \triangledown$$
$$- \cup - - - \cup \cup - \cup - \triangledown$$
$$- \cup \cup - \triangledown$$

It has been frequently tried in English, both as burlesque and seriously.   For the former use (as in Canning's immortal " Needy Knife-Grinder ") it is, like most classical metres, well suited, though the true Greek and even Latin rhythm is generally (*v. sup.* p. 1 2 4) violated.   In serious verse Mr. Swinburne has produced exquisite and others (as Watts and Cowper) respectable examples ; but even the best is a *tour de force* only.

SECTION.—A term not useless in its general sense as denoting verse divisions larger than a foot ; but now prejudicially preoccupied by Guest (*v. sup.* p. 2 54, *note*) and others.

SEPTENAR.—A word applied (very undesirably) by most German and a few English writers to the fourteener or seven-foot iambic.

SEPTET.—A verse or stanza of seven lines.

SESTET, also SIXAIN.—A verse or stanza of six lines.

SESTINE, SESTINA.—A very elaborate measure invented by the Provençal poet Arnaut Daniel, imitated by Dante and other Italians, tried inexactly by Spenser, and sometimes recently attempted in English.

SHORT MEASURE ("S.M.").—The split-up poulter's measure or quartet of 6, 6, 8, 6.

SINGLE-MOULDED.—The term used in this book to describe the early blank-verse line, which appears to be constructed complete in itself, without any expectation of, or preparation for, continuance.   See END-STOPPED.

SKELTONIC.—The peculiar kind of (generally short) line used by Skelton.   Its commonest form is an anapæstic monometer (*i.e.* two feet), often much further cut down by dissyllabic and monosyllabic substitution or by catalexis, but sometimes extended. It is always rhymed ; sometimes on the same rhyme for several lines together. Though usually called "doggerel," it is in fact.rather a hybrid between two kinds of that stuff defined as *sub voce.*

SLUR.—See ELISION.

SONNET.—A word sometimes, in former days, loosely applied to any short poem, especially of an amatory nature ; often nowadays almost as improperly limited to a special Italian form of the true sonnet. This latter is a poem of fourteen lines, of the same length generally and (except by exception) decasyllables (originally, of course, *hen*decasyllables) arranged in varying rhyme-schemes. Its exact origin is unknown ; but it is first found in Italian-Sicilian poets of the thirteenth century, and it became enormously popular in Italy very soon. It did not spread northward for a considerable time, the first French sonnets occurring not very early in the sixteenth century ; the first English, not till near its middle. A great sonnet-outburst took place at the end of that century with us ; but the form fell into disuse in the seventeenth, though championed by Milton ; and it was not till the extreme end of the eighteenth century that it became, and has since remained, something of a staple. Partly the absence of the Italian plethora of similar endings, and partly something else, made the earliest English practitioners select an arrangement with final rhymed couplet, the twelve remaining lines being usually arranged in rhymed, but not rhyme-linked, quatrains : and this form, immortalised by Shakespeare, is probably the best suited to English. It is, at any rate, absolutely genuine and orthodox there. But Milton, Wordsworth, and especially Dante and Christina Rossetti, have given examples of the sonnets which, divided mostly into octave and sestet, have this latter arranged in intertwisted rhymes. This form is susceptible of great beauty, but has no prerogative, still less any primogeniture, in our poetry.

SPENSERIAN.—See Origin-List.

SPONDEE.—A foot of two long syllables (– –). Its

presence in English has been denied, but most strangely; its condition is, in fact, exactly opposite to that of the dactyl. In single and separate words its representatives are chiefly compounds like "moonshine," "humdrum," etc. But, as formed out of different words, it is frequent.

STANZA or STAVE.—A collection of lines arranged in an ordered batch and generally on some definite rhyme-scheme. Also designated by one of the loose senses of "verse."

STRESS.—Generally, though not universally, used as synonymous with accent, but somewhat differently applied, "accent" being regarded as something more or less permanent in the word, "stress" something added specially in the verse. By extension of this, numerous arbitrary and fanciful systems of prosody have been recently devised.

STRESS-UNIT.—A recent instance, and one of the worst, of the new terms invented to avoid the use of "foot." For, almost more than any other, it ignores the importance of non-stressed syllables.

STROPHE.—The stanza-unit of Greek odic or choric arrangement. The system is triple—strophe, antistrophe, and epode—and will be found fully illustrated and scanned from Gray (*v. sup.* pp. 89-91).

SUBSTITUTION.—See EQUIVALENCE.

SYNALŒPHA.⎫
SYNCOPE. ⎬—See ELISION.
SYNIZESIS.⎭

SYZYGY.—A term of classical prosody which has a perfectly strict meaning—the yoking of two feet into a metrical batch (see DIMETER). It has, in some recent cases, been rather unfortunately extended to other forms of combining syllables, sounds, etc. As thus used it is not needed, and is likely to cause confusion.

TAILED SONNET.—An Italian lengthening of the sonnet to eighteen or twenty lines, sometimes practised in English, the best known example being Milton's; but not very admirable in our language, and not at all necessary. Even in Italian the use is largely burlesque.

TERCET.—A group of three lines like TRIPLET, but specially limited to that used in TERZA RIMA.

TERZA RIMA.—A verse-arrangement by which, in a group of three lines, the first and third rhyme together, while the middle is left to rhyme with the first and third of the next batch. This arrangement, very effective in Italian, and undoubtedly one of the chief elements of the magnificence of Dante's prosody, has never been really successful in English. Some of the best examples are Shelley's ; the earliest, after some fragments in Chaucer, are Wyatt's ; the largest continuous employment is in Canon Dixon's *Mano.*

TETRAMETER.—A term improperly applied to the octosyllable ; properly to divers long lines of eight iambs, anapæsts, or trochees.

THESIS.—See ARSIS.

TIME.—A "word of fear" in prosody, as it is almost always a "voice prophesying war." Used merely in the sense of "rhythm," it is quite innocuous ; and construed generally, as when Southey says that "two short syllables take up only the time of one," there need be no harm in it. But when absolute "duration" is insisted on, and people discuss whether this can be given by that or the other means, great and unnecessary mischief is likely to be done.

TRIBRACH.—A foot of three short syllables ($\cup \cup \cup$). Very frequent in later English, perhaps less so in earlier.

TRIOLET.—A short French form of the rondeau, in the most common variety of which the first of eight lines is repeated in the fourth and seventh, the second being also repeated in the eighth, so that there are only *five* lines of independent sense.

TRIPLE.—See DUPLE.

TRIPLET.—A group of three lines ; most commonly used of three which rhyme together. See TERCET.

TROCHEE.—A foot of two syllables—long, short ($- \cup$). The complement - contrast of the iamb ; an invaluable variant upon it ; the best introducer (by admitting it as

a substitute) of the dactyl in English ; and very effective
by itself when properly managed.

TRUNCATION.—The lopping off of a syllable at beginning
or end of line. This in the latter case equals what is
here called CATALEXIS (*q.v.*), and in the former is often
better accounted for by a monosyllabic foot. But there
are cases, as in Chaucer's "acephalous" lines, where it is
not inapplicable.

TUMBLING VERSE.—A phrase of King James the Sixth
(First) in his prosodic treatise, which has caused, or at least
been connected with, difficulties (see CADENCE). He seems
to have meant by it nothing more than the loose half-
doggerel anapæsts which were so common in the first two-
thirds of the sixteenth century.

TURN OF WORDS.—A phrase specially used in the
seventeenth century for the repetition, identically or with
little change, of the same words at the end of a line and
the beginning of the next.

VERSE.—A word used with unfortunate, though perhaps unavoidable, ambiguity. It is employed first (and
best) of writing in general as opposed to prose ; secondly,
of a single line of poetry ; thirdly, of a batch of lines ; while
there is even a fourth use, now obsolete, but common in
the Elizabethans, by which it applied to classical unrhymed
metres in English. This last, one may hope, will never be
revived. Of the others, the first and third are indispensable
and can cause no real confusion. But, though a fairly
strong case can be made out for "verse" in the sense of
"line," the inconvenience and confusion of this use should
be held to prohibit it.

VERSE PARAGRAPH.—A very important development of
blank verse, ensuring to it almost all the advantages of
stanza in some ways, and more than all in others. First
reached by Shakespeare in drama, and by Milton in non-
dramatic verse, it consists in so knitting a batch of blank-
verse lines together by variation of pause, alternate use of
stop and enjambment, and close connection of sense, that

neither eye nor voice is disposed to make serious halt till the close of the paragraph is reached. Thus an effect of concerted music is produced through the whole of it. No one has ever been a great master of blank verse without being a master of this device ; but perhaps the most special and elaborate command of it has been Tennyson's.

VOWEL-MUSIC.—In a certain sense vowel-music may be said to be, and always to have been, a main, if not the main, source of the pleasure given to the ear by poetry. Nor, it may also be said, can any accomplished poet ever have been indifferent to it. Deliberate attention to it, however, has varied much at different times of English poetry, and was perhaps at its lowest in the eighteenth, at its highest in the nineteenth, century.

WEAK ENDING.—A technical term used by not a few prosodists, but not adopted in this book, for redundance. As a matter of fact a line is often much stronger for the extra syllable.

WRENCHED ACCENT.—A term applied, by accentual prosodists, sometimes to signify removal of accent on a word from the usual place ; sometimes to the presence of an unaccented syllable where they expect an accented, or the reverse. In the first sense it is unobjectionable ; in the second, always unnecessary, and often suggestive of misdescription of the results of ordinary substitution.

CHAPTER II

REASONED LIST OF POETS WITH SPECIAL REGARD TO THEIR PROSODIC QUALITY AND INFLUENCE

ARNOLD, MATTHEW (1822-1888).—Made various attempts (outside of his classical drama *Merope*) at rhymeless metres in English. Countenanced the English hexameter. Also made, but abandoned, experiments in the enjambed couplet, which anticipated William Morris.

BARHAM, RICHARD H. ("Thomas Ingoldsby") (1788-1845).—Showed the greatest proficiency in light, loose metres of the anapæstic division, and exercised much influence by them, owing to the wide and long-sustained popularity of the *Ingoldsby Legends* (1840, but earlier in magazines).

BEAUMONT, SIR JOHN (1583-1623).—One of the earliest (before 1625) practitioners, and perhaps the very earliest champion in verse itself, of the stopped couplet exactly arranged.

BLAKE, WILLIAM (1757-1827).—Although Blake's immediate and direct influence must have been small, there is hardly any poet who exhibits the tendency of his time in metre more variously and vehemently. In his unhesitating and brilliantly successful use of substitution in octosyllabic couplet, ballad measure, and lyrical adjustments of various kinds, as well as in *media* varying from actual verse to the rhymed prose of his "Prophetic" books, Blake struck definitely away from the monotonous and select metres of the eighteenth century, and anticipated the liberty, multiplicity, and variety of the nineteenth. And he differed, almost equally, from all but one or two of his older contemporaries, and from most of his younger for many years, in the colour and "fingering" of his verse.

BOWLES, WILLIAM LISLE (1762-1850).—A generally mediocre poet, who, however, deserves a place of honour here for the sonnets which he published in 1789, and which had an immense influence on Coleridge, Southey, and others of his juniors, not merely in restoring that great form to popularity, but by inculcating description and study of nature in connection with the thoughts and passions of men.

BROWNE, WILLIAM (1591-1643).—A Jacobean poet of the loosely named Spenserian school—effective in various metres, but a special and early exponent of the enjambed couplet.

BROWNING, ELIZABETH BARRETT (1806-1861).—Remarkable here for her adoption of the nineteenth-century principle of the widest possible metrical experiment and variety. In actual *metre* effective, though sometimes a little slipshod. In rhyme a portent and a warning. Perhaps the worst rhymester in the English language—perpetrating, and attempting to defend on a mistaken view of assonance, cacophonies so hideous that they need not sully this page.

BROWNING, ROBERT (1812-1889).—Often described as a loose and rugged metrist, and a licentious, if not criminal, rhymester. Nothing of the sort. Extraordinarily bold in both capacities, and sometimes, perhaps, as usually happens in these cases, a little too bold ; but in metre practically never, in rhyme very seldom (and then only for purposes of designed contrast, like the farce in tragedy), overstepping actual bounds. A great master of broken metres, internal rhyme, heavily equivalenced lines, and all the *tours de force* of English prosody.

BURNS, ROBERT (1759-1796).—Of the very greatest importance in historical prosody, because of the shock which his fresh dialect administered to the conventional poetic diction of the eighteenth century, and his unusual and broken measures (especially the famous Burns-metre) to its notions of metric. An admirable performer on the strings that he tried ; a master of musical "fingering" of verse ; and to some extent a pioneer of the revival of substitution.

BYRON, GEORGE GORDON, LORD (1788-1824).—Usually much undervalued as a prosodist, even by those who admire him as a poet. Really of great importance in this respect, owing to the variety, and in some cases the novelty, of his accomplishment, and to its immense popularity. His Spenserians in *Childe Harold* not of the highest class, but the light octaves of *Beppo* and *Don Juan* the very best examples of the metre in English. Some fine but rhetorical blank verse, and a great deal of fluent octosyllabic couplet imitated from Scott. But his lyrics of most importance, combining popular appeal with great variety, and sometimes positive novelty, of adjustment and cadence. Diction is his weakest point.

CAMPBELL, THOMAS (1777-1844). — Not prosodically remarkable in his longer poems, but very much so in some of his shorter, especially "The Battle of the Baltic," where the bold shortening of the last line, effective in itself, has proved suggestive to others of even better things, such as the half-humorous, half-plaintive measure of Holmes's "The Last Leaf" and Locker's "Grandmamma."

CAMPION, THOMAS (?-1619).—Equally remarkable for the sweetness and variety of his rhymed lyrics in various ordinary measures, and as the advocate and · practitioner of a system of rhymeless verse, different from the usual hexametrical attempts of his contemporaries, but still adjusted to classical patterns.

CANNING, GEORGE (1770-1827).—Influential, in the general breaking-up of the conventional metres and diction of the eighteenth century, by his parodies of Darwin and his light lyrical pieces in the *Anti-Jacobin*.

CHAMBERLAYNE, WILLIAM (1619-1689).—Remarkable as, in *Pharonnida*, one of the chief exponents of the beauties, but still more of the dangers, of the enjambed heroic couplet; in his *England's Jubile* as a rather early, and by no means unaccomplished, practitioner of the rival form. To be carefully distinguished from his con-temporary, Robert Chamberlain (*fl. c.* 1640), a very poor poetaster who wrote a few English hexameters.

CHATTERTON, THOMAS (1752-1770).—Of some interest here because his manufactured diction was a protest against the conventional language of eighteenth-century poetry. Of more, because he ventured upon equivalence in octosyllabic couplet, and wrote ballad and other lyrical stanzas, entirely different in form and cadence from those of most of his contemporaries, and less artificial even than those of Collins and Gray.

CHAUCER, GEOFFREY (1340?-1400).—The reducer of the first stage of English prosody to complete form and order; the greatest master of prosodic harmony in our language before the later sixteenth century, and one of the greatest (with value for capacity in language) of all time; the introducer of the decasyllabic couplet—if not absolutely, yet systematically and on a large scale—and of the seven-lined "rhyme-royal" stanza; and, finally, a poet whose command of the utmost prosodic possibilities of English, at the time of his writing, almost necessitated a temporary prosodic disorder, when those who followed attempted to imitate him with a changed pronunciation, orthography, and word-store.

CLEVELAND, JOHN (1613-1658).—Of no great import-ance as a poet, but holding a certain position as a com-paratively early experimenter with apparently anapæstic measures in his "Mark Antony" and other pieces.

COLERIDGE, SAMUEL TAYLOR (1772-1834).—In the *Ancient Mariner* and *Christabel*, the great instaurator of equivalence and substitution; a master of many other kinds of metre; and an experimenter in classical versing.

COLLINS, WILLIAM (1721-1759).—Famous in prosody

for his attempt at odes less definitely "regular" than Gray's, but a vast improvement on the loose Pindaric which had preceded; and for a remarkable attempt at rhymeless verse in that "To Evening." In diction retained a good deal of artificiality.

CONGREVE, WILLIAM (1670-1729). — Regularised Cowley's loose Pindaric.

COWLEY, ABRAHAM (1618-1667).—The most popular poet of the mid-seventeenth century; important to prosody for a wide, various, and easy, though never quite consummate command of lyric, as well as for a vigorous and effective couplet (with occasional Alexandrines) of a kind midway between that of the early seventeenth century and Dryden's; but chiefly for his introduction of the so-called Pindaric.

COWPER, WILLIAM (1731-1800).—One of the first to protest, definitely and by name, against the "mechanic art" of Pope's couplet. He himself returned to Dryden for that metre; but practised very largely in blank verse, and wrote lyrics with great sweetness, a fairly varied command of metre, and, in "Boadicea," "The Castaway," and some of his hymns, no small intensity of tone and cry. His chief shortcoming, a preference of elision to substitution.

DONNE, JOHN (1573-1631).—Famous for the beauty of his lyrical poetry, the "metaphysical" strangeness of his sentiment and diction throughout, and the roughness of his couplets. This last made Jonson, who thought him "the first poet in the world for some things," declare that he nevertheless "deserved hanging for not keeping accent," and has induced others to suppose a (probably imaginary) revolt against Spenserian smoothness, and an attempt at a new prosody.

DRAYTON, MICHAEL (1563-1631).—A very important poet prosodically, representing the later Elizabethan school as it passes into the Jacobean, and even the Caroline. Expresses and exemplifies the demand for the couplet (which he calls "gemell" or "geminel"), but is an adept in stanzas. In the *Polyolbion* produced the only long English poem in continuous Alexandrines before Browning's *Fifine at the Fair* (which is very much shorter). A very considerable sonneteer, and the deviser of varied and beautiful lyrical stanzas in short rhythms, the most famous being the "Ballad of Agincourt."

DRYDEN, JOHN (1630-1700).—The establisher and master of the stopped heroic couplet with variations of triplets and Alexandrines ; the last great writer of dramatic blank verse, after he had given up the couplet for that use ; master also of any other metre—the stopped heroic quatrain, lyrics of various form, etc.—that he chose to try. A deliberate student of prosody, on which he had intended to leave a treatise, but did not.

DIXON, RICHARD WATSON (1833-1900).—The only English poet who has attempted, and (as far perhaps as the thing is possible) successfully carried out, a long poem (*Mano*) in *terza rima*. Possessed also of great lyrical gift in various metres, especially in irregular or Pindaric arrangements.

DUNBAR, WILLIAM (1450 ?-1513 ? or-1530 ?).—The most accomplished and various master of metre in Middle Scots, including both alliterative and strictly metrical forms. If he wrote "The Friars of Berwick," the chief master of decasyllabic couplet between Chaucer and Spenser.

DYER, JOHN (1700 ?-1758 ?).—Derives his prosodic importance from *Grongar Hill*, a poem in octosyllabic couplet, studied, with independence, from Milton, and helping to keep alive in that couplet the variety of iambic and trochaic cadence derived from catalexis, or alternation of eight- and seven-syllabled lines.

FAIRFAX, EDWARD (d. 1635).—Very influential in the formation of the stopped antithetic couplet by his use of it at the close of the octaves of his translation of Tasso.

FITZGERALD, EDWARD (1809-1883).—Like Fairfax, famous for the prosodic feature of his translation of the *Rubáiyát* of Omar Khayyám. This is written in decasyllabic quatrains, the first, second, and fourth lines rhymed together, the third left blank.

FLETCHER, GILES (1588-1623), and PHINEAS (1582-1650).—Both attempted alterations of the Spenserian by leaving out first one and then two lines. Phineas also a great experimenter in other directions.

FLETCHER, JOHN (1579-1625).—The dramatist. Prosodically noticeable for his extreme leaning to redundance in dramatic blank verse. A master of lyric also.

FRERE, JOHN HOOKHAM (1769-1846).—Reintroduced the octave for comic purposes in the *Monks and the Giants* (1817), and taught it to Byron. Showed himself a master of varied metre in his translations of Aristophanes. Also dabbled in English hexameters, holding that extra-metrical syllables were permissible there.

GASCOIGNE, GEORGE (1525?-1577).—Not unremarkable as a prosodist, from having tried various lyrical measures with distinct success, and as having given the first considerable piece of non-dramatic blank verse ("The Steel Glass") after Surrey. But chiefly to be mentioned for his remarkable *Notes of Instruction* on English verse, the first treatise on English prosody and a very shrewd one, despite some slips due to the time.

GLOVER, RICHARD (1712-1785).—A very dull poet, but noteworthy for two points connected with prosody— his exaggeration of the Thomsonian heavy stop in the middle of blank-verse lines, and the unrhymed choruses of his *Medea*.

GODRIC, SAINT (? - 1170). — The first named and known author of definitely English (that is Middle English) lyric, if not of definitely English (that is Middle English) verse altogether.

GOWER, JOHN (1325?-1408).—The most productive, and perhaps the best, older master of the fluent octosyllable, rarely though sometimes varied in syllabic length, and approximating most directly to the French model.

HAMPOLE, RICHARD ROLLE OF, and commonly called

by the place - name (1290? -1347).—Noteworthy for the occasional occurrence of complete decasyllabic couplets in the octosyllables of the *Prick of Conscience.* Possibly the author of poems in varied lyrical measures, some of great accomplishment.

HAWES, STEPHEN (d. 1523 ?).—Notable for the contrast between the occasional poetry of his *Pastime of Pleasure* and its sometimes extraordinarily bad rhyme-royal—which latter is shown without any relief in his other long poem, the *Example of Virtue.* The chief late example of fifteenth-century degradation in this respect.

HERRICK, ROBERT (1591 - 1674).—The best known (though not in his own or immediately succeeding times) of the " Caroline " poets. A great master of variegated metre, and a still greater one of sweet and various grace in diction.

HUNT, J. H. LEIGH (1784-1859).—Chiefly remarkable prosodically for his revival of the enjambed decasyllabic couplet; but a wide student, and a catholic appreciator and practitioner, of English metre generally. Probably influenced Keats much at first.

JONSON, BENJAMIN, always called BEN (1573 ?-1637). —A great practical prosodist, and apparently (like his successor, and in some respects analogue, Dryden) only by accident not a teacher of the study. Has left a few remarks, as it is, eulogising, but in rather equivocal terms, the decasyllabic couplet, objecting to Donne's "not keeping of accent," to Spenser's metre for what exact reason we know not, and to the English hexameter apparently. His practice much plainer sailing. A fine though rather hard master of blank verse ; excellent at the couplet itself ; but in lyric, as far as form goes, near perfection in the simpler and more classical adjustments, as well as in pure ballad measure.

KEATS, JOHN (1795-1821).—One of the chief examples, among the greater English poets, of sedulous and successful study of prosody ; in this contrasting remarkably with his contemporary, and in some sort analogue, Shelley. Began by much reading of Spenser and of late sixteenth- and early seventeenth - century poets, in following whose enjambed couplet he was also, to some extent, a disciple of Leigh Hunt. Exemplified the dangers as well as the beauties of this in *Endymion*, and corrected it by stanza-practice in *Isabella*, the *Eve of St. Agnes*, and his great Odes, as well as by a study of Dryden which produced the stricter but more splendid couplet of *Lamia*. Strongly Miltonic, but with much originality also, in the blank verse of *Hyperion* ; and a great master of the freer sonnet, which he had studied in the Elizabethans. Modified the ballad measure in *La Belle Dame sans Merci* with astonishing effect, and in the " Eve of St. Mark " recovered (perhaps from Gower) a handling of the octosyllable which remained undeveloped till Mr. William Morris took it up.

KINGSLEY, CHARLES (1819-1875).—A poet very notable, in proportion to the quantity of his work, for variety and freshness of metrical command in lyric. But chiefly so for the verse of *Andromeda*, which, aiming at accentual dactylic hexameter, converts itself into a five-foot anapæstic line with anacrusis and hypercatalexis, and in so doing entirely shakes off the ungainly and slovenly shamble of the *Evangeline* type.

LANDOR, WALTER SAVAGE (1775-1864).—A great master of form in all metres, but, in his longer poems and more regular measures, a little formal in the less favourable sense. In his smaller lyrics (epigrammatic in the Greek rather than the modern use) hardly second to Ben Jonson, whom he resembles not a little. His phrase of singular majesty and grace.

LANGLAND, WILLIAM (fourteenth century).—The probable name of the pretty certainly single author of the remarkable alliterative poem called *The Vision of Piers Plowman*. Develops the alliterative metre itself in a masterly fashion through the successive versions of his poem, but also exhibits most notably the tendency of the line to fall into definitely metrical shapes—decasyllable, Alexandrine, and fourteener,—with not infrequent anapæstic correspondences.

LAYAMON (late twelfth and early thirteenth century).— Exhibits in the *Brut*, after a fashion hardly to be paralleled elsewhere, the passing of one metrical system into another. May have intended to write unrhymed alliteratives, but constantly passes into complete rhymed octosyllabic couplet, and generally provides something between the two. A later version, made most probably, if not certainly, after his death, accentuates the transfer.

LEWIS, MATTHEW GREGORY (1775-1818).—A very minor poet, and hardly a major man of letters in any other way than that of prosody. Here, however, in consequence partly of an early visit to Germany, he acquired love for, and command of, the anapæstic measures, which he taught to greater poets than himself from Scott downwards, and which had not a little to do with the progress of the Romantic Revival.

LOCKER (latterly LOCKER-LAMPSON) FREDERICK (1821-1895).—An author of "verse of society" who brought out the serio-comic power of much variegated and indented metre with remarkable skill.

LONGFELLOW, HENRY WADSWORTH (1807-1882).—An extremely competent American practitioner of almost every metre that he tried, except perhaps the unrhymed *terza rima*, which is difficult and may be impossible in English. Established the popularity of the loose accentual hexameter in *Evangeline*, and did surprisingly well with unvaried trochaic dimeter in *Hiawatha*. His lyrical metres not of the first distinction, but always musical and craftsmanlike.

LYDGATE, JOHN (1370-1450?).—The most industrious and productive of the followers of Chaucer, writing indifferently rhyme-royal, "riding rhyme," and octosyllabic couplet, but especially the first and last, as well as *ballades* and probably other lyrical work. Lydgate seems to have made an effort to accommodate the breaking-down pro-

nunciation of the time—especially as regarded final *e*'s—
to these measures; but as a rule he had very little success.
One of his varieties of decasyllable is elsewhere stigmatised.
He is least abroad in the octosyllable, but not very effective
even there.

MACAULAY, THOMAS BABINGTON (1800-1859).—Best
known prosodically by his spirited and well beaten-out
ballad measure in the *Lays of Ancient Rome.*   Sometimes,
as in "The Last Buccaneer," tried less commonplace
movements with strange success.

MAGINN, WILLIAM (1793-1842).—Deserves to be
mentioned with Barham as a chief initiator of the earlier
middle nineteenth century in the ringing and swinging
comic measures which have done so much to supple
English verse, and to accustom the general ear to its
possibilities.

MARLOWE, CHRISTOPHER (1664-1693).—The greatest
master, among præ-Shakespearian writers, of the blank-
verse line for splendour and might, as Peele was for sweetness and brilliant colour.   Seldom, though sometimes, got
beyond the "single-moulded" form; but availed himself
to the very utmost of the majesty to which that form
rather specially lends itself.   Very great also in couplet
(which he freely "enjambed") and in miscellaneous
measure when he tried it.

MILTON, JOHN (1608-1674).—The last of the four
chief masters of English prosody.   Began by various
experiments in metre, both in and out of lyric stanza—
reaching, in the "Nativity" hymn, almost the maximum
of majesty in concerted measures.   In *L'Allegro, Il
Penseroso,* and the *Arcades* passed to a variety of the
octosyllabic couplet, which had been much practised by
Shakespeare and others, but developed its variety and
grace yet further, though he did not attempt the full
Spenserian or *Christabel* variation.   In *Comus* continued
this, partly, with lyrical extensions, but wrote the major part
in blank verse—not irreminiscent of the single-moulded

form, but largely studied off Shakespeare and Fletcher, and with his own peculiar turns already given to it. In *Lycidas* employed irregularly rhymed paragraphs of mostly decasyllabic lines. Wrote some score of fine sonnets, adjusted more closely to the usual Italian models than those of most of his predecessors. After an interval, produced, in *Paradise Lost*, the first long poem in blank verse, and the greatest non-dramatic example of the measure ever seen—admitting the fullest variation and substitution of foot and syllable, and constructing verse-paragraphs of almost stanzaic effect by varied pause and contrasted stoppage and overrunning. Repeated this, with perhaps some slight modifications, in *Paradise Regained*. Finally, in *Samson Agonistes*, employed blank-verse dialogue with choric interludes rhymed elaborately—though in an afterthought note to *Paradise Lost* he had denounced rhyme—and arranged on metrical schemes sometimes unexampled in English.

MOORE, THOMAS (1779-1852).—A very voluminous poet in the most various metres, and a competent master of all. But especially noticeable as a trained and practising musician, who wrote a very large proportion of his lyrics directly to music, and composed or adapted settings for many of them. The double process has resulted in great variety and sweetness, but occasionally also in laxity which, from the prosodic point of view, is somewhat excessive.

MORRIS, WILLIAM (1834-1896).—One of the best and most variously gifted of recent prosodists. In his early work, *The Defence of Guenevere*, achieved a great number of metres, on the most varied schemes, with surprising effect; in his longer productions, *Jason* and *The Earthly Paradise*, handled enjambed couplets, octosyllabic and decasyllabic, with an extraordinary compound of freedom and precision. In *Love is Enough* tried alliterative and irregular rhythm with unequal but sometimes beautiful results; and in *Sigurd the Volsung* fingered the old four-teener into a sweeping narrative verse of splendid quality and no small range.

ORM.—A monk of the twelfth to the thirteenth century, who composed a long versification of the Calendar Gospels in unrhymed, strictly syllabic, fifteen-syllabled verse, lending itself to regular division in eights and sevens. A very important evidence as to the experimenting tendency of the time and to the strivings for a new English prosody.

O'SHAUGHNESSY, ARTHUR W. E. (1844-1881).—A lyrist of great originality, and with a fingering peculiar to himself, though most nearly resembling that of Edgar Poe.

PEELE, GEORGE (1558?-1597?).—Remarkable for softening the early "decasyllabon" as Marlowe sublimed it.

PERCY, THOMAS (1729-1811).—As an original versemaker, of very small value, and as a meddler with older verse to patch and piece it, somewhat mischievous; but as the editor of the *Reliques*, to be hallowed and canonised for that his deed, in every history of English prosody and poetry.

POE, EDGAR (1809-1849).—The greatest master of original prosodic effect that the United States have produced, and an instinctively and generally right (though, in detail, hasty, ill-informed, and crude) essayist on points of prosodic doctrine. Produced little, and that little not always equal; but at his best an unsurpassable master of music in verse and phrase.

POPE, ALEXANDER (1688-1744).—Practically devoted himself to one metre, and one form of it—the stopped heroic couplet,—subjected as much as possible to a rigid absence of licence; dropping (though he sometimes used them) the triplets and Alexandrines, which even Dryden had admitted; adhering to an almost mathematically centrical pause; employing, by preference, short, sharp rhymes with little echo in them; and but very rarely, though with at least one odd exception, allowing even the possibility of a trisyllabic foot. An extraordinary artist on this practically single string, but gave himself hardly a chance on others.

PRAED, WINTHROP MACKWORTH (1802-1839).—An

early nineteenth-century Prior. Not incapable of serious verse, and hardly surpassed in laughter. His greatest triumph, the adaptation of the three-foot anapæst, alternately hypercatalectic and acatalectic or exact, which had been a ballad-burlesque metre as early as Gay, had been partly ensouled by Byron in one piece, but was made his own by Praed, and handed down by him to Mr. Swinburne to be yet further sublimated.

PRIOR, MATTHEW (1664-1721).—Of special prosodic importance for his exercises in anapæstic metres and in octosyllabic couplet, both of which forms he practically established in the security of popular favour, when the stopped heroic couplet was threatening monopoly. His phrase equally suitable to the *vers de société* of which he was our first great master.

ROBERT OF GLOUCESTER (*fl. c.* 1280).—*Nomen clarum* in prosody, as being apparently the first copious and individual producer of the great fourteener metre, which, with the octosyllabic couplet, is the source, or at least the oldest, of all modern English forms.

ROSSETTI, CHRISTINA GEORGINA (1830-1894) and DANTE GABRIEL (1828-1882).—A brother and sister who rank extraordinarily high in our flock. Of mainly Italian blood, though thoroughly Anglicised, and indeed partly English by blood itself, they produced the greatest English sonnets on the commoner Italian model, and displayed almost infinite capacity in other metres. Miss Rossetti had the greater tendency to metrical experiment, and perhaps the more strictly lyrical gift of the song kind; her brother, the severer command of sculpturesque but richly coloured form in poetry.

SACKVILLE, THOMAS (1536-1608).—One of the last and best practitioners of the old rhyme-royal of Chaucer, and one of the first experimenters in dramatic blank verse.

SANDYS, GEORGE (1578-1644).—Has traditional place after Fairfax and with Waller (Sir John Beaumont, who ought to rank perhaps before these, being generally omitted) as a practitioner of stopped heroic couplet. Also used *In Memoriam* quatrain.

SAYERS, FRANK (1763-1817).—An apostle, both in practice and preaching, of the unrhymed verse—noteworthy at the close of the eighteenth century—which gives him his place in the story.

SCOTT, SIR WALTER (1771-1832).—The facts of his prosodic influence and performance hardly deniable, but its nature and value often strangely misrepresented. Was probably influenced by Lewis in adopting (from the German) anapæstic measures; and certainly and most avowedly influenced by Coleridge (whose *Christabel* he heard read or recited long before publication) in adopting equivalenced octosyllabic couplet and ballad metres in narrative verse. But probably derived as much from the old ballads and romances themselves, which he knew as no one else then did, and as few have known them since. Applied the method largely in his verse-romances, but was also a master of varied forms of lyric, no mean proficient in the Spenserian and in fragments, at least, of blank verse.

SHAKESPEARE, WILLIAM (1564-1616).—The *catholicos* or universal master, as of English poetry so of English prosody. In the blank verse of his plays, and in the songs interspersed in them, as well as in his immature narrative poems and more mature sonnets, every principle of English versification can be found exemplified, less deliberately "machined," it may be, than in Milton or Tennyson, but in absolutely genuine and often not earlier-found form.

SHELLEY, PERCY BYSSHE (1792-1822).—The great modern example of prosodic inspiration, as Keats, Tennyson, and Mr. Swinburne are of prosodic study. Shelley's early verse is as unimportant in this way as in others; but from *Queen Mab* to some extent, from *Alastor* unquestionably, onwards, he displayed totally different quality, and every metre that he touched (even if possibly suggested to some extent by others) bears the marks of his own personality.

SHENSTONE, WILLIAM (1714-1763).—Not quite unimportant as poet, in breaking away from the couplet; but of much more weight for the few prosodic remarks in his *Essays*, in which he directly pleads for trisyllabic (as he awkwardly calls them "dactylic") feet, for long-echoing rhymes, and for other things adverse to the "mechanic tune by heart" of the popular prosody.

SIDNEY, SIR PHILIP (1554-1586).—A great experimenter in Elizabethan classical forms; but much more happy as an accomplished and very influential master of the sonnet, and a lyric poet of great sweetness and variety.

SOUTHEY, ROBERT (1774-1843).—A very deft and learned practitioner of many kinds of verse, his tendency to experiment leading him into rhymelessness (*Thalaba*) and hexameters (*The Vision of Judgment*); but quite sound on general principles, and the first of his school and time to champion the use of trisyllabic feet in principle, and to appeal to old practice in their favour.

SPENSER, EDMUND (1552 ?-1599).—The second founder of English prosody in his whole work; the restorer of regular form not destitute of music; the preserver of equivalence in octosyllabic couplet; and the inventor of the great Spenserian stanza, the greatest in every sense of all assemblages of lines, possessing individual beauty and capable of indefinite repetition.

SURREY, EARL OF, the courtesy title of HENRY HOWARD (1517-1547).—Our second English sonneteer, our second author of reformed literary lyric after the fifteenth-century break-down, and our first clearly intentional writer of blank verse.

SWINBURNE, ALGERNON CHARLES (1837-1909).—Of all English poets the one who has applied the widest scholarship and study, assisted by great original prosodic gift, to the varying and accomplishing of English metre. Impeccable in all kinds; in lyric nearly supreme. To some extent early, and, still more, later, experimented in very long lines, never unharmonious, but sometimes rather compounds than genuine integers. Achieved many triumphs with special metres, especially by the shortening of the last line of the Praed-stanza into the form of " Dolores," which greatly raises its passion and power.

TENNYSON, ALFRED (1809-1892).—A poet who very nearly, if not quite, deserves the position accorded here to Chaucer, Spenser, Shakespeare, and Milton.   Coming sufficiently late after the great Romantic poets of the earlier school to generalise their results, he started with an apparent freedom (perfectly orderly, in fact) which puzzled even Coleridge.   Very soon, too, he produced a practically new form of blank verse, in which the qualities of the Miltonic and Shakespearian kinds were blended, and a fresh metrical touch given.   All poets since—sometimes while denying or belittling him—have felt his prosodic influence ; and it is still, even after Mr. Swinburne's fifty years of extended practice of it, the pattern of modern English prosody.

THOMSON, JAMES (1700-1748).—The first really important practitioner of blank verse after Milton, and a real, though rather *mannerised*, master of it.   Displayed an equally real, and more surprising, though much more unequal, command of the Spenserian in *The Castle of Indolence*.

TUSSER, THOMAS (1524?-1580).—A very minor poet —in fact, little more than a doggerelist ; but important because, at the very time when men like Gascoigne were doubting whether English had any foot but the iambic, he produced lolloping but perfectly metrical continuous anapæsts, and mixed measures of various kinds.

WALLER, EDMUND (1606-1687).—A good mixed prosodist of the Caroline period, whose chief traditional importance is in connection with the popularising of the stopped couplet.   His actual precedence in this is rather doubtful ; but his influence was early acknowledged, and therefore is an indisputable fact.   He was also early as a literary user of anapæstic measures, and tried various experiments.

WATTS, ISAAC (1674-1741).—By no means unnoteworthy as a prosodist. Followed Milton in blank verse, early popularised triple-time measures by his religious verse, evidently felt the monotony of the couplet, and even attempted English Sapphics.

WHITMAN, WALT[ER] (1819-1892).—An American poet who has pushed farther than any one before him, and with more success than any one after him, the substitution, for regular metre, of irregular rhythmed prose, arranged in versicles something like those of the English Bible, but with a much wider range of length and rhythm, the latter going from sheer prose cadence into definite verse.

WORDSWORTH, WILLIAM (1770-1850).—Less important as a prosodist than as a poet; but prosodically remarkable both for his blank verse, for his sonnets, and for the "Pindaric" of his greatest Ode.

WYATT, SIR THOMAS (1503?-1542).—Our first English sonneteer and our first reformer, into regular literary verse, of lyric after the fifteenth-century disorder. An experimenter with *terza*, and in other ways prosodically eminent.

CHAPTER III

ORIGINS OF LINES AND STANZAS

(IT has seemed desirable to give some account (to an extent which would in most cases be disproportionate for the Glossary) of the ascertained, probable, or supposed origin of the principal lines and line-combinations in English poetry. The arrangement is logical rather than alphabetical. Slight repetition, on some points, of matter previously given is unavoidable.)

A. LINES

I. ALLITERATIVE.— Enough has probably been said above of the old alliterative line and its generic character; while the later variations, which came upon it after its revival, have also been noticed and exemplified. Its origin is quite unknown; but the presence of closely allied forms, in the different Scandinavian and Teutonic languages, assures, beyond doubt, a natural rise from some speech-rhythm or tune-rhythm proper to the race and tongue. It is also probable that the remarkable difference of lengths —short, normal, and extended—which is observable in O.E. poetry is of the highest antiquity. It has at any rate persevered to the present day in the metrical successors of this line; and there is probably no other poetry which has — at a majority of its periods, if not throughout — indulged in such variety of line-length as English. Nor, perhaps, is there any which contains, even in its oldest and roughest forms, a metrical or quasi-metrical arrangement more close to the naturally increased, but not

denaturalised, emphasis of impassioned utterance, more
thoroughly born from the primeval oak and rock.

II. "SHORT" LINES.—Despite the tendency to variation
of lines above noted, A.S. poetry did not favour *very* short
ones ; and its faithful disciple and champion, Guest,
accordingly condemns them in modern English poetry.
This is quite wrong. In the "bobs" and other examples
in Middle English we find the line shortened almost, if
not actually, to the monosyllable, and this liberty has
persisted through all the best periods of English verse
since, though frequently frowned upon by pedantry. Its
origin is, beyond all reasonable doubt, to be traced to
French and Provençal influence, especially to that of the
short refrain ; but it is so congenial to the general
tendency noted above that very little suggestion must
have been needed. It must, however, be said that very
short lines, in combination with long ones, almost neces-
sitate rhyme to punctuate and illumine the divisions of
symphonic effect ; and, consequently, it was not till rhyme
came in that they could be safely and successfully used.
But when this was mastered there was no further difficulty.
In all the best periods of English lyric writing—in that
of *Alison* and its fellows, in the carols of the fifteenth
century, in late Elizabethan and Caroline lyric, and in
nineteenth-century poetry—the admixture of very short
lines has been a main secret of lyrical success ; and in
most cases it has probably been hardly at all a matter of
deliberate imitation, but due to an instinctive sense of the
beauty and convenience of the adjustment.

III. OCTOSYLLABLE.—The historical origin of the octosyllabic (or, as the accentual people call it, the four-beat
or four-stress line) is one of the most typical in the whole
range of prosody, though the lesson of the type may
be differently interpreted. Taking it altogether, there is
perhaps no metre in which so large a body of modern,
including mediæval, poetry has been composed. But,
although it is simply dimeter iambic, acatalectic or
catalectic as the case may be, it is quite vain to try to

discover frequent and continuous patterns of origin for it in strictly classical prosody.[1] Odd lines, rarely exact, in choric odes prove nothing, and the really tempting

$$\text{Ἄμμων Ὀλύμπου δέσποτα}$$

of Pindar is an uncompleted fragment which might have gone off into any varieties of Pindaric. There are a few fragments of Alcman—

$$\text{Ὧρας δ' ἔσηκε τρεῖς, θέρος}$$

and of the genuine Anacreon—

$$\text{Μηδ' ὥστε κῦμα πόντιον,}$$

in the metre, while the spurious verse of the " Anacreontea," a catalectic form with trisyllabic equivalence, seems to have been actually practised by the real poet. *Alternately* used, it is, of course, frequent in the epodes of Horace, in Martial, etc. But the fact remains that, as has been said, it is not a classical metre to any but a very small extent, though those who attach no value to anything but the "beats" may find it in bulk in the *anapæstic* dimeter of Greek and Latin choruses. It is in the Latin hymns—that is to say, in Latin after it had undergone a distinct foreign admixture —that the metre first appears firmly and distinctly established. In the fourth century, St. Ambrose without rhyme, and Hilary with it, employ the iambic dimeter, and it soon becomes almost the staple, though Prudentius, contemporary with both of them and more of a regular poet, while he does use it, seems to prefer other metres. By the time, however, when the modern prosodies began to take form, it was thoroughly well settled ; and every Christian nation in Europe knew examples of it by heart.

[1] The longest passage that my memory (assisted in this case by the kindness of my friend and colleague Professor Hardie) supplies is in Aristophanes, *Eq.* 911-940. And it is not insignificant that this not only becomes (and seems actually to be started by) a burlesque repetition—

$$\text{A. ἐμοῦ μὲν οὖν.}$$
$$\text{K. ἐμοῦ μὲν οὖν,}$$

but can only be made out by constantly breaking words, as in

$$\text{εἰς ἣν ἀναλῶν οὐκ ἐφέ-}$$
$$\text{ξεις οὐδὲ ναυπηγούμενος.}$$

It still, however, remains a problem exactly why this particular metre should, as a matter of direct literary imitation, have commended itself so widely to the northern nations.   They had nearly or quite as many examples in the same class of the *trochaic* dimeter

Gaude, plaude, Magdalena

and they paid no attention to this, though their southern neighbours did.   They had, from the time of Pope Damasus[1] downwards, and in almost all the hymn-writers, mixed dactylic metres to choose from; but for a staple they went to this.   It seems impossible that there should not have been some additional and natural reasons for the adoption—reasons which, if they had not actually brought it about without any literary patterns at all, directed poets to those patterns irresistibly.   Nor, as it seems to the present writer, is it at all difficult to discover, as far at least as English is concerned, what these reasons were.

The discovery might be made "out of one's own head"; but here as elsewhere Layamon is a most important assistant and safeguard.   A mere glance at any edition of alliterative verse, printed in half lines, will show that it has a rough resemblance on the page to octosyllabics, though the outline is more irregular.   A moderately careful study of Layamon shows, as has been indicated, that, in writing this verse with new influences at work upon him, he substitutes octosyllabic couplet for it constantly.   And the history in the same way shows that this occasional substitution became a habitual one with others.   Not that there is any mystical virtue in four feet, despite their frequency in the actual creation : but that, as an equivalent of the old half line, the choice lies practically between three and four.   Now a three-foot line, though actually tried as in

---

[1] Stirpe decens, elegans specie,
Sed magis actibus atque fide,
Terrea prospera nil reputans
Jussa Dei sibi corde ligans.

This, which is still fourth century, is important as showing *couplet* rhyme. Hilary had rhymed in *fours*.

the *Bestiary* and in parts of *Horn*, is, as a general norm, too short, is ineffective and jingly, brings the rhyme too quick, and hampers the exhibition of the sense by a too staccato and piecemeal presentment. The abundant adoption of the octosyllable in French no doubt assisted the spread in English. But it is not unimportant to observe that English translators and adapters of French octosyllabic poems by no means always preserve the metre, and that English octosyllables often represent French poems which are differently metred in the original.

IV. DECASYLLABLE.—A connected literary origin for this great line—the ancient staple of French poetry, the modern staple of English, and (in still greater modernity) of German to some extent, as well as (with the extension of one syllable necessitated by the prevailing rhythm of the language) of Italian throughout its history—has always been found extraordinarily difficult to assign. That some have even been driven to the line which furnishes the opening couplet of the Alcaic

Quam si clientum longa negotia,

or

Vides ut alta stet nive candidum,

an invariably *hen*decasyllabic line of the most opposite rhythm, constitution, and division, will show the straits which must have oppressed them. The fact is that there is nothing, either in Greek or Latin prosody, in the least resembling it or suggestive of it. To connect it with these prosodies at all reasonably, it would be necessary to content ourselves with the supposition, not illogical or impossible, but not very explanatory, that somebody found the iambic dimeter too short, and the iambic trimeter too long, and split the difference.

In another way, and abandoning the attempt to find parents or sponsors in antiquity for this remarkable foundling, a not wholly dissimilar conjecture becomes really illuminative—that the line of ten syllables (or eleven with " weak ending ") proved itself the most useful in the

modern languages.   As a matter of fact it appears in the
very earliest French poem we possess—the tenth- or
perhaps even ninth-century *Hymn of St. Eulalia* :

> Bel auret corps, bellezour anima,

and in the (at youngest) tenth-century Provençal *Boethius* :

> No credet Deu lo nostre creator.

If it still seem pusillanimous to be content with such an
explanation, one can share one's pusillanimity with Dante,
who contents himself with saying that the line of eleven
syllables "seems the stateliest and most excellent, as well
by reason of the length of time it occupies as of the
extent of subject, construction and language of which it is
capable."   And in English, with which we are specially,
if not indeed wholly, concerned, history brings us the
reinforcement of showing that the decasyllable literally
forced itself, in practice, upon the English poet.

This all-important fact has been constantly obscured
by the habit of saying that Chaucer "invented" the heroic
couplet in English—that he, at any rate, borrowed it first
from the French.   Whether he did so as a personal fact
we cannot say, for he is not here to tell us.   That he need
not have done so there is ample and irrefragable evidence.
In the process of providing substitutes for the old unmetrical line, it is not only obvious that the decasyllable—
which, from a period certainly anterior to the rise of
Middle English, had been the staple metre, in long
assonanced *tirades* or batches, of the French *Chansons de
geste*—must have suggested itself.   It is still more certain
that it did.   It is found in an unpolished and haphazard
condition, but unmistakable, in the *Orison of our Lady*
(early thirteenth century); it occurs in *Genesis and
Exodus*, varying the octosyllable itself in the middle of
that age; it is scattered about the Romances, in the
same company, at what must have been early fourteenth
century at latest; it occurs constantly in Hampole's *Prick
of Conscience* at the middle of this century; and there are

solid blocks of it in the Vernon MS., which was written (*i.e.* copied from earlier work), at latest, before Chaucer is likely to have started the *Legend of Good Women* or the *Canterbury Tales.* That his practice settled and established it — though for long the octosyllable still outbid it in couplet, and it was written chiefly in the stanza form of "rhyme-royal" — is true.   But by degrees the qualities which Dante had alleged made it prevail, and prepared it as *the* line-length for blank verse as well as for the heroic couplet, and for the bulk of narrative stanza-writing.   No doubt Chaucer was assisted by the practice of Machault and other French poets.   But there should be still less doubt that, without that practice, he might, and probably would, have taken it up.   For the first real master of versification— whether he were Chaucer, or (in unhappy default of him) somebody else, who must have turned up sooner or later— could not but have seen, for his own language, what Dante saw for his.

V. ALEXANDRINE.—The Alexandrine or verse of twelve syllables, iambically divided, does not resemble its relation, the octosyllable, in having a doubtful classical ancestry ; or its other relation, the decasyllable, in having none.   It is, from a certain point of view, the exact representative of the great iambic trimeter which was the staple metre of Greek tragedy, and was largely used in Greek and Roman verse.   The identity of the two was recognised in English as early as the *Mirror for Magistrates*, and indeed could escape no one who had the knowledge and used it in the most obvious way.

At the same time it is necessary frankly to say that this resemblance—at least, as giving the key to origin—is, in all probability, wholly delusive.   There are twelve syllables in each line, and there are iambics in both.   But to any one who has acquired—as it is the purpose of this book to help its readers to acquire or develop — a "prosodic" sense, like the much-talked-of historic sense, it will seem to be a matter of no small weight, that while the cæsura (central pause) of the ancient trimeter is

penthemimeral (at the fifth syllable), or hepthemimeral
(at the seventh), that of the modern "Alexandrine" is,
save by rare, and not often justified, license, invariably at
the sixth or middle—a thing which actually alters the
whole rhythmical constitution and effect of the line.[1] Nor,
is the *name* to be neglected. Despite the strenuous effort
of modern times to upset traditional notions, it remains a
not seriously disputed fact that the name "Alexandrine"
comes from the French *Roman d'Alexandre*, not earlier than
the late twelfth century, and itself following upon at least
one *decasyllabic* Alexandreid. The metre, however, suited
French, and, as it had done on this particular subject,
ousted the decasyllable in the *Chansons de geste* generally;
while, with some intervals and revolts, it has remained the
"dress-clothes" of French poetry ever since, and even imposed itself as such upon German for a considerable time.

In English, however, though, by accident and in special
and partial use, it has occupied a remarkable place, it has
never been anything like a staple. One of the most
singular statements in Guest's *English Rhythms* is that the
"verse of six accents" (as he calls it) was "formerly the
one most commonly used in our language." The present
writer is entirely unable to identify this "formerly": and
the examples which Guest produces, of single and occasional
occurrence in O.E. and early M.E., seem to him for the
most part to have nothing to do with the form. But it
was inevitable that on the one hand the large use of the
metre in French, and on the other its nearness as a
metrical adjustment to the old long line or stave, should
make it appear sometimes. The six-syllable lines of the
Bestiary and *Horn* are attempts to reproduce it in halves,
and Robert of Brunne reproduces it as a whole.[2] It
appears not seldom in the great metrical miscellany of the
Vernon MS., and many of Langland's accentual-alliterative

---

[1] It may be added that while the ancient trimeter is very largely patient
of substitution, the French Alexandrine positively refuses any, and the
English is, for an English line, distinctly intolerant of it.

[2] And somewhat of that tree, they bond until his hands.

lines reduce themselves to, or close to it; while it makes
a fugitive and unkempt appearance very often in fifteenth-
century doggerel. Not a few of the poems of the *Mirror
for Magistrates* are composed in it, and as an alternative
to the fourteener (this was possibly what Guest was thinking
of) it figures in the "poulter's measure" of the early and
middle sixteenth century. Sidney used it for the sonnet.
But it was not till Drayton's *Polyolbion* that it obtained the
position of continuous metre for a long poem : and this
has never been repeated since, except in Browning's *Fifine
at the Fair*.

So, the most important appearances by far of the Alexandrine in English are *not* continuous ; but as employed to
vary and complete other lines. There are two of these
in especial : the first among the greatest metrical devices in
English, the other (though variously judged and not very
widely employed) a great improvement. The first is the
addition, to an eight-line arrangement in decasyllables, of
a ninth in Alexandrine which constitutes the Spenserian
stanza and will be spoken of below. The other is the
employment of the Alexandrine as a variation of decasyllable in couplet, in triplet and singly, which is, according
to some, including the present writer, visible in the "riding-
rhyme" of Chaucer; which is often present in the blank
verse of Shakespeare; not absent from that of Milton in
his earlier attempts ; employed in decasyllabic couplet by
Cowley, and (with far greater success) by Dryden; gradually
abandoned and unfavourably spoken of by Pope; but
revived with magnificent effect by Keats in *Lamia*.

VI. FOURTEENER.—On this, as indeed on most of these
heads, it will be well to compare the continuous survey of
scanned examples and the remarks there. This line (or
its practical equivalent under the final *e* system, the *fif*teener)
is probably the oldest attempt to get a single metrical
equivalent for the old divided stave. Its own equivalents
exist, of course, both in Greek and Latin, but it is rather
doubtful whether these had much or anything to do with
its genesis. A more probable source, if any source of the

kind is wanted, has been suggested in the peculiar Latin
*thir*teener so popular in the Middle Ages, and best known
by the lines attributed to Mapes—

> Meum est propositum in taberna mori.

With a "catch" syllable at each half[1] you get the full
accentual iambic *fif*teener, and the *four*teener follows.

Perhaps, though it is difficult to recognise the fourteener-
rhythm attributed by Guest and others to Cædmon and
later A.S. writers, it is not necessary to look for any
foreign sources as other than auxiliary to the development
of the metre in English. So soon as a definite iambic
mould, with or without trochaic and anapæstic substitution,
began to be impressed on the language, the amount of
stuff usual in a full line would naturally fall into fourteener
shape. It did so, we know, as early as the *Moral Ode* at
least; and barely a century later, it showed its popularity
by the abundant use of Robert of Gloucester and the
Saints' Lives writers. Nor, although the inevitable and
fortunate break-up into ballad eight-and-six encroached on
its rights to a large extent, and the alliterative revival still
more, did it lose its attraction, as *Gamelyn* and other things
show, till it got half drowned in the doggerel welter of the
fifteenth century. From this the earlier Elizabethans
fished it out, cleaned and mended it for practice both independently and as part of the "poulter's measure," while
the finest example existing was given by Chapman's *Iliad*
in the early seventeenth century. More recently, except
in the *Sigurd* variety, it has been seldom used for long
poems, but has served as the vehicle of many of the finest
short pieces in the poetry of the nineteenth century.

VII. DOGGEREL.—In the sense (see Glossary) in which
this ambiguous word applies to *line*, it is very important to
acquire some notion of its meaning, but rather difficult
to put that notion except very hypothetically. It is, in
this use, conveniently applied to an enormous mass of

---

[1] As thus :
  [*Et*] me|um est | propo|situm | [*hac*] in | taber|na mori.

verse—sometimes hardly deserving that name, but principally produced in the fifteenth and early sixteenth centuries
—which refuses, except occasionally, to adjust itself to any
standard, even liberally equivalenced, of iambic octosyllable,
decasyllable, Alexandrine, and fourteener, or of the trochaic
and anapæstic metres corresponding to some of these,
though it comes nearest to the anapæstic division.   The
pure accentualist may dismiss it as lines of so many
irregular beats, and trouble himself no farther.   But that,
on the principles of this book, will not do.   An exceedingly
interesting parallel between it (as well as one of its regularised forms, the anapæstic dimeter) and the Spanish long
line, or "Arte Mayor," has been drawn by Professor Ker.
(See Bibliography.)   But, without either taking or opposing
his view, there is no doubt of the existence of this *mare
magnum* of imperfect versification.   It seems to have been
fed by various streams.   In the first place, as we see from
the *Gamelyn* metre, and from some nursery songs (which,
though they cannot be older than formed Middle English,
may be nearly as old), like "The Queen was in the Parlour,"
the fourteener had a tendency to break itself into roughly
balanced halves of sometimes different rhythm.   The Alexandrine, never quite at home in English, would naturally
bulge and straddle in the same way.   On the regular and
continuous anapæstic swing nobody had yet hit for long,
though it probably arose in part from this very chaos.
But perhaps the most abundant source of all was the
attempt to write Chaucerian decasyllables with a constantly altering pronunciation, and the break-down in it.
Examples of various forms of doggerel, with their corresponding metres, are given below.[1]

[1] (a) From Heywood :—
(1) Octosyllabic principally :

> And I to every soul again
> Did give a beck them to retain,
> And axèd them this question than,
> If that the soul of such a womàn
> Did late among them there appear ?
>
> *(Four P's.)*

But in close proximity such lines as

VIII. "LONG" LINES.—Beyond the fourteener or fifteener English verse has, until quite modern times, rarely gone. There are *six*teeners to be found in fourteenth-century verse, in the disorderly welter of the fifteenth, and (no doubt deliberately used) in the experiments of the *Mirror for Magistrates*; but neither they, nor any longer still, commended themselves much to any English poet before Mr. Swinburne. His experiments are famous, and some examples of them are given elsewhere. Their spirit and sweep has made not a few

and
> But Lord ! how low the Souls made curtesy,

> 'Christ, help,' quoth a soul that lay for his fees,

make their appearance.

(2) Hawesian or Barclayan decasyllables staggering into Alexandrine or anapæstic doggerel :

> How can he have pain by imagination,
> That lacketh all kinds of consideration ?
> And in all senses is so insufficient
> That nought can he think in ought that may be meant
> By any means to devise any self thing,
> Nor devise in thing past, present, or coming ?
> *(Wit and Folly.)*

(For other passages from Heywood see Scanned Conspectus, § XVIII.)

(*b*) Longer examples :—
(1) With Alexandrine norm :

> Therefore see that all shine as bright as Saint George,
> Or as doth a key newly come from the smith's forge.
> *(Ralph Roister Doister.)*

(2) With fourteener ditto :

D. I know not what a devil thou meanest, thou bringest me mere in doubt.
H. Knowest not on what tom-tailor's man sits broaching through a clout?
> *(Gammer Gurton's Needle.)*

It is curious how closely this unreverend metre sometimes comes to the heroic model of *Sigurd*.

(3) With decasyllabic ditto :

> Housed to say that as servants are obedient,
> To their bodily masters being in subjection,
> Even so evil men that are not content
> Are subject and slave to their lust and affection,

where, once more, the norm may be shifted to the anapæst.

readers look on them with favour ; but it may be questioned
whether any lines beyond seven feet—and whether even
six- and seven-foot lines when trisyllabic feet are allowed
—do not tend to break themselves up in English.   In
Mr. Swinburne's own case certainly, and perhaps in some
others, the seven-foot anapæstic line of Aristophanes gave
the suggestion, while the abundant practice in so-called
English hexameters may also have had not a little to
do with it.

B. Stanzas, etc.

I. Ballad Verse.—A good deal has been said in-
cidentally about this at several points in the preceding text;
but summary, and a little repetition, will not be out of
place here.   There has been an idea with some that it is
a shortened form of the Romance-six (see next article) or
rime couée; but this does not seem to the present writer
nearly so probable as the supposition of a break-up of the
certainly earlier fourteener couplet, which gives it at once.[1]
It is, however, not improbable that the crystallising of this
was assisted by the hesitation, also noticed in text, between
octosyllabic and hexasyllabic couplet.   The indecision and
vacillation, noticeable in such a piece as *Horn*, between the
four- and three-foot line, would easily settle to alternation
more or less regular, and then, with the assistance of the
broken fourteener, into quite regular use.   We do not,
however, find decided examples much before " Judas " and
the *Gospel of Nicodemus* in the late thirteenth century ; it
is not common in the early mysteries, though there are
approaches to it ; and it seems first to have secured the
popular ear in the much-discussed compositions which give
it its name, and which, in English, are very doubtfully to be

(Substitution of individual feet in each case immaterial.)

traced before the late fourteenth century. These, however, "estated" it once for all; though for a long time it was treated with the usual mediæval freedom—wisely restored by Coleridge in the *Ancient Mariner*—and the exact number of four lines, 8, 6, 8, 6, was not adhered to. The further fixed variations, familiar from Psalm- and Hymn-books, of "L.M." (long measure) or octosyllabic quatrain; "C.M." (common measure), the actual 8 and 6; and "S.M." (short measure) 6, 6, 8, 6, date only from Elizabethan times, the last being a breaking-up of the then favourite "poulter's measure" or alternate Alexandrine and fourteener.

II. ROMANCE-SIX or RIME COUÉE.—As in the case of the ballad-four, much has been said about this earlier. In considering its origin it is particularly desirable to distinguish between the possible source of the principle and the probable derivation of the actual form. The term *couée* (*caudatus*), which, as has been pointed out, does not apply very obviously or appropriately to our actual romance-stanza, appears to refer originally to the peculiar jingly infusion of rhyme into Latin hexameters which has been traced back at least to the twelfth century, and the most famous example of which is the original of "Jerusalem the Golden," the *De Contemptu Mundi* of Bernard of Morlaix—

> Hora novissima, tempora pessima sunt, vigilemus—
> Ecce minaciter imminet arbiter ille supremus,

where the rhyme "in the tail" appears clearly enough. It is also not inappropriate to the form in which Robert of Brunne writes his verse of the kind, as in Guest's example :

> When ye have the prize of your enemies, none shall ye save :
> Smite with sword in hand ; all Northumberland with right shall ye have.

Sometimes, however, he also batches the two first divisions :

> For Edward's good deed ⎱ a wicked bounty.
> The Balliol did him meed ⎰

But it came generally to be written in short lines straight on after the form now familiar. How or why it became so favourite a measure for romance is not, I believe, known.

Direct French influence could certainly have had little to do here; for though the six-line measure appears in Marot (early sixteenth century), it is not common earlier, and I am not even aware of any perfect example [1] of it, in the abundant variety of French and Provençal lyric during the twelfth and thirteenth centuries; while it is quite unknown to the longer French romances. But it is nearly as easy to remember—or to extemporise in default of memory—as the couplet itself. And it looks as if it were less monotonous; though—as those who drew down on it the lash of *Sir Thopas*, and *Sir Thopas* itself, show—nothing can be more monotonous in actuality. Its extensions and variations, and its migration from long narrative to short lyrical use, have been noticed already. *These* may have been to some extent influenced by the great popularity of Marot's *Psalms*, though the metre had long been naturalised.

III. Octosyllabic and Decasyllabic Couplet.—Of the two great couplet metres in English, the octosyllabic requires little notice, because it is almost indissolubly connected with the octosyllabic *line*. As soon as rhyme appears, the old iambic dimeter, four-accent line, or whatever you like to call it, *must* fall into this shape, and does. There remains indeed the problem why we have no period, in French, of octosyllabic *tirade* or batch-writing as we have (see immediately below) of decasyllabic. [2] But it is certain that the octosyllabic couplet established itself very early in French, and that at the important nick of time, when English

---

[1] The nearest is probably No. 28 in Bartsch, *Romanzen und Pastourellen*, "Volez vos que je vos chante," with its famous verse about the nightingale and the mermaid. But there is a perpetual tendency to cut the eights to sevens and the sixes to fives, as thus:

> Li rosignox est mon pere
> Qui chante sur la ramee
> El plus haut boscage.
> La seraine ele est ma mere
> Qui chante en la mer salee
> El plus haut rivage.

[2] There are examples, as in the *Vie de Saint Léger* and in Alberic of Besançon's fragmentary poem on Alexander, but few of them, and the couplet soon conquers.

prosody was being formed late in the twelfth century, this couplet came to Layamon and others as a great influence in determining the shape which alteration of the old long line or halved stave should take in their hands.

Decasyllabic couplet, on the other hand, has a much more tardy and uncertain history; though, again, much that has to be said about it has been said in reference to the single line. As soon as that line makes its appearance, in the "Saint Eulalia" hymn, it does indeed make its appearance in couplet, rhymed or assonanced.[1] But the attraction of the longer batches in identical rhyme or assonance seems, however surprisingly,[2] to get the better; and this is the form that it takes in the Provençal *Boethius* and the French *Saint Alexis*. In fact, as has been hinted above, our own scattered decasyllabic couplet rather precedes the French, though Guillaume de Machault has the credit, rightly or wrongly, of teaching it to Chaucer. After Chaucer, at any rate, there needed nobody to teach it to Englishmen; although it underwent various vicissitudes, which are duly traced elsewhere.

IV. QUATRAIN.—At a very early period, indeed as soon as they appear, Latin accentual rhythms have a tendency to batch themselves in four; as had, earlier still, Greek and Latin stanzas, Sapphic, Alcaic, and what not. The development of alternate rhyme in the octosyllabic quatrain or (*v. sup.*) ballad metre was certain to lead to a similar arrangement of *deca*syllables; and when rhyme-royal became popular the first four lines were so arranged, and might easily be broken off for separate use, as there is little doubt that the final couplet was. "Fours" of various arrangement are also abundant in lyric and in drama from the thirteenth to the fifteenth century. But the greatest

---

[1] Buona pulcella fut Eulali*a*,
   Bel auret corps, bellezour anim*a*. } *rhyme.*
   Voldrent la veintre li deo inim*i* } *assonance.*
   Voldrent la faire diaule serv*ir*.

[2] Not to the present writer, nor, he thinks, to any one who is really familiar with the *Chansons de geste*.

impulse was probably given to the alternate decasyllabic form by its adoption for the bulk of the English sonnet; and from this to separate use, which became common in the later Elizabethan poetry, there is but a very short step. The metre has always been a popular one since, and, in the hands of Dryden and Gray especially, is very effective. But a certain grave monotony about it has constantly invited modifications, of which the greatest and most successful, without altering the line-length, are those of FitzGerald in *Omar Khayyám*[1] and Mr. Swinburne in *Laus Veneris*;[2] with altered line-lengths, those of Tennyson in "The Poet,"[3] "The Palace of Art," and "A Dream of Fair Women." It was also tried in the seventeenth century as what may be called by anticipation "long *In Memoriam* measure"—that is to say, with the rhymes arranged *abba*.

V. IN MEMORIAM METRE itself may have been suggested quite casually in the endless rhyme-welter of mediæval experiment. For instance, it occurs in lines 3 to 6 of Chaucer's nine-line stanza[4] in the *Complaint of Mars*, and

[1] A book of verses underneath the bough,
A jug of wine, a loaf of bread—and thou
   Beside me singing in the wilderness—
Oh! wilderness were Paradise enow!

[2] I seal myself upon thee with my might,
Abiding always out of all men's sight,
   Until God loosen over sea and land
The thunder of the trumpets of the night—

The only difference of these is that FitzGerald, following, I believe, his Persian original, left the third lines quite blank, while Mr. Swinburne rhymed these in adjacent stanzas.

[3] For examples see above, Book II. Chap. VI. pp. 209, 210.

[4] To whom shal I then pleyne of my distresse?
Who may me helpe? Who may my harm redresse?
Shall I compleyne unto my lady fre? }
Nay, certes! for she hath such hevynesse, }
For fere, and eek for wo, that, as I gesse, }
In litil tyme it wol her bane be. }
But were she sauf, it were no fors of me!
Alas! that ever lovers mote endure,
For love, | so ma|ny a pe|rilous a|venture!

(ll. 191-199.)

the last eight of his ten-line in the *Complaint to his Lady*,[1] with decasyllabic lines, of course.   It occurs also, with six-syllable lines, in the last halves of the octaves of No. XIX. of the *York Plays*.[2]   Sidney has it as a "sport" or chance. But the first person to use it regularly and with octo-syllables was Ben Jonson,[3] who was followed by Lord Herbert of Cherbury and George Sandys.   Yet it was not widely taken up, though few measures could better have suited the "metaphysical" poets ; and after that genera-tion it remained unused till Tennyson, and by unwitting coincidence Rossetti, hit upon it just before the middle of the nineteenth century.   Rossetti has also a very effective extension of it to seven lines *abbacca*.[4]

[1] My dere herte and best beloved fo,
   Why liketh yow to do me al this wo,
      What have I doon that greveth yow, or sayd,
      But for I serve and love yow and no mo ?
      And whilst I lyve I wol ever do so;
         And therefor, swete, ne beth nat yvel apayd.
      For so good and so fair as [that] ye be ⎫
         Hit were right grete wonder but ye hadde ⎪
         Of alle servantes, bothe of goode and badde ; ⎬
      And leest worthy of alle hem, I am he. ⎭

Not dissimilar suggestions may be found in Dunbar's *Golden Targe*.

[2] We heard how they you hight,
      If they might find that child,
   For to have told you right,
      But certes they are beguiled.
   ⎧ *Swilk tales are not to trow,*
   ⎪   *Full well wot ilka wight,*
   ⎨   *Thou shall never more have might*
   ⎩ *Ne maistery unto you.*

[3] Who, as an offering at your shrine,
      Have sung this hymn and here entreat
      One spark of your diviner heat
   To light upon a love of mine.

[4] Consider the sea's listless chime,
      Time's self it is, made audible :
      The murmur of the earth's own shell—
   Secret continuance sublime
         Is the sea's end ; our sight may pass
         No furlong further.   Since time was
   This sound hath told the lapse of time.
                              (*The Sea Limits.*)

VI. RHYME-ROYAL.—However much doubt there may be about the directly imitative origin of things like couplets, or even quatrains (which might, and almost certainly would, suggest themselves without pattern), the case is different with such a thing as the permutation of rhyme in a fixed order of sevens *ababbcc*. It may, therefore, be very likely that Chaucer took this from Guillaume de Machault, a slightly older French poet (1284?-1377), with whom he was certainly acquainted. If so, it is unlikely that Machault invented it, though he may have done so ; for there is almost every possible cross-arrangement of rhymes in the enormous wealth of French and Provençal lyric from the eleventh to the fourteenth century. But it was certainly not a frequent metre before. On the other hand, Chaucer's *Troilus* made it the most fashionable metre in English throughout the fifteenth century for long narrative poems, and it was splendidly written by Sackville in the mid-sixteenth, but thereafter succumbed to the octave. The last considerable example of it, in the larger Elizabethan period, was the *Leoline and Sydanis* of Sir Francis Kynaston, a great admirer of Chaucer, who actually also translated part of *Troilus* into Latin rhyme-royal. But it was revived in the worthiest fashion by the late Mr. William Morris.

VII. OCTAVE. — There are two principal eight-line stanzas of decasyllables used in English. The oldest form, employed by Chaucer, appears to have been derived from the French, as it is certainly used by Deschamps, and may have been by Machault. Here the rhymes are arranged *ababbcbc*. By addition of an Alexandrine this arithmetically makes the Spenserian (*v. inf.*). The other—later, but much more largely used—is derived from the Italian *ottava rima*, the rhyme order of which is *abababcc*. This is the kind employed by Fairfax (with great results, though rather in the direction of its final couplet than as a whole) in his translation of Tasso (1600), and (with a comic bent also directly imitated from Italian) by Frere in *The Monks and the Giants*, and (after him) by Byron in *Beppo* and *Don*

Juan. The greatest modern serious employment of it is in Shelley's *Witch of Atlas.*

VIII. SPENSERIAN.—The Spenserian stanza of nine lines—eight decasyllables and an Alexandrine, rhymed *ababbcbcc*—is entirely the invention of Edmund Spenser. It is false to say that it was " taken from the Italians "; for there is no such stanza in Italian, and the octave-decasyllabic part of it is rhymed differently from the Italian octave. It is irrelevant to say that it is the Chaucerian octave with an Alexandrine added; for it is exactly in the addition of the Alexandrine that the whole essence and the whole beauty of the stanza consist. It is still more irrelevant, though true, to assert that there had been a few attempts (as by More) to add an Alexandrine to other stanzas or to lengthen out their last line into one; for it is of *this* stanza that we are talking, and not of something else. Therefore it is sufficient to say once more that the Spenserian stanza is the invention of Emund Spenser, and one of the greatest inventions known in prosody.

IX. BURNS METRE.—This arrangement is found first in the verse of the Provençal prince, William IX. Count of Poitiers (poems about 1090).

> Pus oezem de novelh florir
> Pratz e vergiers reverderir
> Rius e fontanas esclarrir
> Auras e vens
> Beu deu quas des lo joy jourir
> Dou es jauzens.

He has it also in a seven-line form, with four instead of three eights to start with; while the shorter variety is repeated in Northern France, as in the beautiful song of "Bele Aeliz." It appears in one English romance, *Octovian Imperator*, and largely in the Miracle plays; but later seems to have been preserved only in Scotland, where Burns gave it once more world-wide vogue.

X. OTHER STANZAS.—Of the numerous other forms of what some improperly call "irregular verse"—what King James the Sixth (First) showed himself much more of a

Solomon in calling "broken and cuttit," and adding, "quhairof new formes are daylie inventit according to the Poëtes Pleasour"—it is impossible to give an exhaustive account, or even to supply a mere list with examples of the "formes."[1] It is sufficient to say that when the new English prosody was in making there were already extensive patterns of such verse in French and Provençal poetry; that these were freely imitated and improved upon. In the present writer's larger *History* the passages dealing with the contents of MS. Harl. 2253, with the Vernon MS., and with the Miracle plays will be found to contain specifications of almost every form, and examples of not a few. This liberty continued in the lyrics of the Elizabethan period in the larger sense, being especially manifested in the later Elizabethan miscellanies of the time proper, and in the Caroline poets; but was discontinued in practice, and frowned upon in principle, during the eighteenth century. It was revived in the nineteenth by the great poets of the first Romantic period to some extent, but to a much greater degree by some of their "intermediate" successors, like Beddoes and Darley; while, from Tennyson and Browning onward, it has been the delight of almost every poet worthy of the name to add to the variety.

[1] For instance, Coleridge has shown, in the *Ancient Mariner*, that the ballad or common measure of four lines, 8, 6, 8, 6, *abab*, can be extended to any number of lines up to *nine* (*v. sup.* p. 97), with the number and order of each rhyme-end varied to suit, and yet without overrunning, or loosening the general grip and character of the stanza. Now the smallest knowledge of mathematics will show the enormous number of combinations—five-, six-, seven-, eight-, and nine-lined, with the *a* and *b* rhymes variously grouped—that would require tabulation even up to this limit. And it would argue utter insensibility to the qualities and capacities of English poetry to deny that, on the morrow of this classification, a poet might arise who would give the same solid effect to *ten* or more lines with still more endlessly varied rhyme-permutation. Instead, therefore, of attempting a hopeless and even mischievous task (for these classifications always generate the idea that whatsoever is outside of them is bad), it has seemed better to lay down, and to illustrate largely and variously, the principles on which all such legitimate combinations have been formed hitherto, but on which they may legitimately be formed anew *ad infinitum*. And this, it is hoped, has been done sufficiently here.

CHAPTER IV

BIBLIOGRAPHY

(THE following list contains almost everything with which
any student, who is not making the subject one of exhaustive and practically original research, need make himself
acquainted ; while it will carry him pretty far even in that
direction.   Further information will be found in the works
of Mr. T. S. Omond, *English Metrists* (Tunbridge Wells,
1903), and *English Metrists of the Eighteenth and Nineteenth
Centuries* (Oxford and London, 1907), as well as in the
present writer's larger *History of English Prosody*.   Several
of the works hereinafter catalogued will be found collected
in Professor Gregory Smith's *Elizabethan Critical Essays*
(2 vols., Oxford, 1904), and extracts from not a very few
of them in the present writer's *Loci Critici* (Boston, U.S.A.,
and London, 1903).)

ABBOTT, E. A.   *Shakesperian Grammar* (London, 1869),
and (with J. R. Seeley) *English Lessons for English People*
(London, 1871).   Reissued frequently.

ALDEN, R. M.   *English Verse* (New York, 1904), and
Introduction to Poetry (New York, 1909).

[BLAKE, J. W.]   *Accent and Rhythm explained by the
Law of Monopressures* (Edinburgh, 1888).

BREWER, R. F.   *Manual of English Poetry* (London,
1869).   Reissued and enlarged later as *Orthometry*
(London, 1893).

BRIDGES, R. S.   *Milton's Prosody* (Oxford, 1889).
Frequently reissued, especially in 1901, with important
additions on stress-prosody.

BYSSHE, EDWARD.   *The Art of English Poetry* (London,

337

1702). Frequently reprinted throughout the eighteenth century, the best edition being that of 1708.

CALVERLEY, C. S. *On Metrical Translation*, originally in a magazine. Reprinted in *Works* (London, 1901).

CAMPION, THOMAS. *Observations in the Art of English Poetry* (London, 1602). Reprinted in Gregory Smith's *Elizabethan Essays*, in Bullen's *Works* of Campion (London, 1889), and in the Oxford edition of these *Works* (1910).

CAYLEY, C. B. *Remarks and Experiments on English Hexameters* (*Transactions of Philological Society*, Berlin, 1861), and Preface to translation of Æschylus's *Prometheus Bound* (London, 1867).

COLERIDGE, S. T. Preface to *Christabel*. Almost any edition of *Poems*.

CONWAY, GILBERT. *A Treatise of Versification* (London, 1878).

CROWE, WILLIAM. *A Treatise on English Versification* (Oxford, 1827).

DANIEL, SAMUEL. *A Defence of Rhyme* (London, 1603?-1607). In Gregory Smith, and in all reprints of Daniel's *Works*, as well as among the *Poems* in Chalmers's *Poets*.

DRYDEN, JOHN. No single concentrated treatment, but interesting glances, some of which will be found in *Loci Critici* (*v. sup.*), and all of which can be easily traced in Professor Ker's edition of the *Critical Essays* (2 vols., Oxford, 1908).

GASCOIGNE, GEORGE. *Certain Notes of Instruction in English Verse* (London, 1575). Reprinted in Gregory Smith, in Arber's English reprints (London, 1868), etc.

GOLDSMITH, OLIVER. *Essay on Versification* (*British Magazine*, London, 1763). Reprinted in all editions of his *Works* as " Miscellaneous Essays, No. 18."

GUEST, EDWIN. *History of English Rhythms* (2 vols., London, 1838). Reprinted and edited in one vol. by Professor Skeat (London, 1882).

HODGSON, SHADWORTH. "English Verse" in *Outcast Essays*, etc. (London, 1881).

HOOD, T. (the younger). *The Rules of Rhyme* (London, 1869).

JENKIN, FLEEMING. Papers on Metre in *Saturday Review* for 1883. Reprinted in *Memoir and Remains* (Edinburgh, 1887).

JOHNSON, SAMUEL. Papers chiefly in *The Rambler* (London, 1750). To be found partly in *Loci Critici*, and completely in all editions of the *Rambler* itself. A few remarks on prosody are in the " Grammar " accompanying the *Dictionary*, and many scattered over the *Lives of the Poets*.

KER, W. P.—*Analogies between English and Spanish Verse* (*Philological Society's Transactions*, London, 1899).

KING JAMES THE FIRST (SIXTH OF SCOTLAND). *Rewlis and Cautelis*. [Full title longer.] (Edinburgh, 1595.) Reprinted by Arber (London, 1869), and in Gregory Smith.

LEWIS, C. M. *The Principles of English Verse* (New York and London, 1906).

LIDDELL, MARK H. *Introduction to the Scientific Study of English Poetry* (New York, 1902).

MASON, JOHN. *An Essay on the Power of Numbers and the Principle of Harmony in Poetical Compositions* (London, 1749).

MASSON, DAVID. Essay on Milton's Versification in edition of *Milton's Works* (London, 1890), vol. iii. pp. 107 *sq.*

MAYOR, J. B. *Chapters on English Metre* (Cambridge, 1886). *A Handbook of English Metre* (Cambridge, 1904).

MITFORD, WILLIAM. *Essay on the Harmony of Language* (London, 1774). Reissued, with large alterations and additions, as *An Enquiry into the Principles of Harmony in Language* (London, 1804).

OMOND, T. S. *A Study of Metre* (London, 1903).

PATMORE, COVENTRY. " English Metrical Criticism," originally in *North British Review* for 1875. Reprinted with *Amelia* (London, 1878), and since in various places of his *Poems* and *Works*.

POE, E. A. *The Rationale of Verse*, originally a magazine essay, 1848. In the various editions of his *Works* (ed. Ingram, 4 vols. ; Edinburgh, 1875, vol. iii. pp. 219-265).

[PUTTENHAM, GEORGE ?] *The Art of English Poesie* (London, 1581). Reprinted by Arber (Birmingham, 1869), and in Gregory Smith.

RUSKIN, JOHN. *Elements of English Prosody* (Orpington, 1880).

SCHIPPER, J. *Englische Metrik* (3 vols., Bonn, 1882-89). *History of English Versification* (Oxford, 1910).

SHENSTONE, WILLIAM. *Essays* in *Works* (3 vols., London, 1764-69). The chief of the few, but very important, prosodic remarks will be found in *Loci Critici*.

SKEAT, W. W. Section on Chaucer's Prosody in *Works of Chaucer*, vol. vi. (Oxford, 1894). Rehandled in paper on the *Scansion of English Poetry* (*Philological Society's Transactions for* 1895-98).

SOUTHEY, ROBERT. Preface of *Vision of Judgment* (London, 1820). A few important remarks (see text) in *Letters* and *Correspondence*.

SPEDDING, JAMES. Review in *Fraser's Magazine*, 1861. Reprinted in *Reviews and Discussions* (London, 1879).

SPENSER, EDMUND. Correspondence with Gabriel Harvey. In full editions of *Works*, or in Gregory Smith.

STEELE, JOSHUA. *Prosodia Rationalis* (London, 1779).

STONE, W. J. *On the Use of Classical Metres in English* (Oxford, 1898). Reprinted, without specimens, together with Mr. Bridges' *Prosody of Milton* (Oxford, 1901).

SYMONDS, J. A. *Blank Verse* (London, 1895).

THELWALL, JOHN. *Illustrations of English Rhythmus* (London, 1812).

VERRIER, M. *Essai sur la métrique anglaise* (3 vols., Paris, 1909).

WADHAM, E. *English Versification* (London, 1869).

WEBBE, WILLIAM. *A Discourse of English Poetry* (London, 1586). Reprinted by Arber (London, 1870) and in Gregory Smith.

INDEX

INDEX

[" Gloss." indicates that the word will be found explained at its alphabetical place in the Glossary.]

341